CAIRO

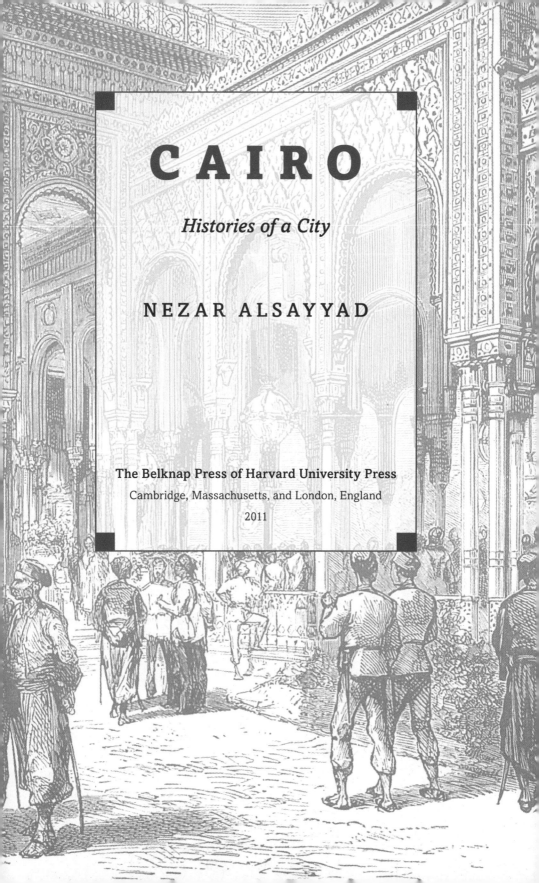

CAIRO

Histories of a City

NEZAR ALSAYYAD

The Belknap Press of Harvard University Press

Cambridge, Massachusetts, and London, England

2011

Library of Congress Cataloging-in-Publication Data
AlSayyad, Nezar.
  Cairo : histories of a city / Nezar AlSayyad. — 1st ed.
    p. cm.
  Includes bibliographical references and index.
  ISBN 978-0-674-04786-0 (alk. paper)
  1. Architecture—Egypt—Cairo—History. 2. Architecture and
society—Egypt—Cairo—History. 3. City planning—Egypt—
Cairo—History. 4. Cairo (Egypt)—Buildings, structures, etc.
I. Title. II. Title: Histories of a city.
  NA1583.A47 2011
  720.962'16—dc22
                          2010041688

Cairo or al-Qahira:
A city whose name means both
the Victorious and the Oppressor.

To those who know Cairo well, hoping
they will find something new here.
And for those who do not know Cairo at all,
hoping they will go out and explore it.

CONTENTS

PREFACE

MY INTEREST IN CAIRO dates to 1973 when, as a student of architecture at Cairo University, I was first exposed to the city's Islamic heritage. Since then, Cairo has continued to fascinate me, although its problems have tempered my exuberant appreciation for the city. This critical view has taken time to develop. When I wrote my first book, *The Streets of Islamic Cairo,* in 1981, I was still under the city's spell. But by 1991, with the publication of *Cities and Caliphs,* which read Fatimid Cairo as a colonial royal compound, my uncritical love affair with the city came to an end. I then spent several years in the 1990s building an elaborate computer model of the city. This ultimately resulted in a successful public television documentary that presented a vivid, simulated image of the development of the medieval city over a five-hundred-year period to the general public and students of architecture and urban history.

Despite all of these engagements, I never really wanted to write an entire book on the history of the city. The task, I thought, was dangerous and impossible, and I had simply assumed that to do it justice would consume my life. So when Dr. Sharmila Sen, a humanities editor at Harvard University Press and a scholar in her own right, proposed the project to me almost four years ago, I must confess that I was reluctant to take it on. However, the words of Janet Abu-Lughod, author of the now-classic *Cairo: 1001 Years of the City Victorious,* who scolded me a decade earlier by asking, "When will you do your book on Cairo?" kept ringing in my ears. Sharmila gave me tremendous freedom to fashion this book in the way that I wanted, which indeed made it very difficult for me to resist. I finally succumbed to the temptation and signed on to do the project.

In embarking on this work, I had already been exposed to most of the primary and secondary sources on the city. Historical treatises on Cairo from Maqrizi to Ali Mubarak were essential in grounding me in the principal texts. The work of Egyptian scholars, from Abdulrahman Zaki to Gamal Hamdan, reminded me of the importance of viewing the city through native eyes. The writings of Max Rodenbeck and Maria Golia, writers and journalists who fell in love with the city, afforded me exposures to different viewpoints. And finally, the work of the prominent contemporary historians of Cairo, Janet Abu-Lughod and André Raymond, provided me with a reliable frame of reference. The work of great novelists who have written about the city rendered significant inspiration. Naguib Mahfouz's *Cairo Trilogy,* from *Palace Walk* (1956) to *Sugar Street* (1957), was the most important. Khairy Shalaby's *Rehalat al-Torshagy al-Halwagy* (translated in English as *The Time-Travels of the Man Who Sold Pickles and Sweets*), a novel in which the author moves historical figures out of their times to meet him in contemporary places, was the most innovative. Alaa Al-Aswany's *The Yacoubian Building* (2002), which captures the history of the city over several decades in the twentieth century in the form of an apartment building, was the bravest. And finally, Gamal al-Ghitani's short and long stories that turn the history of the city into fiction were the most engaging. I am grateful to each and every one of them directly and indirectly. But I would like specifically to single out Gamal al-Ghitani, who walked the streets of Cairo with me and opened his library to me with great generosity, allowing me access to books that have long since disappeared from the public domain.

Some special individuals also deserve specific recognition here, and I offer them my sincere appreciation for helping with the book. Elena Tomlinson, my research assistant, worked on the project for more than a year. She did painstaking library work, read everything that I wrote, traveled with me to Cairo in search of sources and images, and helped package the final manuscript. I have benefited tremendously from her dedication and patience, and I owe her a great debt. David Moffat, my editorial advisor and collaborator for many years, deserves credit for his diligent editorial work on the book. While Ipek Tureli helped me put together the first few chapters of the book, Sylvia Nam helped me finish the last few chapters. They both deserve recognition for setting the manuscript on the right path. Tara Graham and Sylvia Nam were also in charge of revising the final edits, and I am grateful for her critical comments, which required me to rethink how I communicate my ideas to my intended audience of both scholars and the general public, as different as these two groups may be. My staff at the Center for Middle Eastern Studies, Mejgan Massoumi and Priscilla Minaise, and at the International Association for the Study of Traditional Environments, Sophie Gonick and Vicky Garcia, have provided logistical support on more than several occasions. Ayman AlSayyad, Salma AlSayyad, Momen El-Husseiny, and Muna Guvenc helped me find rare illustrations and new images of Cairo, and I am thankful for their work. I am grateful to all of these individuals, and I recognize that any failings of the book are solely my own.

At Harvard University Press, I would like to thank many people who worked on the final stages of the book, specifically Heather Hughes, who coordinated the project at the Press, production editor Elizabeth Gilbert, and manuscript editor Wendy Nelson. Book designer Peter Holm did an excellent job and I am very grateful for his input and cooperation. The final appearance of this book owes as much to them as it does to my work on its content.

Finally, I am grateful to Ananya Roy, who read the book several times in incomplete form and provided a strong dose of criticism that influenced the direction of the project. Without her input, this would have been a different book. In the end, the book did not take over my life, but I am glad it is finished. I do not know if I have done Cairo justice, but time will ultimately tell!

Preamble

Reading and Writing Cairo

This roof, with its inhabitants of chickens and pigeons and its arbor garden, was her beautiful, beloved world and her favorite place for relaxation out of the whole universe, about which she knew nothing.... She was awed by the minarets which shot up, making a profound impression on her. Some were near enough for her to see their lamps and crescent distinctly, like those of Qala'un and Barquq. Others appeared to her as complete wholes, lacking details, like the minarets of the mosques of al-Husayn, al-Ghuri, and al-Azhar. Still other minarets were at the far horizon and seemed phantoms, like those of the Citadel and Rifa'i mosques. She turned her face toward them with devotion, fascination, thanksgiving, and hope. Her spirit soared over their tops, as close as possible to the heavens. Then her eyes would fix on the minaret of the mosque of al-Husayn, the dearest one to her because of her love for its namesake. She looked at it affectionately, and her yearnings mingled with the sorrow that pervaded her every time she remembered she was not allowed to visit the son of the Prophet of God's daughter, even though she lived only minutes away from his shrine.

—Nahguib Mahfouz, *Palace Walk*[1]

THIS IS WHAT NAGUIB MAHFOUZ, Egypt's most distinguished novelist, wrote in the first few pages of *Palace Walk,* the initial volume of the trilogy that won him the Nobel Prize for Literature in 1988.[2] Mahfouz's novels provide a dense commentary on Cairo as it navigated the twentieth century, presented through the life and times of three generations of the Abdel-Jawad family. Through them, Mahfouz accurately documents Egypt's coming of age by tracing the changing social relations in this extended Cairene family. In these three books, he moves us very carefully between the tensions of the emptiness of inherited traditions to the challenges facing a new generation in revolt.

Although Mahfouz wrote his trilogy in the middle of the twentieth century, the dynamics that he describes have existed throughout the history of Cairo. The first volume, *Bayn al-Qasrayn* (translated to English as *Palace Walk*), was written in the first years following the Egyptian Revolution of 1952, Mahfouz having titled it after the famous space in the medieval core of Cairo. But Bayn al-Qasrayn was also witness to the evolution of Cairo for over a thousand years, from its origins as a royal settlement to its development into a dense cosmopolitan city.

There is, however, a lot more to Cairo than Bayn al-Qasrayn—more than the medieval Fatimid city, or the few cities built nearby that preceded it. Indeed, the first settlement in the metropolitan area we now call Cairo was actually known as Memphis, built more than four millennia ago, near the great pyramids of Giza. A serious history of Cairo should indeed start with Memphis, a city that had survived for twice as long as the Cairo of the Arabs.

But what can be said of Cairo and its history that has not already been told? Perhaps little, or nothing at all! For no city has been as studied as Cairo. Travelers to Egypt, even before the time of Christ, had inscribed their impressions of the area on the pyramids of Saqqara and Giza. Throughout medieval times, travelers who visited the Fatimid city wrote extensive accounts of their journeys. Many residents and administrators of Cairo also produced extensive histories and documentations of the city, all the way into the modern era. And in the twentieth century, many scholars have written detailed histories of the city's development, while numerous novelists have used it as a backdrop for their plots.

There are many ways to tell the story of a city, and this book simply offers just one. It starts with the premise that the history of a city is mainly that of specific individuals, places, and events. I thus begin each chapter at a specific place that best represents a period in Cairo's history, and then proceed to describe that time period, telling of the lives of specific individuals, narrating important events, and citing the reports of specific travelers and local residents, all the while attempting to evoke a sense of the evolving spatial order of the city. This approach has its limitations, of course. For example, some chapters deal with two or three centuries of the city's history, while others deal with only two decades. This treatment is justified, however, because certain events and individuals are indeed more consequential to the development of the city than are others. Similarly, I proceed from the premise that all historical periods are usually uncovered and articulated as clearly bracketed eras not at the time in which they transpire but after many decades or centuries have passed. For this reason, I often narrate the history of a period by relating it in terms of the time of its discovery. I do not, however, let my method dominate my narrative; when the method cannot accommodate historical evidence, I leave it behind.

Not only has this book required me to delve into many histories and different historical methods—it has also forced me to adjust my role as a historian. The choices I have made, in terms of which historical periods to cover (although I try to cover most of the significant ones), which historical characters to single out (again, I try to include all of the noteworthy figures, at least as far as the development of the city is concerned), and in which places to anchor my stories (and here I have had to leave out many), are all part of a broader historical method, rather than just a style of writing. This book, in turn, has convinced me that there is no history without historians—with all the biases, frailties, and limitations of their methods. It also reminds me of an old conviction: history is always written from the present moment, and possibly in the service of it. As such, there is no history that is innocent of contemporary demands. From this perspective, history is neither simply the knowledge of things that have occurred in the past nor the memory of these past events, but rather, it is the convergence of these events with certain individuals and in specific places, as discussed and interpreted by others removed from the time and place in which the events occurred.

An underlying assumption behind this work is a fundamental belief that the institutional structure of a society, based on who governs it and how, is often reflected in the places this society produces. Again, this assumption affords methodological limits, because urban form is very complex and cannot be looked upon simply as a language that can just be read. Such reading would be meaningless without the qualifications of social and economic history. At best, the shape of a city becomes a road map for deciphering its history.

Under the best possible conditions, the act of writing history consists of piecing together fragments. The process unavoidably leads to resolving contradictions between bits of evidence to arrive at a reasonably substantial version of what has occurred. We inevitably exercise judgment in qualifying which sources are more reliable than others. All these problems are compounded when, as historians, we set out to construct a narrative whose strength lies in its ability to convey precise representations of urban form and space. But in the final analysis, we must remember that the writing of history will always be, first and foremost, an art of interpretation, not a science of representation. The stories that we depict will change from time to time and from place to place to reflect the intentions of those who tell them and the interests of the people for whom they are written. The challenge in the telling of history today perhaps lies in reversing the equation and finding the proper balance between what I call the science of interpretation and the art of representation.

In this work, I have attempted to let the multiple histories of Cairo speak for themselves.[3] I am, however, very conscious of how this exercise is enmeshed in a politics of representation in which I play a part. Because I operate mainly in the space between the words and the images, I am perhaps another Baudelairean flâneur who wanders through the city's history with his mind instead of seeing its actual streets with his eyes. The great novelist Italo Calvino once wrote that cities are like dreams: their rules seem absurd, their perspectives are often deceitful, and everything in them conceals something else. He tells us that we should take delight not in a city's wonders, whether these number seven or seventy, but in the answers a city can give to questions we pose, or in the questions it asks us in return. It is only in the context of this wisdom that I have attempted to write this history of Cairo.[4]

Road map

The author generated this table to conceptualize the various chapters of the book. The table may also serve as a road map of the book for its readers. For each chapter, the road map indicates the time covered, the physical location from which the chapter starts, and the main event(s) that shaped the city during that period. Another set of columns provide information on the main historical figures whose actions were critical to the formation of the city, as well as the places created, with mention of the various travelers and commentators whose narration of the city made the writing of this book possible.

Chapter	Time Frame	Starting Location	Main Event(s)	Figures and Actors	Travelers or Commentators	Places Told
Chapter 1 Memphis: The First Cairo	4000 BC to 331 BC	Foothill of the Giza Pyramids	The discovery of ancient Egypt	Khafra; Khufu; Menkaura	Auguste Mariette; Manetho; Herodotus; Khaemwaset	Nile River; Giza; Saqqara; Danshur
Chapter 2 From Ancient Egypt to the Coptic Enclave	331 BC to 640	Fortress of Babylon; Coptic Museum	The Arab conquest of Christian Egypt	Markus Simaika; 'Amr ibn al-'As; Comité de Conservation des Monuments de l'Art Arabe; Patriarch Cyrus; Benjamin; Heraclius	Diodorus; John of Nikiu; Ibn Duqmaq; Diodorus Siculus	From Babylon to Alexandria; Babylon fort; Coptic Church; Coptic Museum
Chapter 3 Fustat-Misr: The City of Arab Islam	640 to 969	Minaret of Ibn Tulun Mosque	Lajin takes refuge in the Mosque of Ibn Tulun	Husan al-Din Lajin; 'Amr ibn al-'As; Ahmad ibn Tulun	Mohammed Abul-Kassem ibn Hawqal	Fustat to al-Qata'i; Mosque of 'Amr; Mosque of Ibn Tulun
Chapter 4 Al-Qahira: A Fatimid Palatial Town	969 to 1169	Minaret of al-Hakim Mosque	The Bohras' restoration of Fatimid architecture	Caliph Muizz; Jawhar al-Siqilli; Badr al-Jamali; Al-Hakim	Nasir-i Khusraw	Central al-Qahira; Fatimid palaces; Mosques of al-Azhar, al-Hakim, al-Aqmar
Chapter 5 Fortress Cairo: From Salah al-Din to the Pearl Tree	1169 to 1250	The Citadel; Shagarat al-Durr and the tomb of al-Salih Najm al-Din	Shagarat al-Durr conceals the death of al-Salih	Salah al-Din; Shagarat al-Durr; Louis IX; Izz al-Din Aybak; Turan Shah	Ibn Sa'id; Abdel Latif al-Baghdadi; Ibn Jubayr	From the Citadel to the tomb of Shagarat al-Durr; madrasa of al-Salih; mausoleum of al-Shafi'i
Chapter 6 The Bahri Mamluks: The City of the Slave Sultans	1250 to 1382	Sultan Hasan Mosque and minaret	Qalawun establishes the longest-lasting Mamluk dynasty	Al-Zahir Baybars; Al-Mansur Qalawun; Al-Nasir Muhammad; Sultan Hasan	Ibn Battuta; 'Emanuel Piloti; Ibn Khaldun	Mosques of Baybars, Nasir Muhammad, and Sultan Hasan; Qalawun's complex

Chapter	Date	Landmark	Event	People	Chroniclers	Sites
Chapter 7 Governing from the Tower: The Burji Mamluks	1382 to 1517	Bab Zuwayla; Mosque of Shaiykh Mu'ayyad	Rise of the Circassians	Al-Zahir Barquq; Faraj ibn Barquq; Al-Mu'ayyad Shaiykh; Al-Asharaf Qaytbay; Al-Asharaf Qansuh al-Ghuri	Taqi al-Din al-Maqrizi	Bab Zuwayla; Mosques of Barquq, Shaiykh Mu'ayyad; complex of Qaytbay and al-Ghuri; house of Maqrizi
Chapter 8 A Provincial Capital under Ottoman Rule	1517 to 1799	Ottoman Palaces; Madrasa of Khair Bey; Mosques of Sinan and Abu Dahab; sabil-kuttab of Katkhuda al-Sihaymi	Fall of the Mamluks	Selim Bey; Khair Bey; Ridwan Bey; Ali Bey al-Kabir; Muhammad al-Dahab; 'Abd al-Rahman Katkhuda; Ibrahim Bey; Murad Bey	Carsten Niebuhr; Jean de Thevenot	Mosque of Sinan; Al-Alfi house; Mosque of Khair Bey; sabil-kuttab of Katkhuda; Mosque of Abu al-Dahab; house of al-Harawi
Chapter 9 A Changing City: From Napoleon to Muhammad Ali	1799 to 1854	Mosque of Muhammad Ali	Arrival of Napoleon in Egypt and the rise of Muhammad Ali	Napoleon; Muhammad Ali	'Abd al-Rahman al-Jabarti; David Roberts; Jean-Léon Gérôme; Edward William Lane	Mosque of Muhammad Ali; House of al-Alfi; Azbakiya Lake; Shubra Palace
Chapter 10 Modernizing the New, Medievalizing the Old: The City of the Khedive	1854 to 1952	Cairo Marriott in Gezira	Suez Canal	Khedive Ismail; Khedive Abbas; King Farouk	Francis Firth; Ali Mubarak	Abdin Palace; Suez Canal; Pyramid Street; Qasr al-Nil barracks and bridge; Opera House; Muhammad Ali Road; Egyptian Museum
Chapter 11 The Arab Republic and the City of Nasser	1952 to 1970	Cairo tower, looking east to the Arab Socialist Union, the Nile Hilton, and the Arab League	Building the Aswan High Dam and the nationalization of the Suez Canal	Gamal Abdul Nasser	Naguib Mahfouz	From Cairo Tower to Nasser's tomb; Cairo Tower; Nile Hilton; Arab Socialist Union; Nasr City; Mohandeseen; public housing
Chapter 12 Escaping the Present, Consuming the Past	1970 to 2009	Sadat's Tomb	Ramadan War or Yom Kippur War of 1973	Anwar Sadat; Hosni Mubarak	Alaa Al Aswany	Tomb of Sadat; City Stars Mall; 6th of October City; gated community of Rehab; medieval Cairo as museum

CAIRO

Memphis: The First Cairo

THE CITY OF CAIRO has been more than twenty-five centuries in the making. It took the efforts of many unlikely characters over time to turn a small residential cluster on the west bank of the Nile into the mammoth metropolis we know today. This chapter tells the story of the first Cairo, a story involving a Frenchman by the name of Auguste Mariette, a man whose life and work helped uncover this first city.

Mariette was born in 1821 in Boulogne-sur-Mer in France, and grew up cultivating a talent and interest in drawing, which he later coupled with an ability to write. He found footing in the writing vocation around 1843 as editor of a local newspaper.[1] However, when he was commissioned to review the papers of a recently deceased cousin and Egyptologist, Nestor L'Hôte (1804–1842), he quickly became charmed by the stories of ancient Egypt. Egyptology soon became his hobby. For the following seven years, Mariette spent his spare time studying the few ancient artifacts in the Boulogne Museum, trying to decipher hieroglyphs.

At the time, the most valuable contribution to the knowledge of ancient Egypt was a fine granite tablet, discovered by the French army engineer Captain Pierre-François Bouchard in the upper Nile Delta city of Rosetta in 1799 during Napoleon Bonaparte's Egyptian campaign. The Rosetta Stone, as it became known, reached England as part of the spoils of the Anglo-French War (1793–1802). Because it contained the same decree in three languages—ancient Egyptian, Demotic, and Greek (which was still commonly learned in the nineteenth century)—it was assumed that deciphering the stone would be easy. But scholars remained baffled by the fact that each hieroglyphic sign appeared to have a different meaning each time it was used. The Demotic script did not offer any additional help in solving this riddle of ancient Egyptian writing.

Twenty-three years later, on September 27, 1822, the French classical scholar Jean-François Champollion (1790–1832), who had worked for many years to decipher hieroglyphic texts, addressed the French Royal Academy of Letters. In his speech Champollion outlined his discovery that hieroglyphics involve an intricate combination of phonetic and ideographic symbols. He further explained that Demotic writing was simply a vernacular form of hieroglyphics; not in itself a discrete alphabetic script.

Champollion embarked on a trip to Egypt in 1828, which allowed him and his assistant, the aforementioned L'Hôte, to assemble a record of inscriptions that were meant to expand knowledge of ancient Egypt beyond the Rosetta Stone. However, Champollion died in 1832 at the age of forty-two, leaving much of Egyptian history yet to be deciphered. L'Hôte returned to Egypt after Champollion's death to complete the work, but he too died prematurely from heatstroke. L'Hôte's father inherited his son's documents and, for lack of better use, turned them over to one of the few men in his town with a literary background, Auguste Mariette.

Figure 1.1 *The Pyramids of Giza* **by David Roberts, 1854.**

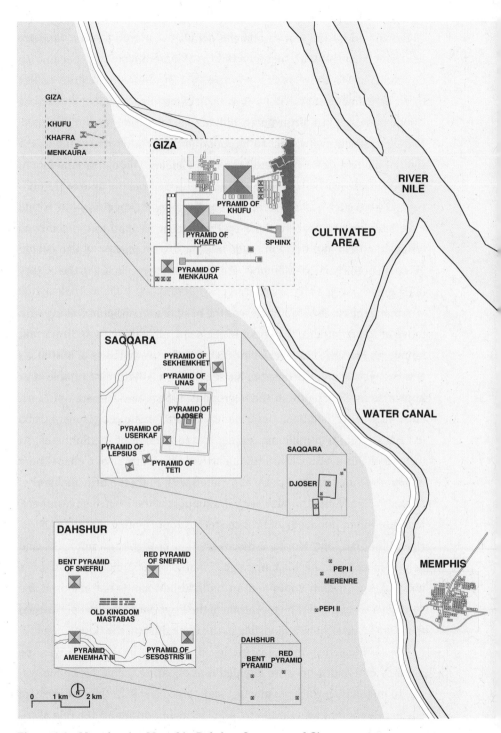

Figure 1.2 Map showing Memphis, Dahshur, Saqqara, and Giza.

Fascinated by the stories and the details in L'Hôte's papers, Mariette became consumed with hieroglyphics and, quite unwittingly, became an Egyptologist. He took his first trip to Egypt in the fall of 1850 to collect rare Coptic manuscripts.[2] But this mission came to an abrupt end when the Coptic patriarch in Cairo refused him access to ancient texts. Frustrated, Mariette turned his interest to Egyptian antiquity after marveling at the sight of the first Cairo from atop the Giza Plateau. There, from the foot of the pyramids—which had been known in Europe from the time of Herodotus and were later "rediscovered" by the Napoleonic expedition—he would have been able to observe the Step Pyramid in Saqqara to the south, as well as the Bent and Red Pyramids in Dahshur. He may have also caught glimpses of the ruins of Memphis, the longest-serving capital in the history of Egypt as well as in the world.[3]

Among the ruins of Memphis was the head of a small sphinx, along with those of fifteen others, rising out of the sand, all leading to an important temple, as Mariette discovered in 1850. This became the site of Mariette's first excavation and the onset of his search for a labyrinthine temple later known as the Serapeum in the necropolis at Saqqara. The area of Mariette's excavation had been described by the Ptolemaic geographer Strabo (64 BC–AD 23) two millennia earlier as the Avenue of the Sphinxes. At the end of this avenue, Mariette unearthed the doorway of a chapel built in honor of Apis, the bull deity associated with Ptah, the principal god of Memphis.[4] Four months later, with the support of the French government, Mariette found hundreds of bronze statues representing the gods Osiris, Apis, Ptah, Isis, and Horus, a discovery that brought him notoriety and helped to consolidate his campaign. Finally, in 1851, he penetrated the tomb of Apis, which contained an undisturbed vault that enclosed the sarcophagus of a bull. The footprints of the Egyptians who had performed the sacred burial were still visible in the thick dust on the floor.

One of Mariette's most fascinating discoveries in the tomb was the mummy of a man who wore a gilded mask bearing the name Khaemwaset. In millennia past, Khaemwaset had played a role in the discovery of ancient Egypt that was similar to, and just as important as, the role Mariette was now playing.

The history of Egypt extends back to the fourth millennium BC. The earliest records show that it was divided into two kingdoms, extending north and south of the city of On, which served as "the locus of a solar cult and center of astronomical observation."[5] Upper Egypt stretched south along the Nile Valley toward Aswan, while the kingdom of Lower Egypt occupied a marshy delta in the north.[6] The site of today's Cairo, situated between these areas, witnessed a long, drawn-out struggle between these two kingdoms, which concluded only in 3100 BC with the conquest of the Nile Delta by the king of Upper Egypt.[7]

Ancient Egyptian myth tells of a god-king, named Menes, who made this unification possible. Menes, who is believed to have been born in the vicinity of Abydos in Upper Egypt, was a skillful warrior and a vigorous administrator. He was able to gather the resources to invade and conquer the delta and merge the two kingdoms into one nation, completing a process of integration that had been under way for many centuries.[8] For his stronghold in the area, Menes did not choose On, known today as Heliopolis, on the right bank of the Nile, because of its vulnerability to attack from the east. Instead, he chose a virgin site on the left bank, thirty-two kilometers south and just upstream from the forking of the delta, which became the site of the city of Memphis.

It is essential to remember that Egypt's history is so long that it was studied by its own historians and archaeologists during the many millennia in which it flourished, long before the advent of what we deem modern civilization. Thus, a man living in Upper Egypt close to the temple of Abu Simbel when it was finished circa 1224 BC during the reign of King Ramses II would have considered the pyramids very old. Indeed, the pyramids for that person would have been "more than two thousand years away from him, more remote in time than Jesus Christ is from us."[9] We know much of this history because of three important men: Khaemwaset, Manetho, and Herodotus.

Khaemwaset, who was the high priest of Memphis for some time and also one of the sons of Ramses II (who reigned from 1279 to 1213 BC), was one of the most important builders of ancient Egypt. He passed much time wandering the Memphis necropolis, reading the inscriptions on tombs and temples. His reputation as an antiquarian was so great that his stories spread widely through the writings of later scribes. Known as one of the first Egyptologists, Prince Khaemwaset would inspect the tombs at Giza, and, if information was lacking, would have his men carve hieroglyphs on the entrances identifying the rulers for whom the tombs had been built. One could consider these inscriptions the precursor to the modern museum's technique of classification. Twenty-five centuries later, Mariette found a papyrus containing a few of Khaemwaset's tales. He, too, benefited from Khaemwaset's inscriptions, which are still visible today in many parts of the Memphis necropolis.

In contrast, we know very little of Manetho's origins except that he was born in a small town in the delta. He was a priest educated in the old scribal tradition and, around 280 BC, became the first person to write a condensed indigenous history of ancient Egypt in Greek. Manetho's approach to history was principally one of chronicling the activities of the divine pharaohs and stressing their central mystical role in the life of the people. No original copy of Manetho's work has been found, but references to it abound in the scholarship of historians who came centuries later. More importantly, his compilation is considered to be the most authoritative list of the ancient Egyptian kings.[10] Indeed, Manetho's list enabled modern Egyptologists, including Mariette, to identify and date major monuments of ancient Egyptian history.

The third figure, Herodotus, is often considered the father of modern history. A Greek, he visited Egypt from about 460 to 455 BC during the country's occupation by the Persians, nearly two centuries before Manetho, and wrote the first comprehensive account of its ancient civilization. He characterized the Nile as the regulator and predictor of Egyptian life and the maker of a unique Egyptian culture. According to Herodotus, the Nile brought floods, which spoiled crops and caused droughts; the latter were the source of long famines. The Nile also, however, sustained the prosperity of Egypt. Egyptians adapted to it by staying in its proximity, without building their dwellings on its floodplains. The constant shifting of the Nile also determined the locations of the many different settlements that constituted Cairo throughout its history.

Mariette never accepted Herodotus's account of the area as substantive or definitive. He even scorned what he considered Herodotus's silliness in his choice of historical evidence and the ancient Egyptian monuments he chose to describe. Frustrated with what could have been a better source for his work, Mariette once commented in a letter to a friend,

> I detest this traveler who came to Egypt at a time when the Egyptian language was spoken, who with his eyes saw all the temples still standing, who only had to ask the first comer the name of the reigning king, who only had to refer to the first temple for the history, religion, and everything of interest concerning the most fascinating country in the world. And who instead tells gravely of (unworthy) stories. … This is not what one should expect of Herodotus, and as for me, I look upon him as a real criminal. He who could have told so much tells us only stupidities. Consider the great number of mistakes in Herodotus … would it not have been better for Egyptology had he never existed?[11]

Despite such an opinion, Mariette's lifelong engagement with Egypt united the previous works of Khaemwaset, Manetho, and Herodotus into one cohesive account.

The connection between Mariette and Memphis was formidable. Mariette left his family in France to begin work there in 1850. Although he was not the first to excavate in the area, his life and his discoveries became inextricably intertwined with it. Convinced that he was going to stay for an extended period of time, Mariette soon built a little home to shelter himself and to house his discoveries. In his early years, Mariette faced obstacles posed by an Egyptian administration hostile to his mission, and several attempts were made to expel him and confiscate his findings. Eventually, to secure some protection for himself and his mission, he hoisted the French flag over his house and called his work an expedition. Seven years after his arrival, in 1857, Mariette moved his family there.

In the ensuing years, Mariette experienced a number of demoralizing tragedies, though they never defeated him in his larger intellectual quest. His loyal assistant Bonnefoy died of heatstroke in 1859; his daughter Josephine died two years later; and his wife Elenore suffered an unknown malady and died in 1865. All were buried in Cairo.[12]

According to Mariette's reading of Herodotus, Menes built a great dam to change the course of the Nile to make way for the new city of Memphis. At the time the stronghold was known not as Memphis but as the White Wall; this invoked the name of the White Kingdom—white being the royal color of Upper Egypt.[13] As the new seat of government, Memphis was surrounded by battlements and strategically situated at the junction between the two former kingdoms. We do not know whether Menes intended to establish the city as a capital or as a fortress to secure the unity of his country. Some scholars also doubt that Memphis was the capital throughout the entire period of the Old Kingdom (2750–2250 BC). Nevertheless, for more than four centuries it was the most important city in the region.[14]

The importance of Memphis was, to a considerable extent, based on its religious role. Most accession ceremonies were performed there, as was the Heb-Sed festival, a reenactment of the coronation that restated the supernatural powers of the king. Although it was not directly on the Nile, Memphis was connected to it by a canal, and the city likely emerged as an important commercial center.

Specific quarters of the city were named after the foreign colonies of peoples—slaves, prisoners of war, merchants, and so forth—who resided there. A section was called the Field of the Hittites after a group of invaders of Egypt. In later periods, sections inhabited by Carians and Phoenicians were also named thus. Interestingly, this pattern of planning and naming quarters after particular ethnic groups reappeared in the cities of the region during the Islamic period.

From Memphis, Menes extended his reign over a great expanse of Egyptian territory. He also carried his arms southward against northern Nubia, which extended below the first cataract as far as Edfu.[15] In the thousand years after Menes, Egyptian civilization blossomed. It was an era that saw the establishment of state administration, court ritual, legal practice, and religious doctrine.

At the end of the Old Kingdom, however, Memphis suffered from political and social upheaval, and its prominence decreased until the Second Intermediate Period (1648–1539 BC). But with the start of the New Kingdom (1539–1070 BC) and until the end of the Pharaonic Era (332 BC), it regained its status as one of the foremost cities in Egypt, possibly serving as its political capital, even at a time when Thebes, further south down the Nile, functioned as its religious center. All told, the city lasted through three millennia and thirty-four dynasties, and remained a vibrant urban center for most of that time.

Even during the Ptolemaic Period (332–330 BC), Memphis retained its cosmopolitan character. Its original name had been Men-efer, meaning lasting and beautiful.[16] The Greeks changed its name to Memphis. Hellenistic rule also brought with it a sizable Greek population. The continued racial diversity of its population was depicted in a series of striking terracotta statues in town.

Today the few remaining ruins of Memphis make it difficult to form an idea of the nature of ancient Egyptian dwellings. Some coffins crafted in the form of houses from the Old Kingdom hint at their formal particularities. These buildings had a rather ordinary character, and the numerous representations in Memphite tombs indicate that their details were often arbitrary. They were built with mud bricks and often adorned with bright colors and ornaments. Pillars projected slightly from the walls to support beams, which supported their flat roofs. The broader piers were hung with carpets, each with its own pattern and color. Representations of doors similar to those of ancient homes were also found in tombs in Memphis—some simple, others ornamented, but all in bright colors.

The detailed reliefs in some of these tombs include scenes of daily life and give some idea of the costumes and occupations of the royal court. Often the dwellings of the rich were built with stone. They might take the form of either detached or semidetached, two-story townhouses in urban settlements; or if they were built on agricultural estates, they might be larger country houses with clerestory windows. Some granaries in the form of mud-brick silos were found in larger houses, and storehouses appear to have been spread throughout. Two types of palaces served the royalty. One was the residential palace in the capital, from which much of the government was administered. The second type was built within or attached to temples that were used by the kings in festivals and other religious rituals.[17]

Although ancient Egypt was predominantly a rural society throughout much of its history (despite minor competition from Thebes), Memphis was its chief city. But it is important to remember that very little physical evidence of its daily life remains, except what can be gathered from the reliefs on ancient temples. Smaller cities, such as Deir el-Medina and the worker town of Amarna, provide much of what we know about ancient Egyptian settlements. Those towns demonstrate a simple planning scheme, often consisting of a central street flanked on each side by a row of contiguous, uniformly laid houses.[18]

Today the site of the ancient city of Memphis lies near the village of Mit Rahina. At the beginning of the twentieth century, some of its ruined walls were still visible, but these have now disappeared. The only monument above ground is a colossal statue of Ramses II, which had once adorned the great temple of Ptah. Ramses II erected several colossi in the temple. Some believe that the Serapeum, dedicated to the cult of Apis, the bull-god, and built in the form of a labyrinth, was begun under Khaemwaset, the son of Ramses II, when he was the high priest of Ptah at Memphis.

A fundamental aspect of ancient Egyptian culture was a belief in the afterlife. This governed the daily life of both rich and poor and shaped the ancient Egyptian city and village. Unfortunately there is little evidence that allows us to speculate on the experience of average urban residents, because there is nothing left of the spaces they inhabited. Archaeological investigations have instead centered on the temples, tombs, and pyramids of the greater Memphis region. However, it would be a mistake to try to understand this huge necropolis, extending from Memphis to Giza in the north and Darshur in the south, simply known as the City of the Dead. The City of the Living or Thebes and the City of the Dead should rather be looked upon as an integral unit. Together, these different environments tell us about the culture of ancient Egypt—that is, the beliefs and values of its citizens and rulers.

It is critical to understand how much of ancient Egyptian urban civilization was based on erecting and maintaining monumental structures of the necropolis. The majority of ancient Egyptians lived their entire lives in the shadows of these large-scale construction projects. And once these projects were complete, scores of others were required to service them. Throughout its history—as one of the longest inhabited sites in the history of the world—the Memphis region has witnessed numerous rises and falls in population, and these have often corresponded with the need for workers at its nearby pyramids and other funerary complexes.

Most of the burials that took place in the necropolis of Memphis were held in the two main cemeteries at Giza and Saqqara, but many of the kings of the later dynasties built their pyramids and temples midway between these locations. The earliest tombs at Saqqara were built out of mud brick and had a rectangular layout with a flat roof and slightly sloping walls. These structures are known today as *mastaba,* an Arabic term meaning bench. The part of the structure that stood above ground was usually a storeroom stocked with objects for the afterlife.

The oldest of these pyramids was built circa 2600 BC by King Djoser and his chief architect, Imhotep. During the rule of Djoser, a change in the techniques of construction brought a major transformation to the Saqqara necropolis. To distinguish his tomb from earlier monuments, Djoser ordered that the traditional mud bricks be replaced by cut stone. Thus, the Egyptian historian Manetho attributed the invention of building in stone to Imhotep, the king's legendary chief counselor and architect. It is believed that Imhotep revised the design of the tomb six times, the final version resembling six mastabas stacked on top of one other. The Step Pyramid, as it came to be known, was the tallest pyramid at the time, rising to 62 meters and measuring 118 by 140 meters at its base. It brought its architect the praise and admiration of the entire kingdom, and led to his later deification and identification with the Greek demigod Asclepios.[19]

Saqqara is an extensive stretch of land overlooking the city of Memphis at the edge of the western desert. It is considered the largest cemetery of Egypt. Altogether, its necropolis includes about twenty pyramids and

Figure 1.3   The Step Pyramid of Djoser.

royal tombs along with hundreds of mastabas and private tombs scattered around the Step Pyramid, its most important monument. Fifty years after Djoser's death, however, another massive pyramid, the Pyramid at Meidum, was constructed sixty-four kilometers south of Saqqara and Memphis. Although it is believed this pyramid was originally built by King Huni, it was his son-in-law, King Snefru, the founder of the Fourth Dynasty (2675–2565 BC) of the Old Kingdom, who is credited with covering it with granite. This innovation created the first of what would be considered archetypal pyramids of Egypt. King Snefru also built two more pyramids, the Red Pyramid and the Bent Pyramid, south of Memphis at Darshur.

Tourist visits to the pyramids are not just a phenomenon of recent history. As early as the New Kingdom, Egyptian travelers were visiting these sites and other ancient temples in what is now the Cairo area. Inscriptions found carved in the stone of the monuments bear evidence to these ancient tourists. In one inscription, "Ahmose, son of Iptah," who visited the Step Pyramid of Saqqara around 1600 BC, writes that the monument looks as though heaven were within it. Another visitor, "Hednaks, son of Tewosret," expresses his admiration for the pyramids, asking the gods

Figure 1.4   The Red (above) and Bent (below) Pyramids of Snefru.

to allow him "a full lifetime in serving your good pleasure" and a "good burial after a happy old age."[20]

King Khufu, Snefru's successor (also known as Cheops) returned north to a prominent site on the plateau of Giza to build his pyramid. This site was also later used by two kings, Khafra and Menkaura of the Fourth Dynasty, and became the best-known pyramid complex in the world. The three pyramids at Giza were arranged in chronological order from northeast to southwest, descending in volume, size, and level of perfection.[21] The size and grandeur of Khufu's pyramid in Giza can be taken as reflections of the overall strength, comprehensive centralization, and effectiveness of his rule. The Great Pyramid of Khufu originally stood 147 meters high. It is estimated to contain 2.3 million limestone blocks, averaging 2.5 tons each, and covering an area of thirteen hectares—equivalent to nearly eighteen soccer fields.[22]

Figure 1.5　The Great Pyramids at Giza in the nineteenth century.

Herodotus reported that this pyramid demanded the labor of one hundred thousand men over a period of twenty years, and its construction a labor site comparable to a small city. The sheer size of such an enterprise makes it arguably one of the most formidable building projects in the history of humanity.[23] Some of its masonry was executed with such finesse that blocks of considerable weight were set together with lengthy joints only a ten-thousandth of an inch wide completed with exquisitely fine edgework. The entire monument was made of limestone, though the main sepulchral chamber was made of granite.

The Pyramid of Khafra or Khefron (and sometimes spelled Chephron), as it became known, is situated to the southwest of Khufu's pyramid. While actually two and a half meters shorter, it gives the impression of being taller because it is built on slightly higher ground. Its related funerary temples have now been mostly destroyed, except for the granite temple that stands near the Sphinx, the most essential ceremonial structure of the complex. The third pyramid of Giza, built by Menkaura (or Mycerinus), occupies less than half the area taken by the Great Pyramid and is only sixty-six meters high. However, its placement and proportions are what give the Giza complex its distinctive aesthetic identity.

The Giza Sphinx is not only the oldest sphinx in Egypt, but also the largest.[24] Beyond it lies the Sphinx Temple, which is made entirely of limestone. Khufu's descendant Menkaura ordered the work on the colossal sphinx, which has Khafra's features and royal headdress but the body of a lion. Historians believe that the Great Sphinx is actually Khafra transformed into Horus, the ancient Egyptian god of kingship, giving offerings to the god Re. According to the legend, an Arab ruler who was not fond of the Sphinx's smile destroyed its nose, although another story attributes its destruction to Napoleon's cannons during the Battle of the Pyramids against the Mamluks.[25] It is likely, however, that the Sphinx's nose and beard no longer exist simply due to wear and tear over time.

The last of the Egyptian pyramids was erected about three centuries after those at Giza. King Pepi II, who was the last to rule over centralized Egypt, erected the last Old Kingdom pyramid at Saqqara.

Over the past fifty years, the Egyptian government has labored to

Figure 1.6   The Sphinx and the Pyramid of Khafra in the nineteenth century. ━━━━━

prevent any development on the Giza Plateau. However, one major activity that can be observed near there is the construction of the Grand Egyptian Museum. Nearby, to the northeast, one can also see a number of modern structures, most of which are hotels for foreign tourists. The most prominent of these is the Mena House Hotel, built to house visitors for the opening of the Suez Canal in 1869. On the southeastern side sits the village of Nazlet al-Samman, now a bustling informal settlement whose residents cater primarily to tourists, Egyptian visitors, and students who wish to experience the Great Pyramids.

This brings us to the end of our first story. Although criticized for his methods, Mariette, who helped discover and bring the sites of ancient Egypt to life, had always insisted on preserving ancient Egyptian monuments. It was he who convinced the ruler of Egypt at the time to ban the trade of ancient Egyptian antiquities. Without Mariette, Egypt would not have discovered the importance of its monuments during the time of its modern nation-building project.

Later in life, Mariette spoke of "the Egyptian decoy duck, who welcomes you blithely, but if you let yourself be duped by his innocent air, you are lost! One peck and he injects his venom, and there you are, an Egyptologist for the rest of your life."[26] Due to his efforts, along with those of younger Egyptian Egyptologists, the country has one of the most elaborate and exquisite museums of ancient history and art in the world. For this, Mariette was accorded the prized title *pasha*.

It is perhaps the ultimate irony that all of these developments occurred at the height of European colonial expansion into the Middle East. The preservation of Egypt's ancient legacy required a man from France to follow in the footsteps of another Frenchman, Napoleon. Napoleon had conquered Egypt six decades earlier. His interest in the country was not only about empire, it was also fueled by his fascination with the Egyptian people. This fascination ultimately prompted the West's rediscovery of Egypt. Mariette's obsession with Egypt, on the other hand, was marked by a desire to collect and preserve ancient historical artifacts. Both men were driven by what they viewed as a mission to civilize; but only one, Mariette, ended up believing that he had, in turn, been civilized by Egypt's past.

Even when Egypt fell to the British Empire and became one of its colonies, Mariette continued with his work for a few more months. His commitment to Egypt's ancient monuments served as his method of repayment. His efforts enabled Egypt to recognize its own ancient past, which later helped the country define itself as a new nation-state after achieving independence from the British. Indeed, many empires have often seen themselves as the keepers of universal heritage, particularly when their colonial subjects have not understood the significance of such heritage.

Accidents of history have allowed for the preservation of much of Egypt's ancient heritage, which was neither the focus nor the passion of many of its rulers, let alone much of its population from the end of the Pharaonic Era until present time. Perhaps colonial ideas, later adopted by the nation-state, were what allowed many ancient Egyptian monuments to escape the fate of the Buddhas in Bamian in Afghanistan, which were destroyed under the Islamic orthodox regime of the Taliban at the beginning of the twenty-first century.

At the beginning of the twentieth century, Egypt, a new semi-independent kingdom, mourned Mariette's death and rendered him near-royal in its honors to him. He was buried at the very entrance to his museum at Bulaq, in a tomb of white marble with a bronze statue. The following words are engraved on the pedestal: "À Mariette Pacha, l'Égypte Reconnaissante."[27] When the museum moved to its current location in downtown Cairo, Mariette's grave was moved along with it. Now that the Grand Egyptian Museum is under construction at the foot of the Giza Plateau, it is poetic justice that Mariette, who spent most of his productive life excavating the great treasures of ancient Egypt in that area, will finally return home.

Figure 1.7   Tomb of Auguste Mariette at the Egyptian Museum, Cairo.

From Ancient Egypt
to the Coptic Enclave

MOST TOURISTS TO MODERN CAIRO are advised by guidebooks to visit the pyramids in Giza and the bazaars in the medieval quarters of the city, often referred to as Islamic Cairo. If time allows, they are then encouraged to visit Coptic Cairo, the Christian urban enclave that existed at the time of the Arab Islamic takeover of Egypt in the second half of the seventh century. After all, the people of Egypt were among the first in the world to adopt Christianity.

Today, an intriguing building stands among the few remains and the multiple reconstructions of this Coptic town. This is the Coptic Museum, a structure of little architectural significance, but one that captures the spirit of a time long gone. The museum stands partly on the ruins of a large round tower. Looking west, where the current Mar Girgis Station of the Cairo Metro lies, one sees a place where the Nile once flowed; and looking east, one can see the area where the Arabs settled on barren land following their conquest of Egypt. At that time, cultivated land existed both north and south of the city.

The tower is part of what remains of the historic fortress of Babylon, which is to play a central role in our story. The museum itself exists due to the efforts of a few individuals, notably Markus Simaika, an Egyptian Copt who was as essential to the discovery and remaking of a Coptic Cairo as Auguste Mariette was to the rediscovery and imagining of ancient Egypt. Following the Arab conquest, the Copts, or *Qibt*, lived as a segregated religious minority that was merely tolerated by Egypt's Muslim majority. But in the early twentieth century, they emerged as the proud inheritors of Egypt's ancient civilization. Simaika's work contributed to both this

Figure 2.1   The Coptic Museum.

development and the consequent preservation of Coptic Cairo, a small district in the city that claims to represent Coptic life and culture of the seventh and eighth centuries.

Markus Simaika (1864–1944) grew up in the predominantly Coptic quarter north of Ezbekiyeh in Cairo. He attended the Coptic school founded by Patriarch Cyril VI—the first of such schools that shaped the identity of a generation of Copts. Simaika was a pioneer in arousing enthusiasm for Coptic history, and his interest in the archaeology of Coptic settlements both emerged from and contributed to his advocacy of social reform in the way Copts viewed both their past and their modern identity during a period of dramatic transition.[1]

Simaika gave an account in his memoirs of an encounter he had with Patriarch Cyril in the winter of 1908.[2] For fundraising purposes, the patriarch considered melting silver gospel covers and church vessels bearing fifteenth-century inscriptions. Simaika, then vice president of the Coptic Community Council, offered to pay above market value for the silver. In doing so, he preserved the objects and began a collection that was later housed in Cairo's Coptic Museum.[3] It is interesting that this seemingly incidental strategy was almost identical to that employed by Mariette with regard to ancient Egyptian artifacts a few decades earlier.

During the British occupation of Egypt, colonial authorities often relied on the Christian minorities, mainly Armenians and Copts, to bridge the divide between the British and the predominantly Muslim population. But Copts, who had a longer history in the region and spoke Arabic as their mother tongue, also claimed solidarity with the Muslim majority by rejecting collaboration with the British Empire. Indeed, Coptic intellectuals later played an important role in the Egyptian nationalist movement and the making of the new nation-state in the twentieth century.

In 1881, one year prior to the British invasion of Egypt, the Comité de Conservation des Monuments de l'Art Arabe, known more commonly as the Comité, was established. A private, government-supported group of prominent Egyptians and resident Europeans, it claimed responsibility for the protection and conservation of the historic monuments of Cairo. The Comité was in charge of creating an inventory of these monuments and of evaluating the degree of care needed to preserve and restore ailing buildings. Coptic participation in the Comité began when Simaika and others argued that Cairo's Coptic monuments should also be placed under the Comité's jurisdiction. This constituted an important political step toward integrating the built heritage of the Coptic community with that of the rest of the Egyptian nation. The history of Coptic Cairo, however, cannot be told without a larger reflection on the developments that attended the slow disintegration of Egypt's ancient civilization and the emergence of Christianity in its place.

A country that has existed as long as Egypt encompasses not only multiple histories but also many chapters in the histories of other civilizations. Ancient Egyptian civilization, which lasted three millennia, did not die abruptly. It did, however, undergo considerable transformation when Alexander the Great conquered its lands in 332–331 BC. That conquest, which was followed by nearly three centuries of Greek control, gave rise to the Ptolemaic dynasty and resulted in the establishment of Alexandria as Egypt's new capital. In the centuries that followed, Egypt would become part of the Roman and Byzantine empires. These later occupations would be superseded by the Arab conquest, which would bring a total transformation of Egypt through its absorption into Arab Islamic civilization.

Egyptians often proudly speak of their country as "the tomb of all conquerors." Although the reality of conquest is more complicated, there is some truth to this epigram. Most of those who have conquered Egypt have found it convenient, desirable, or necessary to change their own habits, customs, and even religions to fit the Egyptian mold or to adopt Egyptian identity altogether as a means of governing the territory.

In this respect, the history of Coptic Cairo remains one of the least researched aspects of the city. This is partly the result of the paucity of physical evidence that can be tied to the stories and myths of this period, as Cairo is not often thought of as a Christian city. Nevertheless, it is important to recognize that Christianity was the main religion of the region for a good half millennium before the Arab conquest. And the most pivotal and long-lasting expression of that identity has been the Coptic Church.

The words *Copt* and *Egypt* are most likely derived from the ancient Egyptian *hi-ka-Ptah,* which means "the house of the spirit of Ptah." Ptah was the god of the ancient Egyptian city of Memphis. Prior to Alexander's invasion, the Greeks may have pronounced *Hikaptah* as "Aigyptos," which ultimately became "Egypt." The Arabs initially referred to the inhabitants of Egypt as the Qibt. But by the time of their invasion, they used the word settlement, or *misr,* to describe all of Egypt, and specifically the dense urban settlements of the Nile Delta. It was a term they used to describe many conquered lands, and today Egyptians from all over the country refer to Cairo simply as Misr.

During this period, Cairo's development was intertwined with that of the city of Alexandria. When the Greeks conquered Egypt, they were already familiar with the area of the Nile Delta along the Mediterranean through the writings of Homer. In 331 BC, Alexander took the notable step of founding a city there. According to the historian Diodorus Siculus, Alexander himself specified the layout and orientation of its streets. He then ordered that Alexandria be developed according to a mix of Egyptian traditions, local knowledge, and distinctively Greek features.[4]

Following Alexander's death in 323 BC, one of his generals became ruler of Egypt. Assuming the title of king under the name Ptolemy Soter in 306 BC, he was eventually crowned pharaoh in 304 BC.[5] Under a succession of Ptolemaic rulers, Alexandria continued to grow through the first century BC, achieving great prominence in the eastern Mediterranean.

During the rule of the last Ptolemaic monarch, Cleopatra VII, Egypt became the object of desire of an imperially aspiring Rome. When Cleopatra became queen in 51 BC, Alexandria was the only city in the Mediterranean region that rivaled Rome. The subsequent historical accounts of Cleopatra's involvement with Julius Caesar and Mark Antony relay interesting details about Alexandria and the everyday life of its people.

After Julius Caesar conquered Egypt, Cleopatra realized that she would need his protection to remain ruler. When she offered her political support to Caesar, she not only gained him as an ally but also became his mistress. In the years to follow, she would rule Egypt along with her brother, Ptolemy XIV, and eventually give birth to a son, Ptolemy Caesar. Although the name suggests a blood tie, it has not been confirmed that the child was the son of the Roman. After Caesar's assassination in Rome in 44 BC, Mark Antony became Caesar's successor, and later also Cleopatra's ally and lover. He once again allowed her to rule, not as protected sovereign but as an independent monarch.[6]

The demise of Cleopatra and Mark Antony in the year 30 BC is described in great detail in Plutarch's biography of Mark Antony. He relates that when the queen heard of the defeat of Mark Antony by the Roman emperor Octavian, she took refuge in her tomb. Believing that Cleopatra was no longer alive, Mark Antony took his own life. Soon afterward, Cleopatra committed suicide as well, putting an end to almost three centuries of Ptolemaic pharaohs, and marking the start of direct Roman rule of Egypt.[7]

The Roman military presence in Egypt originally consisted of three legions: one in Alexandria, one in Thebes in Upper Egypt, and a third across the Nile from Memphis in a fortress named Babylon, parts of which still stand in old Cairo.[8] During this period, Alexandria remained the administrative center of Egypt, but Babylon became the Roman

Empire's most strategic outpost.[9] It is believed that Emperor Trajan built the fortress of Babylon in 98. He may have used an earlier garrison site dating back to a Babylonian occupation of Egypt, either during the time of Nebuchadnezzar or Cambyses; and it is possible that the fortress took its name from that history. But it is equally possible the name derived from *Bab-li-on,* meaning "the gate to On," which was the biblical name of the nearby ancient city of Heliopolis.[10]

During the third century, under the pressures of invasions and economic instability, the Roman Empire started to crumble. Its decline culminated in 476 when the last emperor of its western territories, Romulus Augustus, was deposed by the German general Odoacer, who became the first non-Roman ruler of Italy. More than a century before, in 330, the Byzantine Empire had been born when Constantine moved the capital of Rome's eastern territories to Byzantium.[11] That city, on the site of modern-day Istanbul, was first known as New Rome; its name later changed to Constantinople.

The rise of Constantinople corresponds with the spreading influence of the Byzantine Empire, which lasted for a millennium following the fall of Rome. The city quickly grew to eclipse Alexandria as a center of power, culture, and commerce, and in the years to follow, Egypt would come under its control.[12] During this time, Constantinople also became an important religious center, contributing to the spread of Christianity, which had been legalized by Constantine in 313. However, Egypt considered itself the true cradle of Christianity. Egypt was where the Holy Family had sought refuge in its flight from Judea, and it was a prominent location for Christian institutions. Most Christian theological doctrines were also born in Egypt, particularly following an early dispute over the nature of the origins of Christ.

The dispute originated in 325 in Nicaea when an Egyptian presbyter, Arius, declared his thesis that God, the Father, was divine, eternal, and without beginning, and that Jesus, the Son, was simply his begotten human extension, born in time and place. Influenced by Athanasius, another Alexandrian theologian, the Nicaea Council rejected Arius's doctrine and declared that Jesus was of the same substance as God. Athanasius's view was eventually adopted as orthodoxy by the Christian Church and led to the consolidation of orthodox Christian views in the Nicene Creed.

The dispute continued to simmer until the Second Ecumenical Council of Constantinople, which mandated that all parts of the empire accept the orthodox position. In 381, as a result of this discord, the Egyptian Church based in Alexandria, split from the Byzantine Church. Finally in 451, when the Council in Chalcedon further declared the doctrine of "God as one in two natures," the Egyptian Church, later known as the Coptic Church, rejected the compromise and insisted on the supremacy of Christ's divine nature. This belief, which became known as the monophysite position, fragmented Christians in Egypt into two feuding camps—those, known as the Malekites, who followed Constantinople and accepted the idea of one in two natures, and the Copts, who followed Alexandria.

Egyptian Copts were persecuted for their beliefs under the Byzantine emperor Phocas (602–610) at a time when the Byzantines were at war with the Sassanian Empire of Persia. Heraclius, who had succeeded Phocas, made important institutional and cultural reforms to the Byzantine Empire. For one, Heraclius replaced Latin with Greek as the official language. But such changes were short-lived in the face of military advancements of the Persians, who conquered Egypt in 617, along with Palestine. Within three years the Persians established a dominion there. Although they took significant war spoils from these captured territories, the Persians also tolerated different forms of Christianity.[13] Most significantly, they allowed the Copts to practice their religion independent of Byzantium.

A young priest by the name of Benjamin had proven himself an adept theologian in the Coptic tradition, and in 621, under Persian occupation, he was elected the first patriarch of Alexandria. Through his position, Benjamin consolidated Coptic Christianity and defended Coptic rights over a ten-year period. But in 629, as the result of a major victory by Emperor Heraclius in Persia, the Persian army was forced to retreat. In 631 Cyrus was appointed governor of Egypt and patriarch of Alexandria, replacing Benjamin, thus reestablishing Byzantine authority. He immediately launched a new campaign to enforce religious conformity with Byzantium in Egypt.[14]

During this time, the majority of Egyptians continued to oppose Byzantine rule, and heavy taxation only increased their dissent. In religious terms, the Copts also opposed what they believed to be the heretic beliefs of the Malekites (also known as the Chalcedonians from the time of the Council in Chalcedon). The population of Egypt was further linguistically divided between the elite, predominantly Greek-speaking Malekites, and the majority, mainly Coptic-speaking Copts.[15] In an attempt to unify the empire, Emperor Heraclius tried to impose a new doctrine that decreed that Christ—as the Son of God—had two natures, human and divine, but that he had only one will and one energy. The position became known as the monothelite doctrine. But the Copts, led by their beloved Benjamin, the original patriarch of Alexandria, opposed the imperial edict, and they continued with their dissension.[16]

To enforce the new doctrine, Cyrus was forced to engage in severe persecution of the Copts. He forced Benjamin into exile, and the entire Coptic communion was impelled to operate in secret. After Benjamin fled, his brother joined the rebellion against Cyrus and was eventually captured and executed. The persecution of the Copts continued in succeeding years, as Cyrus confiscated the assets of all who followed Benjamin and turned many of the Coptic churches over to the Malekites.[17]

While these conflicts were playing out within the Christian communities in Egypt, another movement was sweeping westward. Islam, born in Arabia at the beginning of the seventh century, would bring profound change to the entire region. The Islamic conquest did not necessarily bring about immediate destruction of its ancient cities. Indeed, Islamic generals found little resistance from local populations, which were under the rule of the declining Sassanian and Byzantine Empires.

The Arab campaign in Egypt began in the summer of 640. It was led by 'Amr ibn al-'As, one of the Prophet's Companions, who proposed to Caliph Omar a strategy to occupy Egypt as a way to defend against a possible attack from the Byzantine governor of Jerusalem. As 'Amr advanced along the coast into Egypt, he was first able to draw the Byzantine forces into open battle and defeat them. Then, after the remaining Byzantine army sought refuge in the old Roman fortress of Babylon, he turned south to confront them there rather than advance to Alexandria.

Despite his military superiority, 'Amr was not able to attack the fortress directly. Instead, he was forced to engage in a lengthy siege that led to negotiations with Patriarch Cyrus. 'Amr gave Cyrus three options: convert to Islam and be granted social equality; accept religious freedom with second-rank social status in exchange for taxation; or continue with open war.[18] Cyrus chose religious freedom with taxation. Emperor Heraclius, in Constantinople, opposed the compromise. Cast into disgrace with the emperor, Cyrus was recalled to Constantinople. Shortly afterward, however, Heraclius passed away, and the empire was thrown into turmoil.

After seven months of siege and dealing with a destabilized Byzantine regime, the Arabs finally conquered Babylon in the spring of 641. With the fall of the ancient fortress, they set their sights on Alexandria, which was a much more difficult prize. Had it not been for internal Egyptian political divisions, Alexandria would have been impossible to conquer. Cyrus, who believed it was crucial to reach an understanding with the Arab forces to preserve Christianity in Egypt, returned from exile and began secret negotiations with 'Amr. His strategy eventually led to the Treaty of Alexandria, signed in November 641 by Caliph Omar and the son of Heraclius, the new Byzantine emperor, Heraclonas.[19]

The treaty brought with it a complete handover of Egypt to the Arabs, while it preserved the right of resident Jews and Christians to practice their religions freely. After the Arabs occupied Alexandria, with the permission of 'Amr, the Coptic patriarch Benjamin was also allowed to return from exile. Restored to all of the positions from which he had been removed under Cyrus, he was again recognized as the sole representative of the Egyptians. Although the Copts were made to pay higher taxes in exchange for their religious freedom, Benjamin immediately set out to restore their morale and places of worship. He dedicated the remainder of his life to recovering the losses endured from the oppression of Copts and restoring unity to a population fragmented by religious separatism.[20]

As the Arabs consolidated their military rule in Egypt, 'Amr sought advice from the Coptic patriarch. He filled administrative seats with converts to Islam as well as Copts, thereby increasing the latter group's power. However, when Uthman acceded to the caliphate in Medina, 'Amr was abruptly called back to Arabia. By this time, the Arab presence in Egypt had grown into an organized settlement of about ten thousand to fifteen thousand soldiers, from various tribes. Undoubtedly, events in Arabia often had reverberations in Egypt, and vice versa. Thus, when the caliph allowed the new governor of Egypt to raise taxes on the Copts, a revolt ensued, which ultimately resulted in the assassination of Uthman.

During that period, prompted by excessive taxation, the Greeks of Alexandria also asked for help from Byzantium. Emperor Constans sent a fleet, and the Byzantines reconquered the city. However, 'Amr was soon reappointed military commander, and he took back the city from the Byzantine army without any difficulty. Having played a significant role in the founding of the Umayyad caliphate, with Damascus as its capital, 'Amr was then reaffirmed as governor of Egypt in 658, and he ruled until his death in 664.[21]

The Arab military conquest had come during a time of deep political and ethnic conflict among the Egyptian population. In hindsight, it is possible to argue that the religious schism engendered by the debates in the ecumenical councils ultimately allowed for the transformation of Egypt into a Muslim nation. Scholars also believe the Arab conquest would have been impossible without the capture of the fortress at Babylon. Its position on the Nile was of great strategic significance, and it allowed the Arabs to spread their influence over the region.

It was at the site of 'Amr's headquarters during the siege of Babylon that the principal Arab outpost in the region, Fustat, would eventually emerge. Fustat embodied the early Arab settlers' need to distance themselves from the ancient Egyptian city of Memphis across the Nile, which was still partially inhabited. Caliph Omar, ruling from Arabia, was interested in the Babylon area because he wanted to see the canal (established under Trajan) restored, as it linked the Nile to the Red Sea. The canal had once allowed Egypt's crops to be shipped throughout the Roman Empire, and it would have been equally useful for the Arabs, whose homelands were connected to Red Sea ports.

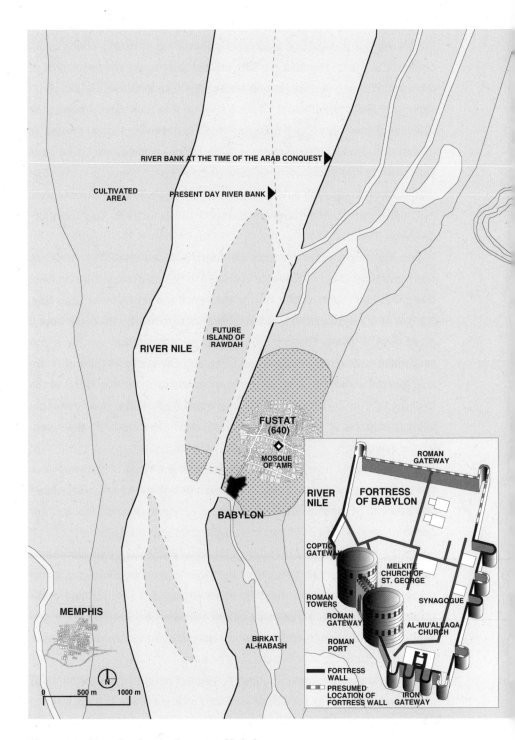

Figure 2.2   Map showing the Fortress of Babylon.

The origins of the modern-day recreation of Coptic Cairo, which incorporates the site of the historic Babylon fortress, is an important part of the story. Throughout Byzantine times, the area enclosed by Babylon's walls was likely small—around six hectares. But there was a large area to its south that was likely occupied by Copts who provided services to its garrison. Around the time of the Arab conquest, the Copts could have called the fortress *Babylon an Khemi*, or Babylon of Egypt. It is possible that this gave rise to the Arabic name *Kasr ash Shama,* or the place of wax. This name, which may have symbolized a fallen fortress, held for many centuries.[22]

During this period of the Arab conquest, Babylon most likely had only one Byzantine church. Little else is known of the edifices that would have stood within it.[23] Meanwhile, during the first three centuries of Arab rule, the site of the old fortress was completely taken over by the local Coptic population, allowing the construction of many new churches there and its transformation into a Coptic town. At least three historic churches are now located within the perimeter of the ancient fortress. The fact that the majority of Coptic churches in this area existed inside the ruins of the old fortress is probably the result of the Arab decision to settle to the northeast at Fustat.

Archaeological investigations indicate that the walls of Babylon were originally over two meters thick and eighteen meters high, interrupted on the south by four tall bastions, of which only two remain. The western portion bears no traces of bastions, indicating that the Nile once flowed under the wall, allowing boats to travel beneath it, while a gate connected two of the bastions on the south wall.[24] The towers were circular, about thirty meters in diameter, and contained complex, winding staircases leading to the top. Ruins of these structures were still in existence at the beginning of the nineteenth century, and were shown in an illustration created during Napoleon's expedition to Egypt.

At the time of the Arab conquest, the view from the top of the bastions must have reached as far as the ancient Egyptian cities of Heliopolis to the northeast and Memphis to the southwest.[25] Arab writers mention that the fortress overlooked the Nile and was accessible through a main

Figure 2.3   The Fortress of Babylon during the time of the Napoleonic expedition (above). Remains of a circular tower at the Fortress of Babylon (below). ━━━━━

entry point, known as the Iron Gate. Records from the time following the conquest also relate that the land east of the fortress was barren and uninhabited, while the northern area was cultivated with vineyards and occupied by several churches. In addition, the fortress was situated near the island of Rawdah, itself surrounded by fortified walls, partially torn down by 'Amr when his army attacked the area. It was precisely Babylon's strategic position close to Rawdah that created a convenient place to cross the Nile, again making it a desirable military asset.

There are two important writers we may draw upon to envision what Babylon looked like at the time of the conquest—the Coptic bishop John of Nikiu, who was a near contemporary of 'Amr; and the Arab geographer Ibn Duqmaq, who lived at the end of the fifteenth century but wrote extensively on the conquest. The account left by John of Nikiu is one of the most influential histories of the Arab conquest of Egypt written from the perspective of a native.[26] He was likely born a few years before these events, and his chronicle, written toward the end of the seventh century, survives today only in its Ethiopian translation. It describes in great detail the capture of Alexandria and Babylon by 'Amr's armies, albeit within a timeline that is contested by some historians.[27]

Eight centuries later, in a book on Egypt, Ibn Duqmaq provided a detailed account of the histories and conditions of contemporary Fustat and Alexandria. In discussing Fustat, he describes how the Roman gateway to the old fortress was still in use in the year 1400. Although the Nile had since retreated from its ruined walls, he tells of boats coming up to an iron gate between its towers and how the gate, which opened onto a quay, served as its main entrance. To pass through, one had to go under the Coptic church of al-Mu'allaqa, or the "hanging church."[28] Ibn Duqmaq also gives a detailed description of the other churches inside the fortress, including explanations of its street and gate names, all of which offer insights into the transformation of Babylon following its conquest by 'Amr and his armies.[29]

Of the three important Christian structures within the remains of the fortress, the church of al-Mu'allaqa, dedicated to the Virgin Mary, is claimed to be one of the oldest Coptic structures in Egypt. It was also

Figure 2.4 The Church of al-Mu'allaqa.

Figure 2.5   The interior of the Church of al-Mu'allaqa.

one of the first churches to follow the basilica typology, with three aisles, a narthex, and a tripartite sanctuary. It was likely begun in the seventh century, probably on the site of another church dating from the third century. The land surface has likely risen by almost six meters since Roman times, diminishing its visual prominence. However, its location in the city is also a subject of debate, because it was built over walls that would have made the use of the river gate impossible—although this may be an indication it was built after the Arab conquest. Ibn Duqmaq describes the church only as it existed in the fifteenth century, and gives no account of its interior except that the main entrance to the fortress passed through the Iron Gate beneath it.[30]

Dedicated to the martyrs Sergius and Bacchus, the church of Abu Serga, or St. Sergius, is the second important Christian monument within the old fortress site. It was built on top of a cave where Copts believe the Holy Family had once stayed. Also dating to the seventh century, the church is mentioned by the nineteenth-century archaeologist Émile Clément Amélineau in a book on the life of Patriarch Isaac. The church is described as having a unique layout, with two aisles and no choir or transept.[31]

The church of St. George is the third major Christian edifice on the fortress site. Today it is the main Greek Orthodox church of Cairo. Built in the tenth century atop a deteriorating Roman tower, it can be reached by a flight of stairs, from which one may find a relief of St. George and the Dragon. The foundations of the church date to the seventh century and are believed to be the remains of the original church built by the wealthy scribe Athanasius in 684, which had burned down. The only section of that original structure that remains today is a rectangular area, known as the Wedding Hall, which still displays the remnants of fresco and stucco decorations.

Another monument that might have existed on the site at the time of the Arab conquest was a synagogue, converted from a Coptic church dedicated to St. Michael, dating from before the time of the conquest. It was demolished in the nineteenth century and replaced with a new Jewish place of worship.[32] Today these structures define an area that is known as Coptic Cairo.

Figure 2.6   The Church of St. George.

Markus Simaika remains the central figure of Coptic heritage, not only by pioneering the search for a Coptic legacy, but also by negotiating between the British, the patriarch, and the Communal Council, and advocating the historic preservation of Coptic monuments.

Returning to where we started, in 1905 Simaika founded the Coptic Museum on the site of old Babylon.[33] Initially arranged in the halls of al-Mu'allaqa church, the collection of Coptic artifacts was eventually moved to an adjacent structure designed by Max Herz. Under the aegis of the Comité, the collection grew in the following years. The building was later expanded by the young architect Achille Patricolo, who also designed a façade that replicated that of the Fatimid mosque of al-Aqmar. The Comité was in charge of administering the museum, while the Coptic patriarchate remained the owner of the collection until the state took it over in 1931.[34]

Throughout its years of operation, the Comité attempted to recast Cairo as a medieval city through the conservation of Muslim monuments and through the revival of Mamluk architectural language. The more refined Mamluk architectural style was deliberately chosen as the means of advancing Egyptian heritage. In contrast, Markus Simaika's Coptic Museum was partially built as a Fatimid revival, a style and historical period that the Comité had largely ignored. Instead of opting for a Mamluk architectural language, as preferred by his colleagues on the Comité, Simaika must have approved of the museum's neo-Fatimid façade. It is possible that he did so in order to counter the stylistic paradigm employed by the Comité for the preservation of Muslim monuments. It is also possible that he favored the Fatimid style because the Fatimids were generous to the Copts when they first conquered Egypt. However, during al-Hakim's rule in the Fatimid period, the Copts were subjected to some of the harshest acts of persecution. Hence this stylistic choice makes Markus Simaika's decision rather paradoxical, resulting in a museum that commemorates Coptic religion and material culture displayed in the aesthetic language of their presumed oppressors.

In the end, Markus Simaika was able to preserve a rich collection of objects possessed by the Coptic Church. Modest at first, the museum gradually became the center of Coptic heritage—and Coptic Cairo emerged as the center of Christian life in the city. Today it remains a pilgrimage site for Cairo's Copts and tourists alike. Without it, the story of Coptic Cairo could easily have been forgotten. Like Mariette, Simaika's project of preserving fragments of history has facilitated the invention of a Coptic Cairo. During much of its existence, however, this historically rich place was not representative of Coptic Christianity but rather simply served as a place to garrison military forces under Roman and Byzantine rule in Egypt.

Fustat-Misr: The City of Arab Islam

THE MINARET OF THE MOSQUE of Ibn Tulun in Cairo is a magnificent, albeit enigmatic structure that rises above the dense fabric of the city. Short and rectangular at the base, its upper levels are wrapped in a spiral staircase that climbs to the sky, as if reaching toward God. In the thirteenth century, an observer ascending this spiral would have enjoyed panoramic views in all directions of the Fustat area. Looking south, this observer would have seen the mosque of 'Amr, possibly in decay but nevertheless an enchanting silhouette on the horizon. Further south one would have seen the walls of Babylon, the former fortress occupied by the Copts, housing their churches. Toward the west would have been the residential structures of an extended Fustat, bordered by the Nile, with the Giza pyramids in the distance. The northern panorama would have revealed the gates of al-Qahira, the Fatimid city, which was by then a well-developed urban center with many structures built by the Ayyubids and Mamluks. And turning slightly east, one would have seen the Citadel of Salah al-Din, the Muqattam Hills, and the eastern desert. This was the magnificent panorama that would have unfolded before the eyes of Lajin, the Mamluk fugitive, who made the mosque of Ibn Tulun a place of refuge.

Husam al-Din Lajin ruled Egypt for only two years (1297–1299), but he left a noteworthy legacy. As a Mamluk he belonged to a clan of soldiers brought up as slaves, whose lives were dedicated to supporting the ruling dynasties of Egypt and much of the central Middle East. Like other members of these clans, however, Lajin acquired his freedom on the battlefield. He had serious ambitions for the throne of Egypt; and as was the case for most Mamluks aspiring to positions of power, his journey required him to engage in conspiracies, deceit, and assassination attempts on a sitting ruler. Indeed, after the Mamluk sultan, al-Ashraf Khalil, defeated European Crusaders in a battle in Palestine, Lajin and some associates conspired to kill him upon his return to Cairo. The assassins were ultimately successful, but the sultan's slaves retaliated and killed all of them. Lajin was the only conspirator who managed to flee.

By the Middle Ages, Cairo had grown substantially to encompass a number of earlier settlements in the region, including the original Arab city of Fustat and its later dynastic extensions, al-Askar and al-Qata'i. But the latter, the home of the large Ibn Tulun mosque, had fallen into grave disrepair. In flight from the massacre of his fellow conspirators, Lajin chose the mosque as a hiding place. He took refuge there for several months, while plotting with his supporters to seize power from Sultan al-Ashraf's younger brother, who had been selected as the sultan's successor. While sheltered in the Ibn Tulun mosque, Lajin is said to have pledged to God that if he were to be saved and succeed in becoming sultan, he would restore the mosque to its former glory. Over the course of a few years, Lajin was able to achieve his goal, and he abided by his pledge to remake the mosque anew.[1]

Today the mosque of Ibn Tulun stands in the southern district of Cairo as a testament of the will of a governor who came to power, as many did in those times, through murder and conspiracy. The story of this mosque, as one of the major buildings in Islamic architecture, is a good place to start this chapter. It is a story, however, that cannot be told without first recounting the history of early Islam, its penetration into Egypt, and the Arab campaigns of the early caliphal regimes.

The birth of Islam occurred in Arabia in the early seventh century. Out of the wilderness of the desert and in a small town called Mecca, Muhammad, its Prophet, began preaching against a culture of pagan belief. He called for the worship of one god—Allah. His fundamental teachings included the belief that human beings must submit to God and observe five specific tenets. These were the *Shahada,* a declaration and acceptance of the oneness of God; the *Salat,* the five daily prayers; the *Siyam,* fasting during the month of Ramadan; the *Zakat,* the giving of alms; and the *Hajj,* the one-time pilgrimage to the Kaaba in Mecca.

The Muhammadan call had a strong hold over its followers, who were urged to spread the word of the new religion. In the decades that followed, the Arabs spread out and conquered the distant lands of other races. They began by unifying themselves in the Arabian Peninsula, a project they achieved while Muhammad was still alive. Then, during the reign of his immediate successors—who were given the title *caliph,* or "successor"— they took over Egypt and Syria from the ailing Byzantine Empire, and Iraq from the equally weakened Sassanian Empire.

The new Islamic Empire was not a monolithic entity. It encompassed different people with distinct cultures, national heritages, geographical conditions, and socioeconomic systems. Nevertheless, by the end of the eighth century, it extended its reach from the area in the east that today is India and China to Spain and Morocco in the west. Beginning with the rule of the Umayyads (661–750), who governed first from Damascus and later from Cordoba, and the Abbasids, who ruled out of Baghdad and later Samarra (759–1258), a new architecture and urbanism emerged commensurate with this new religion. Indeed, a considerable degree of urbanization accompanied its spread; and like any prospering civilization, Islam introduced new functions and activities to the city. Egypt was no exception, and Fustat, as one of these new urban entities, was destined to play a critical role in the history of Cairo.

As described in Chapter 2, the events that gave birth to Fustat began with the Arab military campaign in Egypt led by 'Amr ibn al-'As. 'Amr's advancing forces reached Heliopolis in July 640 and began a siege of the fortress of Babylon in September. After eight months Babylon fell, and soon after 'Amr established the garrison town of Fustat, which was to become the new capital of Egypt, itself a province of the Arab-ruled Islamic Empire.[2]

The occupation of Egypt and the establishment of Fustat must have been a victory of major proportions for the Arabs.[3] Egypt had always played an important role in their imagination; it was known not only as the center of civilization in the ancient world, but also as a place of lush greenery and plenitude—attributes largely missing from the arid lands of Arabia. The term *misr,* often used by the Arabs to describe urban places of some maturity, was later used in the plural, *amsar,* to distinguish their colonial settlements from other towns. In its early years Fustat-Misr grew into a political and administrative center at the junction of several major routes within the new empire, including those linking Upper and Lower Egypt. But the site was also important because of its proximity to the canal that linked the Babylon area to the Red Sea; originally funded by the Roman emperor Trajan, the canal had been restored at the behest of Caliph Omar as a way to link Egypt to the rest of the Islamic Empire.[4]

Garrison towns like Fustat were important creations of early Islam. They reflected the ways in which early Muslim military leaders understood the nature of their mission—namely, to keep the Arabs close to Islamic tradition and ritual. Like Basra and Kufa in Iraq, these settlements were planned and administered according to Islamic ideals of modesty and simplicity and embodied the concerns of a state still engaged in conquest. At their centers they typically included a mosque, a *dar al-imarah,* or governor's residence, and a *sahah,* or square.[5] Yet many other details of their internal organization were negotiated locally between their tribal inhabitants and the military commander or governor in charge.

The basic organizational plan of early Fustat mirrored the diversity and pluralism of Arab society. Its neighborhoods were laid out to accommodate a complicated array of tribal and clan associations.[6] Groups were given portions of land, or *khitat,* whose size reflected their relative ethnic, tribal, and economic status. This spatial arrangement, which reflected some of the values and traditions of Bedouin life in Arabia, initially grew out of the organization of 'Amr's army, which had settled on the site during the siege of Babylon. But over time the tribes mixed, grew in numbers, and began to compete with each other for territory. Gradually the settlement developed into a full-fledged city.[7]

The development of Fustat stretched over several centuries. The Arab army that came to Egypt in the seventh century initially numbered between ten and fifteen thousand soldiers.[8] But by the time they settled in the Fustat area, the soldiers numbered about thirty thousand. In those

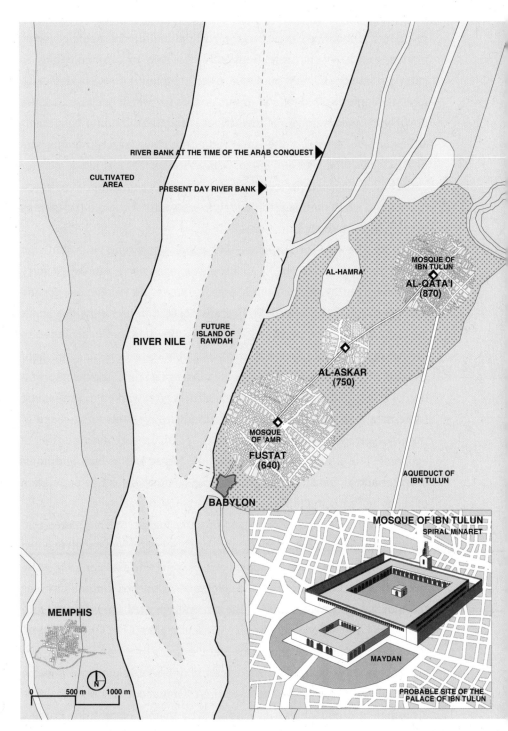

Figure 3.1   A map of Fustat and its surroundings.

years Egypt continued to undergo territorial and demographic transformation, and garrisons were frequently deployed to other locations to carry out minor military missions. After completing these duties, such forces became entitled to land grants, and many warriors chose to settle down with other members of their tribes within the allotted tribal parcels at Fustat.[9] At the peak of the Umayyad period, the central Arab quarters of Fustat near the Nile and surrounding the Babylon fort accounted for about half of Cairo's territory. The rest of the city's population were Egyptian Copts, who continued to occupy areas south of the old fortress, as they had done in Byzantine times.[10]

During the rule of the Umayyad caliph Mu'awiya (661–680), the population of Arabs in the Egyptian *diwan*, or registry, numbered forty thousand.[11] But by the mid-ninth century, when the foundations for the mosque of Ibn Tulun were laid, Fustat's population had grown to about a quarter of a million people. Some of this growth may be attributed to the influx of settlers needed to carry out military actions or implement changes of government. But the rapid increase also reflected the importation of slaves and an influx of foreign settlers who worked as craftsmen, tradesmen, and clerks in support of administrative functions needed in the city. Eventually, toward the end of the ninth century during a time of economic prosperity and political stability, Fustat and its later additions, al-Askar and al-Qata'i, merged into a single metropolis with a population of about half a million inhabitants.[12]

There were two types of streets in early Fustat: thoroughfares that facilitated inner-city circulation, and local access streets that enabled traffic within a given quarter. Main arteries were called *khit* or *tariq,* while smaller connecting streets were called *darb.* At the heart of the city was the mosque of 'Amr ibn al-'As, the general who led the Arab military campaign. 'Amr's mosque came to represent the cradle of Islam in Egypt, permanently associated with 'Amr and the first generation of the Prophet's Companions. Founded in the winter of 641–642, the mosque became the religious center of the city over time.[13] Initially it was built to serve a prominent group of warrior settlers who mainly came from Prophet Muhammad's Quraysh tribe or who were his Medina companions. Known

Figure 3.2   The Mosque of 'Amr ibn al-'As. ■

as Ahl al-Raya, "the people of the banner," they formed the commanding squad of 'Amr's conquering army and were most likely 'Amr's guards.[14] The Ahl al-Raya quarter of Fustat, which was also inhabited by other tribal groups, later became the political, administrative, and commercial nucleus of the city.[15]

As the neighborhoods around the mosque evolved into a prominent urban area, the significance of the mosque of 'Amr grew too.[16] Initially small, the mosque was expanded in stages. The first to undertake such a rebuilding was the governor Maslama ibn Mukhallad, who in 673 increased the size of the mosque and added minarets at its four corners.[17] At a later time, Maslama ibn 'Abd al-'Aziz and his son 'Abd Allah doubled its floor area; and finally, Muhtasib Kurra added a mihrab, or semicircular niche, indicating the qibla, the direction toward Mecca.[18]

During the early years of Islam, control of the cities and territories in the Middle East and Egypt shifted on several occasions. Under the Abbasid dynasty, which came to power in 750 following the collapse of the Umayyads, the center of Arab-Muslim power moved to the newly established city of Baghdad. Meanwhile, after retreating from the central Middle East, the Umayyads created a new center of power in a weak Visigoth state on the Iberian Peninsula, which had come under their control. There they established a new civilization, which was ultimately destined to compete with Baghdad, and which led to the building of such great monuments as the mosque of Cordoba and the Alhambra palace in Granada.

With the rise to power of the new caliphate, the political center in Egypt shifted away from Fustat. The Abbasid governor founded a satellite town called al-Askar, indicating its role as an army encampment, to accommodate his forces. This was situated northeast of Fustat, which was likely in poor shape following a series of raids by the Abbasid army.[19] There are no archaeological remains of al-Askar, but from a few written accounts we know that it had a central mosque and a public square for several decades.

By the ninth century, the Islamic Empire, which extended from the Iberian Peninsula to the borders of China, began to disintegrate into small fiefdoms. Many of these were still, in theory, under the rule of the caliph in Baghdad. But different political and military events led some governors to declare their territories autonomous, while in other regions rebellious groups took over and started entirely new regimes, if not new dynasties.

During this time the gradual rise of Turkish soldiers serving the Abbasids brought personalities such as Ahmad ibn Tulun to the fore. Ibn Tulun's father had been a slave brought to the court of Caliph al-Ma'mun in 815. Yet despite his humble origins, Ibn Tulun benefited from an exceptional education and became one of the most important men in the service of the caliph.[20]

Ibn Tulun received his military training in the Abbasid capital of Samarra in Iraq, where art and architecture flourished under Caliph al-Mu'tasim. A capable commander, he was able to impose his authority on Egypt in 868 after a long period of political instability. Following his military victories, Ibn Tulun was appointed to the post of governor by the Abbasid caliph. During his reign and that of his successors, known as the Tulunid dynasty, Egypt became an autonomous state for the first time since the Roman conquest, although it was nominally still under Abbasid rule.[21]

When Ibn Tulun arrived in Egypt in 870, he moved the seat of government northwest of Fustat and al-Askar to the suburb of al-Qata'i, which in Arabic means "the wards" or "the quarters." Ibn Tulun possibly modeled al-Qata'i after the city of Samarra, which is believed to have influenced his taste in art and architecture.[22] However, like al-Askar before it, al-Qata'i was not truly independent, and relied on Fustat for its economic survival.

Altogether al-Qata'i covered 1.6 square kilometers of land and included a mosque, government buildings, a hippodrome, a palace complex, or dar al-imarah, with views of the Nile and the port in Fustat, and a large square known as the al-Maydan. The palace, where Ibn Tulun established his residence, was built at the foot of a steep rock called Qubat al-Hawa, or the dome of the air, an outcrop later used by Salah al-Din for his citadel. It had nine gates, one of which, Bab as-Salat, or the Gate of Prayer, connected to the mosque via a great thoroughfare, which later became Saliba Street. Ibn Tulun built another house next to the mosque, which he used for ablution before Friday prayer.[23]

During his reign, Ibn Tulun took on infrastructural works that served the population of the area. Among these was a hospital for civilians southwest of al-Askar. He also built an aqueduct to bring water from the Nile to the palace, as the maintenance of such an extensive complex of buildings depended on a constant supply.

It is almost impossible to tell the history of a city that no longer exists, but in the case of al-Qata'i we are left with one of the most remarkable sites of Islamic culture and architecture in Cairo. This is so because the Ibn Tulun mosque, the jewel of al-Qata'i, speaks not only for the city but also for the cultural and political geography of the entire region. For the mosque of Ibn Tulun connects Egypt to Baghdad, Ibn Tulun to the Abbasid caliph, and the architecture of Egypt to major monuments of Abbasid rule, such as the mosque of Samarra. Like the city of Samarra, al-Qata'i did not survive, but the mosque of Ibn Tulun tells us much about the Islamic Empire of the ninth century and the short-lived rule of the Tulunids.

Ibn Tulun built his famous mosque between 876 and 879 on the slopes

Figure 3.3 The Mosque of Ahmad ibn Tulun.

of Jabal Yashkur.[24] The mosque was made of red brick faced with stucco, except for its minaret, which was of limestone. Such materials were new to Cairo, and historians have considered them to be evidence of stylistic influences from Samarra, where building in brick and stucco predates Islam. Although some historians have suggested that the architect of the mosque was from Samarra or Byzantium, it is also possible that he may have been an Egyptian Copt.[25] It is presumed that the architect recommended using rectangular masonry pillars, instead of columns, to build the arcades of the mosque. At the time it was common to reuse columns from churches and other structures taken as part of the spoils of war. The only evidence of this practice in the mosque of Ibn Tulun, however,

Figure 3.4   The interior of the Mosque of Ibn Tulun.

appears to be two pairs of Byzantine-style columns on each side of the prayer niche.

The mosque contained a central courtyard and six prayer halls (although some of them date from various later periods). A main mihrab located in the center of the qibla wall included a Kufic inscription of the Muslim profession of faith, "There is no god but Allah, and Muhammad is the messenger of Allah."[26] On the right side of the mihrab was a door that led to Ibn Tulun's palace, through which he accessed the pulpit.[27]

A perimeter wall created an enclosed court, or *ziyada* (meaning excess or overflow), around the main structure. These outer walls were crowned with a six-and-a-half-foot-high crenellation, whose elaborate

Figure 3.5　The doorway connecting the interior of the Mosque of Ibn Tulun to his palace.

openwork ornament echoed the Samarran motifs that adorned the walls of the mosque.[28] The unique shapes of the crenellation are known as *arias,* and have an unusual anthropomorphic character, resembling paper dolls or abstract human forms. In addition, the upper register of the outside wall had pointed arch openings enclosed with decorative stucco grills featuring elaborate geometric compositions.[29] The arches of the openings were supported by thick columns without capitals, moldings, or decorative borders. In the center courtyard was the *sahn,* once a central washing facility, which burned down in 986.[30]

The limestone minaret of the Ibn Tulun mosque had a three-meter-high rectangular base. But toward its upper portion, its form changed to a nearly circular configuration, wrapped by a counterclockwise spiraling staircase. Some sources connect this shape to that of the Samarran

Figure 3.6 The spiral minaret of the Mosque of Ibn Tulun. ▬▬▬▬▬▬

minaret known as al-Malwiya, although typical Samarran minarets of that time were built of masonry and were entirely circular.[31] Yet several historical texts describe Ibn Tulun arriving at the shape of the minaret by sheer accident.[32] They recount that he had played with a piece of paper by wrapping it around his finger, and when he released the paper, it made a spiral shape, a model that he then ordered his architect to replicate. This anecdote, however, is questionable, because the forty-meter, four-story minaret is not entirely circular.[33]

Many historians now attribute the contradiction in the minaret's form to the fact that it has undergone alterations. Some suggest that the additions made by the Mamluk sultan Lajin are what gave the minaret its final form. Lajin spent lavishly on the reconstruction of the Ibn Tulun mosque soon after coming to power. For the preceding several centuries it had been used as a caravanserai for pilgrims from North Africa on their way to and from Mecca.[34] In his aim to fulfill his pledge, Lajin not only restored the mosque to its former glory but offered funds for the establishment of a madrasa serving the four branches of Islamic theology.[35]

The stucco ornaments of the Ibn Tulun mosque show a distinct Samarran influence.[36] However, the three styles that characterize Samarran ornamentation generally exist separate from one another, but here they merge into a unique composition, primarily evident in the soffits of the arches and the piers. The decoration bordering the arches is formed of continuous bands of vegetal motifs surrounded by geometrical forms. A strip of carved wood molding, bearing inscriptions from the Quran, also runs at the top of the walls in most parts of the mosque. The molding stretches for a distance of almost two kilometers, and popular legend has it that parts of it were made from remnants of Noah's Ark.

Unlike 'Amr's mosque, the mosque of Ibn Tulun seems to have retained the integrity and coherence of its original design for more than a millennium. Although the palace and surrounding structures were mostly destroyed when Abbasid rule came to an end, the mosque has survived to become one of the most important monuments of Islamic architecture.

After Ibn Tulun's death in 884, his twenty-year-old son Khumarawayh kept the Tulunid dynasty in power.[37] Claiming hereditary rights to such an important province as Egypt without the consent of the caliph, however, was unprecedented. In order to preserve Egypt's independence and establish his authority, Khumarawayh had to go to war soon after taking power.[38] Successful military campaigns in Syria and Iraq eventually guaranteed him governance of Egypt. In addition, Khumarawayh strengthened his rule by arranging a marriage between his daughter and Caliph al-Muta'did in Baghdad.

Khumarawayh, according to historical evidence, was known for his extravagant lifestyle. He expanded and embellished the palace built by his father and converted al-Maydan into a lavish garden complex that would fuel the imaginations of writers for centuries to come. The luxurious complex contained not only rare varieties of trees and other plants but also an artificial garden with gilded trees and a menagerie.

Eventually Khumarawayh would be murdered by his eunuchs during a visit to Damascus in 896.[39] His fourteen-year-old son succeeded him in 896, but he too was assassinated after a brief rule. Soon thereafter, the Tulunid dynasty, as well as its built legacy, began its decline. Egypt and the Tulunid dynasty fell to the Abbasid caliph in 905, and al-Qata'i was almost entirely pillaged and destroyed by invading armies. Egypt subsequently underwent a short period of stability when Ikshid (who established the Ikshidi dynasty, the term meaning "king") became governor from 935 to 946. He was succeeded for two years by a regent, an Abyssinian eunuch named Abu' al-Misk Kafur, who was part of his court and the guardian of his two sons. Ikshid's sons, though next in line for the throne, were ultimately judged unfit to rule, and Kafur ruled as governor until 968.

Despite the relative political turmoil of this period, Egypt not only became a center of culture and art, but also was able to expand its territory through successful military campaigns that included the annexation of Syria.[40] In the years that followed, however, Egypt came under the weak rule of the Abbasid caliph and again entered a period of decline, which ended only when Egypt fell to the Fatimids, a Shi'ite clan from North Africa.[41] The traveler and writer Mohammed Abul-Kassem ibn Hawqal wrote about the city of Fustat, which he visited around 960. According to

Ibn Hawqal, Fustat was a thriving city that extended "about two thirds of a *farsang:* it is very well inhabited and supplied with provisions; all their houses are seven or eight stories high." Ibn Hawqal mentions the city's two principal mosques, the mosque of 'Amr and the mosque of Ibn Tulun, and the suburb of al-Qata'i, which Ibn Tulun "called to be built for his troops."[42] A bridge connected Fustat to Gezira, an island in the middle of the Nile.

Here we must return to where we started—to the brief rule of Sultan Lajin. His decision to restore the mosque of Ibn Tulun in the thirteenth century derived from his personal experience as a fugitive. During his brief rule, Egypt underwent a major survey of agricultural holdings in a manner that made the government more aware of the wealth of individuals and families, particularly those of the Mamluks. But like his predecessors, Lajin, too, was ultimately murdered by a competing Mamluk faction. It is a sharp reminder that real political events, personal ambitions, and mere whim often determine urban form.

Al-Qahira: A Fatimid Palatial Town

FROM THE AIR, few mosques compete in size with the mosque of Ibn Tulun, but the mosque of al-Hakim, originally named al-Anwar, or the illuminated, stands out for its size and its expansive interior courtyard. The mosque, located inside the northern gates of Cairo, was built by its namesake, the Fatimid caliph al-Hakim. Standing atop its short minaret today and looking south, one can see the elegant minarets of the al-Azhar mosque, where the Sunni faithful continue to pray a millennium after its founding. Al-Azhar, at its height, was the greatest institution of Islamic learning in the Middle East. During Fatimid times, the mosque became the first Shi'ite mosque in Egypt and the headquarters of Shi'a Islam.[1] Further south, one can also see the twin minarets of the mosque of al-Mu'ayyad built above Bab Zuwayla, or Zuwayla Gate, which had often been used as the gallows for captives and rebellious Mamluks. During the Fatimid period the gate connected the new town to the older city of Fustat, where much of the population resided.

On the horizon are the minarets of the Ibn Tulun and 'Amr mosques, which are obscured behind more-recent developments. These minarets mark the two cities that preceded Fatimid Cairo: al-Qata'i and Fustat. Still looking south, only a couple of hundred yards away and completely hidden from sight, lies the revamped mosque of al-Aqmar. Half of its façade was rebuilt at the end of the twentieth century to match the other half from an earlier Fatimid time. Looking north, one can see a slumlike settlement situated in an area that had been used as a cemetery until a few centuries ago. During Fatimid times, these were fields that provided much of the daily needs of the city. Looking below the minaret in the same direction, one can see Bab al-Futuh, or Conquest Gate, and Bab al-Nasr, or Victory Gate, which were built during Fatimid times and give Cairo its distinctive silhouette. All of these structures become important sites as our story turns to Fatimid Cairo. Indeed, they serve as a stage for some of the most important moments of the city's millennial history. But that is a long story, and this chapter will attempt to describe only its first two centuries.

Today, if one were to descend the minaret to enter the al-Hakim mosque during prayer time, one would be surprised by the uniformity of dress among the majority of believers there: moustached, bearded men in white skullcaps donned in long white shirts over white trousers. Yet both the dress code and the mosque's interior are relatively new additions to Cairo's landscape of piety. If one were to enter the mosque during the festival of Ashura, commemorated by Shi'ites as a day of mourning for the martyrdom of Imam Ali, the cousin and son-in-law of the Prophet, one might come across the same community of believers performing important Shi'ite rituals. Yet if one had visited the same location some forty years ago, the space would have been mere dilapidated ruins partly repurposed as a local primary school standing behind a vegetable market specializing in onions. It was only with the arrival of the Dawoodi Bohra Ismaili community that this milieu changed and gleaming white marble and gold trim were introduced.[2]

The Bohras are practicing Shi'ites who reside primarily in India and had returned to Cairo almost a thousand years after their supposed predecessors, the Fatimids, built the city, which they called al-Qahira. The Bohras came as families dedicated to the mission of reviving this city—which we will refer to from now on as Fatimid Cairo—and began their work by rebuilding its mosques. Eight miles east, in the plush neighborhood of Mohandeseen, there is a palace designed as a strange eclectic mix of Islamic styles that demonstrates this desire to re-create a distant past. It is the palatial home of Syedna Mohammed Burhanuddin, the head of the Bohra community.

Little attention had been paid to the restoration of Islamic monuments in Cairo until 1979, when an application was successfully submitted to the World Heritage Commission to declare "Medieval Cairo" a World

Heritage site. Around the same time, the Bohras secured a concession to restore several Fatimid-era monuments. The Bohra leaders were looking for ways to strengthen their community and anchor it in place, and they decided it was time to return west, to Fatimid Cairo. As many families relocated to Egypt to realize this plan, the Dawoodi Bohra leader issued several pronouncements setting out behavior guidelines for all observant Bohras. In particular, he announced a firman that set a dress code for both men and women during Ashura observances in Cairo in 1981. He also announced a major campaign to restore Fatimid architecture in Cairo to encourage *ziyaret,* a special pilgrimage that is meant to maintain the social cohesion of Bohra communities scattered over several continents.

The restoration of Fatimid architecture by the Bohras created heated debate in Cairo and was denounced by many scholars of heritage preservation.[3] These specialists sought to preserve the "authenticity" of the old core of the city, continuing a project started in the nineteenth century, and the interventions by the Bohras disrupted this vision. The Bohras freely borrowed elements from one structure to apply to another; they introduced new materials; and they removed parts of structures that did not fit their imagining of Fatimid architecture.[4] Ironically, in so doing, they borrowed heavily from Orientalist reconstructions of buildings of this time period. In essence, they sought to redefine and categorize Fatimid architecture as a style that represented them not only historically, but also in the present. But the story of the Bohras in late-twentieth-century Cairo cannot be fully understood without a reflection on events that occurred a millennium earlier in the heart of the Middle East. Because of al-Hakim's significance to their faith, the Bohras' most important project was the restoration of the mosque bearing his name. The story of the Fatimid ruler al-Hakim, as such, starts much earlier.

With the collapse of the central military authority of the Abbasids, who ruled from Baghdad, a series of local dynasties rose to lead the Islamic world. North African principalities were among the first to gain autonomy in the far-flung and loosely controlled empire. In Tunisia, the movement against the Abbasid caliphs, who were perceived as decadent, reached its peak when Sa'id ibn Husain al-Mahdi, an alleged descendant of the

Prophet (through his daughter Fatima—hence the name Fatimid) broke away from the empire and established a Shi'ite caliphate.[5]

The Fatimids were intent on moving eastward, possibly to challenge the Sunni Abbasids. After successive attempts, their movement gathered enough momentum to permit the conquest of Egypt. Al-Mu'izz, who ruled from 953 to 975 as the fourth Fatimid caliph, appointed Jawhar al-Siqilli (928–992) to lead his forces in the Egyptian campaign. Jawhar, whose full name literally means "the Sicilian jewel," was of Christian slave origin.[6] At the time, Egypt was ruled by the Ikhshidi dynasty (935–969), another feudalistic princedom with provincial autonomy from the Abbasids. In 969 the Fatimids easily defeated the Ikhshidis and marched through the cities of Fustat and al-Qata'i.[7]

Almost immediately after his arrival, Jawhar began to search for a site to garrison his troops. According to at least one account, he maintained ideas pertaining to the construction of a new capital based on what al-Mu'izz envisioned as the seat of his caliphate and as a rival to Baghdad.[8] Jawhar established the new city on the only available site in the area, to the north of the existing settlements.[9] Seen in context, this city would add to a sequence of existing cities that bordered the Nile. Continuing what began with Fustat in 640, followed by al-Askar in 750 and al-Qata'i in 870, the new site of Fatimid Cairo would extend along a north–south urban axis and would tie the new city to its predecessors. Jawhar's first step was to establish the boundaries of a city wall, locate its gates, and start construction of two major buildings—the caliphal palace and the mosque.[10] Legend has it that on the following day when a delegation from Fustat arrived to welcome Jawhar, they found the foundation for the entire city had already been marked.[11] Chronicles dating from the period contain no mention of architects or builders involved in this process, leading us to believe that Jawhar's army may have included individuals with specialized skills.

Maqrizi (1364–1442), the renowned medieval historian of Cairo, relates that Jawhar initially planned for the city to follow the shape of a square with sides roughly 1,100 meters long. This defined a total area of about 138 hectares, of which 28 hectares were allotted to the caliphal palace, and another

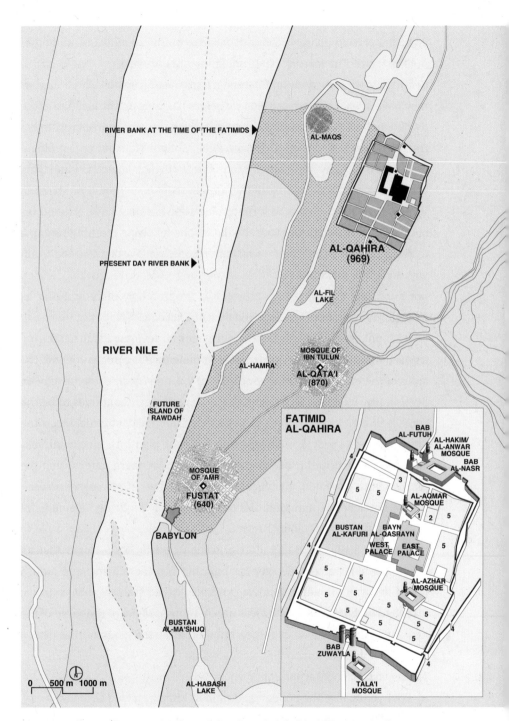

Figure 4.1   Map of Fustat, al-Askar, al-Qata'i, and al-Qahira. (Key: 1. guesthouse; 2. minister's house; 3. stables; 4. gates; 5. residential quarters of different tribes.)

28 hectares to the existing Ikhshidi gardens, al-Bustan al-Kafuri, and other public squares, or *rahbahs*. The remaining area was assigned as *khitat*, or districts, to the twenty or so different groups making up the army.[12] Jawhar may have consulted with astrologers before deciding on the location of the town, if not also the date for executing his plan. Several sources relate that the town was later called al-Qahira after a bright star that an astrologer observed in the sky that night.[13] Maqrizi reports that Jawhar began laying out the town on the evening of a Friday in the Arabic month of Sha'aban in 969. Anxious to implement the project, Jawhar may have ordered his soldiers to carry on throughout the night. The following morning he came to realize that the city outline was built inconsistently, such that the result was a slightly distorted rectangle. According to Maqrizi, Jawhar decided not to correct it, saying that "it was laid out in a holy night and that its irregularity must have been caused by a divine logic."[14]

It is unlikely that the plan could have been so severely distorted during its execution that the envisioned square became a rectangle. Indeed, the sides of the city carried the proportion of 2:3, one not likely to have been achieved by mistake. The original plan, nevertheless, continues to be the subject of controversy. Some believe that Caliph al-Mu'izz designed the city himself and provided Jawhar with a precise plan with specific dimensions and a proposed procedure for execution.[15] Others suggest that the plan of Cairo was initially envisioned along the lines of a Roman *castrum*.[16] Still, other scholars maintain that the plan simply replicated elements of the town of al-Mahdiyah in Tunisia.[17]

Whether it was modeled after a Roman castrum or a North African town, Jawhar started the city by building a palace, a mosque, and a perimeter wall of mud bricks. He originally called the city al-Mansuriya, after a town built by al-Mu'izz's father in Tunisia. Many of the gates of the new city also appear to have been named after the gates of that city in Tunisia—evidence supporting the view that the city was modeled after its North African counterpart.[18]

Four years after the conquest, Caliph al-Mu'izz arrived at the new city, declared it the capital of his caliphate, and changed its name to al-Qahira.[19] The name was later distorted by Italian travelers to *al Cairo*, hence its current English name, Cairo.[20] From the beginning, Caliph al-Mu'izz was intent on creating an imperial capital with an immediate sense of history. From Tunisia he brought three coffins housing the remains of his predecessors and ordered their burial in a site close to his palace. Upon his arrival, the caliph led the first public prayer, prefacing Cairo's role as the religious and intellectual capital of the Muslim world in the years to come.[21] To emphasize the change of dynasty, the Abbasid caliph's name was eliminated from all official records and prayers, and a new coinage was struck. In place of black, the color of the Abbasids, white was pronounced as the new official color of the territory. For the first time in a thousand years, Egypt became a sovereign state headed by one person, the Fatimid caliph, who was its spiritual and political leader.[22]

Maqrizi's description of the urban elements that made up the Fatimid city exceeds a couple of hundred pages, of which a considerable portion is devoted to its palaces. He reports that Jawhar and his forces camped to the south of the proposed site and started the construction of the main caliphal palace in 969.[23] In this account, the palace included several large halls and opened out to the rest of the city through nine gates. It was bordered by the city's central square, or *maydan,* which was later bounded by the addition of another caliphal structure, often called the Western Palace. The maydan acted as a place where the caliph would review his troops. Indeed, it was a monumental space that could accommodate ten thousand soldiers.[24] The caliphal palace was separated from the rest of the city by open spaces and gardens. To its west was al-Bustan al-Kafuri, a large garden established as a retreat during the time of the Ikhshidis. This garden was walled and connected by underground tunnels leading to the palace, and in the early days was exclusively reserved for use by the caliph and his family.[25] Rahbahs on the northern and eastern sides separated the caliphal palace from a guesthouse and the city's residential neighborhoods, respectively. Although the spatial configuration of the caliphal palace appears to be irregular, it nevertheless emulated the concept of isolating the caliph from his surroundings and placing him at the center of the settlement, a precedent set in the first planned Islamic capital, Baghdad.

Figure 4.2 The Mosque of al-Azhar.

Concomitant to the construction of the palace, Jawhar decided to build a congregational Friday mosque to the south of the palace. Initially named Jami' al-Qahira, the mosque soon acquired its present name, al-Azhar—which both means "the magnificent" and is the masculine form of the honorific title *Zahra,* which refers to the Prophet's daughter Fatima. The construction of the mosque began in 970 and was completed three years later. Al-Mu'izz led the first Friday prayer and delivered the *khutbah* sermon on the first Friday of the Arab month of Ramadan in 972.[26]

The original core of the mosque of al-Azhar is today buried under centuries of additions and alterations.[27] The original structure was built of brick, following a simple rectangular plan. One would enter from the northwest through a projecting portal next to a minaret. Inside was the open courtyard, or *sahn,* which featured porticos along both sides. Facing the portal, on the opposite side of the courtyard, was the entry to the hypostyle hall—a hall with a flat ceiling supported by evenly spaced columns—which functioned as the sanctuary, or *haram.* This covered prayer hall consisted of four naves and a transept that terminated in a dome in front of the mihrab on the qibla. Some 150 years after the construction of the mosque, during Caliph al-'Aziz's reign, a new aisle with keel-shaped arches was added all around the courtyard to unify the appearance of the mosque and respond to the social needs of the community.[28] The central transept of the covered prayer hall, indicating the qibla (in this case, southeast toward the holy city of Mecca), was made prominent by the addition of a tall screen wall from the courtyard to the prayer hall. Several domes were added to the mosque in later years.

In its early years al-Azhar served as the only congregational mosque in the city.[29] In 988 the first organized school began there, with thirty-five scholars housed nearby to propagate Ismaili doctrine and train the faith's missionaries. However, al-Azhar lost its status as the Friday mosque to the al-Hakim mosque after the fall of the Fatimid dynasty to the Ayyubids, Sunni Muslims of Kurdish origin who banned Shi'ite doctrines and neglected the building.[30] The layout of the city of al-Mu'izz, at least during its first decade, seems to have been a regular grid with wide streets and large open squares. The city was well fortified, and the Fatimids built most of their buildings inside its walls. In other early Muslim settlements in the region, the cities grew around a core, which was usually a mosque—such as the mosque of 'Amr in Fustat, or the mosque of Ibn Tulun in al-Qata'i. But in Fatimid Cairo this was not the case: palaces were designed to occupy its center, and the mosque of al-Azhar was located off to one side. The central location of the palace no doubt influenced the internal structure of the city and, accordingly, its streets. The major streets of Fatimid Cairo made up a simple network that tied the palace to the city gates. The area between the Eastern Palace (972) and the Western Palace (975–996) has survived to the present, at least in name, as Bayn al-Qasrayn, which means "between the two palaces" or "Palace Walk."[31]

Although it was al-Mu'izz's vision that brought Fatimid Cairo into existence, al-Mu'izz did not live long enough to enjoy his new capital. When he died in 975, his son, al-'Aziz, took over the caliphate and ruled for more than twenty years, until 996. 'Aziz was a great builder, and during his reign several important buildings were added to Fatimid Cairo. Among these were the Western Palace and the al-Hakim mosque.

The small Western Palace, also known as Qasr al-Bahr because it fronted one of the canals connecting to the Nile, came to assume great significance in the city. Initially built as a residence for one of 'Aziz's daughters, it defined the central maydan of Fatimid Cairo and separated it from the caliphal gardens. When al-Mustansir, who ruled for fifty-eight years, ascended to the Fatimid caliphate in 1036, he refurbished the palace in preparation for making it the official residence of the deposed Abbasid caliph. At the time Mustansir sought to bestow greater legitimacy on his own caliphate by offering to relocate the collapsed Abbasid caliphate from Baghdad.[32]

During late Fatimid times, the main artery of the city connected Bab Zuwayla in the south to Bab al-Futuh in the north, passing through the Bayn al-Qasrayn maydan.[33] Entering the city through the southern gate and walking north, a visitor would have passed the al-Azhar mosque on the right before reaching Bayn al-Qasrayn. After passing this maydan, one would have encountered the mosque of al-Aqmar and finally the mosque of al-Hakim before exiting the city through its northern gate.

The rule of Caliph al-'Aziz was followed by the long reign of his eleven-year-old son, al-Hakim, who ruled from 996 to 1021. Al-Hakim's guardian and counselor, the eunuch Barjawan, acted as regent, limiting al-Hakim's authority until he was deemed old enough to rule alone. Four years later al-Hakim had the regent assassinated and began his reign as an absolute monarch at the age of fifteen, limiting the authority of his counselors. Thus began the rule of a controversial figure, whose unpredictable behavior and excesses became the subject of numerous stories and myths. Some of these myths highlight his lavishness and generosity, and others his acts of extreme cruelty against his subjects. Whether it was the sudden execution of a court favorite, or boiling alive a noisy concubine, al-Hakim became known for the arbitrariness of his acts. He supposedly issued decrees ordering the killing of all dogs in Cairo, prohibiting chess, and proscribing the consumption of certain popular foods. Women also appear to have been the target of his laws, as they were under the threat of severe punishment if they wore jewelry or left their homes. To ensure compliance with this latest law, shoe-makers were prohibited from manufacturing women's shoes.[34]

While the Fatimids were tolerant and inclusive of religious minorities such as Christians and Jews, al-Hakim was particularly oppressive and excluded those groups from Egypt's political life. He demolished Jewish and Christian places of worship, including the Church of the Holy Sepulchre in Jerusalem. Though he was particularly hostile to the Sunni, he took the harshest measures against the members and officials of the Christian population. Some he killed; others he forced to either convert to Islam or wear markers of their religion. All were prohibited from owning slaves or horses.[35]

Toward the end of his life, al-Hakim's eccentric behavior became a concern for his officials. His religious fervor increased, and he began to see himself as a prophet, proclaiming his divine nature. This caused the population of Fustat to rise in protest, and in response al-Hakim deployed his forces to attack and quell the city. Yet despite his despotic rule and cruelty, al-Hakim would also be remembered by some as a kind man who cared for the needs of the population, and who often walked the streets and spoke with his subjects, whom he did not allow to address him by

Figure 4.3 The Mosque of al-Anwar, also known as the Mosque of al-Hakim. Before restoration, 1976 (above). After restoration (below).

his royal title. Toward the last years of his rule he led a life of asceticism, with a simple lifestyle, dressing modestly, and generally abstaining from luxury, unlike many of his predecessors. Al-Hakim's death is shrouded in mystery, as it is purported to have occurred during one of his regular solitary trips. He often withdrew for meditation, and one night he rode to the Muqattam Hills, never to return. His bloodstained garb was all that was found of him, which led his followers to believe that he had left the world in order to be resurrected again as the Savior in the future. His followers became known as the Druze, and eventually settled in Lebanon and continued to worship al-Hakim.[36]

The mosque of al-Hakim, as noted earlier, began under the rule of Caliph al-'Aziz to act as a new khutbah mosque to accommodate the Friday sermon and Eid prayers. Maqrizi mentions that 'Aziz prayed in this mosque before it was completed in 995. However, it was finished only after his death by his son al-Hakim.[37] The mosque, which was initially outside Bab al-Futuh (before the city was enlarged and its new stone wall constructed), was the first the Fatimids built outside the city. Its construction, which utilized disassembled building materials from ancient Egyptian temples, also signaled a change in the pattern of religious preaching in Cairo. For a time the Friday khutbah was held in more than one mosque; the mosque of 'Amr, in the city of Fustat, accommodated the Sunni khutbah, while the Shi'ite khutbah was held in the mosques of al-Hakim and al-Azhar.[38]

The mosque of al-Hakim was built to a rectangular plan reminiscent of the previously mentioned mosque of al-Azhar, but it is twice as large. It introduced new features, such as two-corner minarets and, later, a monumental projecting portal in the middle of the entry wall.[39] The two minarets, designed in different shapes, were later encased by rectangular square stone walls during the reign of al-Hakim. Although the al-Azhar mosque was built entirely of brick, the al-Hakim is composed partially of stone. Its minarets are of dressed stone; its exterior walls are made of rough-cut stone. Its interior could be accessed at thirteen different entry points, differentiated by the use of dressed stone, but many of these were later sealed off. Inside the mosque is a Kufic-inscribed frieze composed

Figure 4.4   Gates of Cairo. Bab al-Futuh, 1976 (above, left). Bab Zuwayla, 2010 (above, right). Bab al-Nasr, 2001 (below).

of a band of carved stucco approximately sixty centimeters wide, which ran along the arcades below the beams of the roof. This was the only interior ornamentation that withstood time. At its prime, the mosque also contained silver chandeliers, brocaded curtains, and matting. The interior of the mosque further differs from al-Azhar in that it employed brick piers, rather than columns, to support its wooden roof.

In order to disseminate Ismaili doctrine, al-Hakim commissioned a number of other buildings in the Fatimid city. This included the Dar al-Hikma, or the House of Wisdom (1005). Although no trace of it exists today, it was constructed to the north of the Western Palace and acted as a center of scientific and literary scholarship.[40] In 1068 during Egypt's severe drought, urban order in Cairo deteriorated to such an extent that the caliph at the time, Caliph Mustansir, had to call on his governor in Acre, Badr al-Jamali, to take over the government of Egypt. Al-Jamali was a strong ruler who managed to restore order to the capital and revive the political and religious authority of the Fatimid caliphate, serving as its principal minister, or viziers, from 1073 to 1094.[41] He also sought to renew the appearance of the city. In addition to enlarging the city by building a new stone wall to enclose all of the buildings outside the old wall, al-Jamali built three new gates: Bab al-Futuh (1087) and Bab al-Nasr (1087) on the north wall, and Bab Zuwayla (1092) on the south. Bab Zuwayla was named after the Fatimid soldiers from the Berber al-Zawila tribe who settled near the site of the original gate in 969. All three gates feature pairs of short, bulky towers. Bab al-Nasr's towers are square, while those of Bab al-Futuh and Bab Zuwayla are rounded. In each case the towers frame a recessed gateway constituted of a dome sitting on spherical-triangle pendentives above each entrance passage. This project is said to have been commissioned to three Armenian brothers from Edessa in Turkey by Badr al-Jamali, who himself was also Armenian. As such, the gates have affinities with Byzantine architecture in Syria in terms of style, construction, and materials.

With al-Jamali's interventions, Fatimid Cairo was once again a fortified city. This fortification was accomplished primarily by using recycled stone from nearby ancient Egyptian temples and by importing from Byzantium skilled workers capable of building defensive structures. Badr also built the Dar al-Wizarah, the residence of the vizier, northeast of the central palace. This building acted as the official residence of all Fatimid viziers until the fall of the Fatimid caliphate in 1171.[42]

The mosque of al-Aqmar (*aqmar* means "moonlit," which is why the structure is also known as the Gray Mosque) was built in 1125 during the caliphate of Amir (1101–1130) by his vizier, al-Ma'mun al-Bata'ihi. Constructed of brick with stone facing, al-Ma'mun deviated from the standard rectangular plan by shifting the depth of its entry façade to accommodate existing streets. At ground level the structure contained a series of shops that provided maintenance income; these have since been buried due to the rising ground level. It had a small central courtyard, 12.8 by 9.2 meters, bordered by a portico on all sides.[43] The mosque abutted the Eastern Palace of the caliph and probably served the royal household and the nearby community. The al-Aqmar mosque was much more humble in size than the mosques of al-Azhar and al-Hakim because the political context had dramatically changed. In later years, the Fatimid city would welcome local notables and wealthy merchants to build mansions in the vicinity.

The façade decoration of the mosque of al-Aqmar, moreover, reflected the Fatimid rulers' desire to portray themselves as inclusive. The inscriptions on its façade send a message of tolerance to their subjects through their textual symbolism.[44] This façade has a tripartite composition: in the middle is a protruding portal, and on either side are niches decorated with *muqarnas,* or stalactites. It features three Kufic inscription bands—one at the top, one in the middle, and a third at the level of the door lintel, slightly recessed within the protruding portal. The first two contain information on the foundation and the names of the caliph and the vizier; and the third incorporates inscriptions from the Quran. The portal is decorated as a large keel-arch niche with fluted carvings that emanate from a central medallion over the entrance portal, thereby replicating the sign of Ismailism.[45] The inscriptions speak to a heterogeneous public consisting not only of Fatimid Ismailis but also Ismaili Shi'ites, Sunni Muslims, Christians, and Jews, pronouncing the rulers' concern for tolerance, authority, and stability.[46]

Figure 4.5   The Mosque of al-Aqmar. Before restoration, 1976 (above). After restoration (below).

Outside of the Bab Zuwayla is the last mosque built by the Fatimids, al-Salih Tala'i (1160). It is named after its patron, Tala'i ibn Ruzzik, who was granted the title al-Malik al-Salih, the vizier to the caliphs al-Fa'iz and al-Adid from 1154 to 1161. This mosque is similar to the mosque of al-Aqmar in many respects, including in its scale, decoration, and overall character.[47] It, too, is built over a row of shops and around a courtyard, or sahn, consisting of only three arcades. But the exterior portico, which forms part of the façade, is its most unique feature. Approached from the northwest, the building is accessed by a small staircase several steps up with shops exposed below the street level.

Fatimid Cairo was an impressive city in its heyday. Although initially envisioned as a palatial compound, it quickly developed into a full urban settlement. The Persian scholar and traveler Nasir-i Khusraw (1004–1088), who resided in Cairo from 1047 to 1050, explains that Fatimid Cairo was composed of a large number of detached palaces or houses. "These houses are so magnificent and fine that you would think they were made of jewels, not of plaster, tile, and stone!"[48] Khusraw describes houses five to six stories tall in New Cairo—that is, Fatimid; and houses up to fourteen stories tall, each accommodating up to 350 people, in Fustat, which he calls "Old Cairo."[49] Although Khusraw may have been prone to exaggeration, due to both his conversion to Shi'ite Ismailism during his time in Cairo as well as his support of the regime, his description nevertheless captures travelers' fascination with the city.

Another element of Fatimid Cairo, apparent from examining its plan, was its social hierarchy. The earliest residential quarters, or *haras,* showed strong tribal demarcation, as clearly illustrated by their names.[50] These haras surrounded the palaces in the core of the city and also formed the periphery. Originally there were twenty haras, one for each tribe making up the Fatimid army. The balance achieved between the tribes and their representation in the government of Egypt was of major importance to the existence of the Fatimid city.[51] In the early years, these relatively wealthy groups lived inside the city walls, and the masses, who lived in Fustat, were allowed to enter only with special permission.

Because Fatimid Cairo was a private, princely town, historians originally assumed that it did not have any major markets. After all, it contained only a small, elite population. It is quite possible, though, that during these early days the city did contain warehouses and small neighborhood markets for its residents. Otherwise it would have been inconvenient for the residents to attend to their immediate shopping needs.

In later years this situation changed as the city grew larger and developed a balanced relationship with Fustat, its twin to the south. In his brief description of the extent of trade and commerce inside Fatimid Cairo, Khusraw estimated that there were approximately twenty thousand shops inside the city, accommodating all types of commercial activity.[52] Although that is clearly another embellished figure, shops did indeed exist. These were owned by the caliph and rented to tenants who resided in Fustat. In its first two centuries, no one except for the caliph was allowed to own commercial or residential property in Fatimid Cairo.[53] It is indeed possible to think of al-Qahira during its first century simply as a palatial compound from which a form of colonial or imperial rule was exercised and in which a local population had to abide by the dictates of its foreign rulers.[54]

Commercial activity was closely regulated by the Fatimid caliphate. The various crafts and trades were organized into guilds, and membership in them was compulsory—an organization of labor that also had roots in the Byzantine occupation of Egypt.[55] Urban markets were controlled through the office of the *muhtasib,* a government agent who acted as a market inspector and ranked third among men of the pen.[56] Although that office did not become important until the end of the Ayyubid rule, it may have been part of Cairo's pre-Ayyubid heritage.[57] In any case, the role of the muhtasibs in Fatimid times was limited to controlling market prices, ensuring quality of commodities, and collecting taxes.

In terms of roadwork, Fatimids tended to build broad streets. Recent archeological discoveries suggest that they even widened the narrow streets of Fustat.[58] We can assume that Cairo's streets were at their widest in Fatimid times, although it is difficult to generalize this to all levels. Khusraw and, later, Maqrizi remark specifically on the broadness of Bayn al-Qasrayn and the width of the streets connecting the palaces to the gates of the city.[59]

Before the end of Fatimid rule, the two cities of al-Qahira and Fustat existed side by side and acted as one large settlement that served both the capital of the Fatimid caliphate and the most important city of Islam in the Middle Ages. When the Ayyubids later took over the city in 1171, they opened the city to commoners, who had previously lived outside its walls. It was then that the city's original pattern also started to disintegrate, and al-Qahira began to resemble its older neighbor, Fustat.[60]

Fatimid rule in Egypt ended in the twelfth century after years of political instability brought on by the European Crusaders and the Syrian Seljuks. The burning of Fustat in 1168 is an interesting, albeit puzzling, story to tell here.[61] During the early years of the last Fatimid caliph, Adid, who reigned from 1160 to 1171, a major struggle broke out between his viziers, Shawar and Dirgham, for control of the Fatimid court. When Shawar was removed from power, he struck a deal for support first from Nur al-Din, the ruler of Syria, and then from the Franks—particularly from Amalric, the Crusader king of Jerusalem. Attempting to pit one regional power against the other did not work in Shawar's favor, given that both sides had ambitions to take over Egypt.

As Amalric's forces headed toward Cairo after devastating several unfortified cities in the Nile Delta, Shawar panicked. Fatimid Cairo was a walled city and could protect itself, but much of the urban population resided in unwalled Fustat. Shawar purportedly ordered the population of Fustat to evacuate, and then, according to a tactic employed repeatedly in other parts of the world during premodern times, he ordered Fustat burned to ensure that it would not be used as a base to attack fortified Cairo. Before the Frankish troops could attack Fatimid Cairo, however, the Syrian troops of Nur al-Din ambushed Shawar and killed him.[62]

This story, which has found its way into Cairene myth, is corroborated by eyewitness accounts and some physical evidence. And yet travelers to Fatimid Cairo and Fustat in the succeeding century were able to visit and comment on the mosques, hotels, and even houses that survived from the last two decades of the twelfth century.

Nevertheless, it is likely that when Salah al-Din ibn Ayyub (known in the west as Saladin) took over as vizier and abolished the Fatimid caliphate, Fustat lay in semi-ruins.[63] Its population was either crowded into the former princely city or living in camps outside its walls. It was a ruined city that Salah al-Din took over and had to restore—just as the Dawoodi Bohras set out to remake the ruins of the Fatimid buildings in the 1970s to restore them to their former glory.

Fortress Cairo: From Salah al-Din to the Pearl Tree

LOOKING SOUTH FROM the fortified walls of the Castle of the Mountain, the Arab name for the citadel built by Salah al-Din (known in the West as Saladin), the sultana Shagarat al-Durr would have seen the spiral-shaped minaret of the mosque of Ibn Tulun.[1] Less than a kilometer away, she would have seen the site where she would later choose to build her tomb, which she commissioned during the short time she was the ruling monarch of Egypt. Even further south, she would have seen the mosque of 'Amr standing above the ruins of Fustat.

It would have been difficult during this time to remember the prosperous days of Fustat. All that remained of the old city was decay and rubble, the consequence of vizier Shawar's order, in late Fatimid times, to burn it down in anticipation of a Crusader attack. During the life of Shagarat al-Durr in the thirteenth century, Cairo, or al-Qahira, had replaced Fustat as the thriving urban center of the region. Looking north, she would have seen al-Qahira's gates, walls, streets, and large mosques. In the center of this new capital, she would have seen the square between its two palaces as well as the dome marking where her husband, al-Salih Najm al-Din, would later be buried and commemorated with the al-Salihiya mosque and madrasa bearing his name.

Shagarat al-Durr—whose name literally means "the tree of pearls"—was the first and only woman to rule Egypt during Muslim times. Her audacity and political flair not only influenced the city's destiny at a time when it was threatened by Crusader attacks, but also brought about a dynastic change and a social order based not on hereditary claims to rule but on a system of succession premised on military capability.

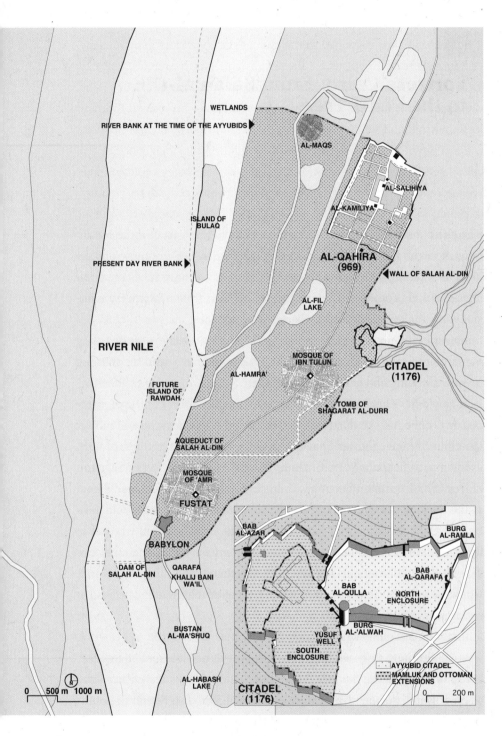

Figure 5.1   Map of Cairo area during the Ayyubid period.

Shagarat al-Durr belonged to the clan of slave-warriors known as the Mamluks. Sent to Egypt as a Christian slave from the remote lands of Armenia, she was converted and brought up in the faith of Islam. The Mamluks—which means "those who are owned"—were valued for their horsemanship and fighting skills, and trained as guards for the Ayyubid rulers of Egypt. Given their indispensable military role, their social status was subject to change over time. From slave soldiers, they could become free men and court favorites, holding important political positions whether as viziers or commanders of army battalions. Mamluk soldiers lived in palaces of their own making and in luxurious barracks built for them on Rawdah Island by the Ayyubid rulers.[2] Their residence on this island in the Nile is the reason they were called the Bahri Mamluks.[3] Eventually the Mamluks became such a dominating and powerful force that no ruler could hold the throne of Egypt without their support.

Shagarat al-Durr had originally been a slave in al-Salih's harem. But after falling in love with her, al-Salih freed and then married her, making her his only wife who held any importance. Soon after, she gave birth to their only son, Khalil. Her story, however, begins somewhat later with the start of the Seventh Crusade, which brought the thirty-year-old King Louis IX of France and his queen, Margaret of Provence, to Egypt. With his allegiance to Christendom, Louis IX sailed from the port of Aigues-Mortes in 1248 with eighteen hundred ships and fifty thousand soldiers. His aim was to occupy Jerusalem and bring it under Christian rule. But to triumph in this holy war, he first had to confront al-Salih, who, as a descendant of Salah al-Din, was sultan of Egypt and Syria and suzerain of Jerusalem. When Louis learned that al-Salih was in poor health and that his eldest son, Turan Shah, who was next in line to the throne, was a weak drunkard, he decided to instead attack al-Salih's homeland of Egypt rather than go directly to Jerusalem.[4]

Al-Salih originally took his troops to Syria to defend against attacks there. But while there, he fell ill with tuberculosis and suffered from an ulcerated leg in the fortress of Homs. Given the considerable threat posed by the Crusaders to the Islamic Empire, the Abbasid caliph could have intervened to support al-Salih, but he decided against taking action.

Thus, in spite of his condition, al-Salih was forced to take his army back to Egypt upon learning of the change in Louis IX's plan. The Crusaders by that point had occupied the coastal town of Damietta. While en route back to Egypt, al-Salih sent a message to Shagarat al-Durr asking that she summon the Mamluks, who, under the leadership of the vizier Fakhr ed-Din, traveled up the Nile to confront an imminent Crusader attack. He also asked her to look into the defense of Cairo, as the capital would likely be one of the next targets of the French Crusaders.[5]

While al-Salih was on his way to Egypt, Shagarat al-Durr became aware that her husband might not live long enough to see his son Turan Shah accede to the throne. Turan Shah was also in Syria, where he was a governor, and he would need time to return to Egypt. Shagarat al-Durr, although a Mamluk herself, was suspicious of her own kin. She was concerned about not only the threat posed by the Crusaders against the city but also the danger that the ambitious, power-coveting Mamluks posed to the throne. Under these circumstances and upon her husband's death in 1249, Shagarat al-Durr hid his body in a castle on Rawdah Island until Turan Shah returned from Cairo and it was safe to give al-Salih a proper burial.

With Egypt still in crisis, caught between the threat of the Crusaders, on the one hand, and the threat of the Mamluks, on the other, Shagarat al-Durr ruled Egypt exclusively, if not secretly, for two months in the interim period between her husband's death and the son's return from Syria. Once Turan Shah returned to Egypt, she handed him the throne. With the aid of the Mamluks, Turan Shah was able to repel the Crusaders, capture Louis IX, and imprison him in Mansoura.[6] There the French king was kept in comfortable quarters in the residence of Dar ibn Lockman until he was ransomed by French officials.[7]

Although Shagarat al-Durr had proven her loyalty to Turan Shah by holding the throne for him, the new sultan did not reward her for ensuring his rise to power. Instead, he had her removed and marginalized, forcing her to ally with the Mamluks for help. The Bahri Mamluks themselves were dissatisfied with the way Turan Shah had failed to acknowledge their role in the war. Consequently a group of Mamluks, led by Baybars, a man who had proven himself in the defeat of the Crusaders, assassinated Turan Shah.

With their consent, Shagarat al-Durr proclaimed herself sultana of Egypt. During the following eighty days of her sovereign rule, she returned King Louis IX to his troops and collected ransom money from Queen Margaret.[8]

Ultimately the Abbasid caliph ruled that a woman could not preside as governor, and Shagarat al-Durr had no choice but to seek other means of retaining power.[9] To gain the consent of the caliph, she married the leader of the Bahri Mamluks, Izz al-Din Aybak, who was declared to be sultan in her place. Although aware of his ambition, she trusted Aybak to maintain his loyalty to her and allow her to rule by his side. She did in fact rule next to her new husband for three years, during which she oversaw the building of an imposing mausoleum for her late husband, al-Salih.[10] Thus Shagarat al-Durr became the first woman ruler of any territory within the Islamic Empire, and the first Mamluk ever to rise to that position. She also inadvertently put an end to the hereditary monarchy of the Ayyubid family, established by Salah al-Din less than a century earlier.

The story of Shagarat al-Durr traces the fall of one regime and the rise of another. The rule of the Ayyubids had begun with the Kurdish soldier Salah al-Din Yusuf ibn Ayyub two centuries prior. Salah al-Din had been a commander in the army of Nur al-Din, who had conquered Egypt in 1171. Nur al-Din was primarily interested in extracting revenue from this newly acquired land while ruling from Syria.[11] Nur al-Din had also succeeded, with the help of Sherako, in overthrowing the Fatimid regime and returning Egypt to the Sunni doctrine. But consolidating his control over Egypt proved challenging, so he sent Salah al-Din to Egypt from Syria with a small military force. In a short time, Salah al-Din was appointed vizier by al-Adid, the last caliph of the Fatimid dynasty.

As vizier, Salah al-Din gradually weakened the Fatimid caliphate until he finally abolished it. At the same time he strengthened his own position by stabilizing a volatile country marked by recurrent rebellions. Although he still deferred authority to Nur al-Din, Salah al-Din succeeded in due time in ruling Egypt alone. This increasing independence did cause concern for his master in Damascus. But a potential power struggle ended before it could begin when Nur al-Din died in 1174.[12] It was then that Salah al-Din made his bid for political autonomy by conquering Syria.

In the wake of his victory to secure the capital, Cairo, Salah al-Din began construction of an extensive fortification wall that would encircle the two cities of Fustat-Misr and al-Qahira. Fustat was then in ruins after being burned to the ground by the last Fatimid vizier. Al-Qahira had also suffered damage in addition to having to accommodate refugees from Fustat. The extension of the northern wall of al-Qahira to the Nile at the port of al-Maqs would allow the city to expand westward onto new land created by changes in the river's course.[13]

Salah al-Din began his ambitious construction project by assigning it to his lieutenant, Baha al-Din Qaraqush. Although he initially set up his rule from the Dar al-Wazir, a palace adjacent to the great Fatimid palace, he also entrusted Qaraqush with the construction of the Citadel on the edge of the Muqattam Hills.[14] Eventually, it was the construction of the Citadel and al-Qahira's new walls that made the city complete and gave it the profile of a fortress. And thus began a process of unifying two discrete cities that had developed under very different political histories.

Before long, Salah al-Din decided to establish his residence in the Citadel, which was completed in 1183. This decision has been interpreted by some as a security concern, if not a desire to visibly manifest the military nature of his regime. Although his choice of a royal residence was a novelty in Egypt, fortified cities with citadels were common in Syria, where he was originally from. The typology also reflected the character of a time marked by a series of invasions and the centuries-long Crusades. Indeed, in medieval times many royal residences in the Middle East were established in fortified enclaves.[15] Construction work on the Citadel thus began in 1176.[16] It was situated on a seventy-five-meter-high platform on the headlands of the Muqattam Hills. This was a strategic location where, according to scholars, the Dome of the Winds, or Qubat al-Hawa, had once existed. There were several other mosques in the general vicinity, including the Sa'a al-Dawla, which was built on the remains of the Dome.

With resources from Salah al-Din, Qaraqush completed the walls of the Citadel with astonishing speed while Salah al-Din traveled between Syria and Egypt during this period. Eventually this Ayyubid dynastic wall would extend fourteen hundred meters, but most of the construction carried on during Salah al-Din's time was probably limited to its northern portions.[17] Older sources, recently contested by scholars, suggest that Qaraqush might have used stone from several small pyramids in Giza to build the walls of the Citadel and the fortifications around al-Qahira and Fustat. One scholar suggests, however, that the stone taken from the pyramids may have instead been used to build a connecting bridge between Fustat and Giza.[18]

The main objective of Qaraqush's plan was the security of the royal residence. His design included a moat around the Citadel's eastern and northern edges along with defensive ramparts and bastions. An inscription on the Bab al-Mudarraj, which is dated 1183, is believed to represent

Figure 5.2 The Citadel of Cairo.

the year when the first stages of construction were completed. The Citadel had several other gates dating from approximately that time as well. These were the Bab al-Qarafa, or the Cemetery Gate, and Burg al-Imam, or the Eastern Gate, located on the south and east sides of the northern enclosure.[19] Circular towers flanked each of these gates.[20] Qaraqush also built other smaller semicircular towers protruding from the defensive wall. Connected by ramparts and interior passages, they were designed as protection.[21]

Because the Citadel was located close to al-Qahira and Fustat, it was easy to supply it with provisions and water from the Nile. Yusuf's Well, a pit excavated ninety meters into the bedrock during Salah al-Din's time, provided a local water supply that would allow the structure to withstand a prolonged siege. The well had two shafts, with the upper shaft wrapped in a spiral staircase accessible to water-carrying cattle. Windows pierced this shaft along the staircase to bring in natural light. The Citadel had an additional source of water from the Nile that was transported through an aqueduct, which was also built during Salah al-Din's time.

After Salah al-Din established his base of power in Cairo, he still had to spend a considerable part of his time fighting the Crusaders, particularly the armies of the Third Crusade led by the king of England, Richard the Lionheart. Salah al-Din's battles against Richard became the subject of a number of myths in the Middle Ages in both Europe and the Middle East. The relationship between the two rulers, which had begun initially in conflict, was ultimately resolved by a treaty that secured the rights of Christians to all the pilgrimage sites in Jerusalem and recognized that the city would continue to exist under Muslim control.[22]

Salah al-Din's fight against the Crusaders, however, drained a considerable part of his energy by forcing him to pay the utmost attention to military activities. Indeed, Salah al-Din's eventual relocation from Egypt to Syria came in response to military demands. Accordingly, the Cairo of Salah al-Din was not defined by new religious or government structures. With the exception of the Citadel and the wall that surrounded Fustat and al-Qahira, the Cairo that emerged from his dynasty was marked by the smaller, albeit important, additions of his successors.[23]

When Salah al-Din died in 1193, his empire was divided between his sons and nephews. The Citadel, which he intended to turn into the seat of Ayyubid rule, was at the time incomplete, with sections of its wall missing. Although some minor work was known to have been carried out during the rule of his immediate successors, there is no account of its extent.[24] When al-Kamil, Salah al-Din's nephew, became viceroy of Egypt in 1200, he chose the Citadel as his official residence and began an extensive program of construction.[25]

The period prior to al-Kamil's rule was also marked by instability and neglect. At the time of Salah al-Din's death, the Citadel was not connected to the neighboring cities of al-Qahira and Fustat, and its defense system was precarious. Because the Citadel was to be the residence of al-Kamil and his court, and the seat of his treasury, it was imperative that the construction work continue. Al-Kamil began by strengthening its fortifications. He then added several towers to the Citadel while retrofitting existing ones, and he built several structures inside the premises.[26] Among the edifices built by al-Kamil were a mosque, a number of palaces, and a library.[27]

Al-Qahira's social structure was transformed under the Ayyubids. Although Salah al-Din initiated the reconstruction of Fustat by building a number of major schools there, little of the area's former population returned. Instead they chose to build on the open spaces and gardens of al-Qahira, in a process similar to squatting. The Citadel pulled some urban development south, specifically once Salah al-Din burned the barracks of the Fatimid Sudanese militia located in the area between al-Qahira and the Citadel, which opened that area to public use.[28]

Salah al-Din's decision to open al-Qahira to general settlement changed the function of the former princely city. Its major palaces were torn down and replaced by mosques and madrasas, and its Fatimid villas were converted to commercial structures.[29] Although the Ayyubids were originally Kurds, they eventually became absorbed into the population they ruled. They managed to reduce the huge divisions among the area's various residents: indigenous Egyptians, Arabs from the early conquest, North Africans who came with the Fatimids, and Sudanese from Black

Africa. The Ayyubids also gradually succeeded in bringing Egypt, whose Muslim population had not fully adopted Shi'a Islam, back into the fold of Sunniism.

When the Ayyubids took control of the Fatimid palaces and converted them into commercial and residential structures, the city's economic life revived. Arab travelers who visited Cairo at the time remarked on the burgeoning of commercial activity at its center. The function of the *muhtasib* was also strengthened at the time. The muhtasib was the office entrusted with police power and the right to supervise markets. To make certain that merchants were fair and honest in their dealings, the muhtasib could punish illegal activities such as price gouging.

The *waqf* system, allowing the endowment of property to support social services, was also introduced under Ayyubid rule. In subsequent years it became common for a wealthy or prominent figure to build a structure or compound, of which a portion would be rented out to generate funds to support other philanthropic activities. For example, the whole of the jewelers district in al-Qahira was deeded to the madrasa of al-Nasiriya, and thirty-two shops in the area of Bab al-Nasr supported the madrasa of al-Siyufiya.[30] Two new types of public structures also evolved during the Ayyubid period: the madrasa, which housed both a school and a mosque; and the *khanqah,* a type of Sufi monastery. Many khanqahs that proliferated at the time of the Ayyubids were completely dependent on waqf endowments. Other public institutions, such as the public hospital located in one of the Fatimids' large palaces, Bimaristan al-Atiq, were also founded during this period.

A map of Cairo at the end of Ayyubid rule would have shown a growing city encircled by suburbs. Al-Qahira, its urban center, was densely populated, expanding south and west of the old Fatimid walls. The city also came to encompass the reconstructed area of Fustat around the mosque of 'Amr, the area near al-Shafi'i's tomb to the south, and the port of al-Maqs on the Nile to the west. The Citadel's new wall and gates were now identifiable landmarks of the city.

Another transformation of the urban landscape that likely took place at the time of the Ayyubids was the narrowing of Cairo's streets. When

Abdel Latif al-Baghdadi, a traveler and scientist from Iraq, visited the city in 1193 at the time of the reign of Salah al-Din, he described al-Qahira as a city of large buildings, green spaces, and wide streets.[31] Yet a traveler from Maghreb by the name of Ibn Sa'id who visited in 1243, when the Ayyubid dynasty had already started its decline, reported that al-Qahira's buildings were tall, its streets narrow, and its traffic unregulated. Indeed, he attributed the frequency of traffic jams and bottlenecks to the narrowness of the streets and their mix of uses. The only place in al-Qahira that did not have such problems and where pedestrians could walk comfortably, he noted, was the area known as Bayn al-Qasrayn situated between the two former Fatimid palaces.[32]

The striking differences in the descriptions provided by two travelers who had visited Cairo only fifty years apart can be explained in several ways. For one, the travelers could have simply perceived the city on personal terms, since they were from different places and may have had dissimilar notions of scale. But their other descriptions of cities besides Cairo indicate this was probably not the case.[33] The more likely explanation is that al-Qahira underwent enormous changes under the Ayyubids. As people moved to al-Qahira and started construction, the wide streets, *maydans*, and gardens of the Fatimid's princely city began to contract and disappear.

Again, the building program of the Ayyubids (other than the Citadel and new fortification walls) was limited in scope relative to that of their predecessors. However, they did build several important madrasas during their eighty years of rule. Most of the Ayyubid buildings were located close to each other in scattered groups along major thoroughfares, mainly within al-Qahira proper. But there were three exceptions: two madrasas in Fustat and a madrasa near the tomb of al-Shafi'i to the south of Cairo.[34]

Muhammad ibn Idris al-Shafi'i (767–820) was a Muslim jurist and a founder of one of the schools of Islamic law.[35] During his time Islamic law, which was based on specific interpretations of the Quran, was still a matter of considerable dispute among scholars. Al-Shafi'i's contribution was to develop a system that brought different readings and competing ideas together. Because his methodology often represented a compromise between opposing schools, his ideas became widely accepted and developed into a separate school of law, or *madhab*. Furthermore, al-Shafi'i developed the science of jurisprudence, and his contributions made him an important figure in the Islamic world.[36]

Under Salah al-Din, whose aim was to reinstate Sunni tradition in Egypt, al-Shafi'i's mausoleum, located in the Southern Cemetery, became a center of pilgrimage.[37] At twenty-nine meters high, its dome was one of the tallest in the Muslim world. The dome sat on a rectangular two-story base and was covered with lead siding. Unlike Fatimid domes, which curved only toward the top of the structure, the dome of this mausoleum began curving at its base.[38] Salah al-Din built a madrasa on one side of the mausoleum, possibly influenced by the building typology of Syrian funerary madrasas, and it was later restored during Mamluk times.

Ibn Jubayr (1144–1217), a traveler who was Salah al-Din's contemporary, reported that the madrasa at the al-Shafi'i tomb had already been completed at the time of his stay in Cairo in 1183. His impressions describe the Southern Cemetery, which also contained the remains of Muhammad's Companions, as one of the wonders of the world. He remarked on the vitality of the place that derived from not only its numerous mosques but also its shrines that lodged strangers, scholars, and men of all social standings. Among all of these monuments, the tomb of al-Shafi'i stood out as the most beautiful and unlike anything he had seen before. He compared the scale of the surrounding madrasa as comparable to that of a town in its own right, noting the presence of a bath annex and other facilities. He also pointed out that construction was still ongoing, and that Salah al-Din had made a generous endowment to the madrasa complex.[39]

In addition to the few mosques built under their tenure, the Ayyubids founded numerous madrasas to advance their religious views, as followers of the Shafi'i rite of Islam. A madrasa was an official institution dedicated to the study of Islamic law. The teaching of theology in mosques had been common since the early days of Islam, but it was usually carried out by private entities. This system of pedagogy changed in Egypt under the Fatimids, who introduced the teaching of Shi'a doctrine into legal and educational institutions.[40]

The madrasa is believed to have been introduced in Persia by a Sufi shaiykh. The first officially approved Sunni madrasa is credited to the Seljuk vizier Nizam al-Mulk, who established one in Baghdad in 1068.[41] Generally, ruling elites would found madrasas and endow them through the waqf system. A given madrasa's theology and law curriculum would then provide the training grounds for future scholars and administrative officials. The Ayyubids introduced the Sunni variant to Egypt.

As a building type, the madrasa differed from the mosque in housing lodgers.[42] It also incorporated the Persian *iwan,* a public and ceremonial hall open at one end, covered by a vault, and dedicated to teaching. Each iwan accommodated one of the four schools of thought in Islam. Usually the largest was dedicated to the preferred madhab, which in the case of Egypt under the Ayyubids was the Shafi'i school.

A unique example of this building type is the funerary madrasa of Sultan al-Salih Najm al-Din, al-Salihiya, which opened its doors in 1242 and was the first madrasa in Cairo to teach all four schools of Islamic law.[43] In 1249, following the death of her husband al-Salih, Shagarat al-Durr added a mausoleum to this complex, thus introducing the tradition of burying benefactors in the establishments they had once funded and of incorporating mausoleums into existing religious institutions.[44]

Al-Salihiya had an inward-facing configuration, its dome and minaret partially obscured by its exterior façade. Its symmetrical plan accommodated two madrasas oriented toward Mecca and separated by a central passage.[45] The angle formed between these buildings and the front façade resulted from a need to reconcile the buildings' orientation toward Mecca with the alignment of the street. The two iwans forming the north and south wings of al-Salihiya stood opposite each other across a courtyard, with multistoried residential buildings on its other sides.[46]

The minaret of al-Salihiya was placed above the entrance passage. Its configuration resembled a *mabkhara,* or incense burner, divided into two tiers separated by a balcony.[47] The lower tier was rectangular, while the upper was octagonal, supporting a ribbed dome. The top was richly

Figure 5.3   The minaret of al-Salih Najm al-Din Ayyub madrasa and funerary complex.

decorated with stalactite ornaments, while the rectangular base was marked by groups of three tall recessed niches, the central one pierced by a window. The octagonal upper register bore lobe-arched windows on each facet of the octagon. The door at the base of the minaret was crowned with a magnificent keel-arched niche carved in stone, which contained a framed inscription in the ornate Naskhi calligraphic style.[48] The flutes radiating from this panel formed a stalactite decoration that echoed the forms of the minaret above.

Figure 5.4   The funerary mausoleum of Shagarat al-Durr.

The mausoleum added to this complex by Shagarat al-Durr had a dome whose configuration was similar to that of the mausoleum of Imam Shafi'i, but which otherwise was entirely unusual at the time. The curvature of the dome began right at its base, transitioning from a circle to an octagonal pedestal. Pointed-arch openings were located in groups of three on every other side of the octagonal base. The interior of the mausoleum was decorated with wood-carved cenotaph doors, while the mihrab wall was decorated with mosaic tiles.

Shagarat al-Durr may have contemplated her own fate when she commissioned her husband's tomb. Standing atop the Citadel looking down toward the city, she must have felt the weight of history and destiny looming in front of her. Difficult times would soon again punctuate her tumultuous life. She lost her only son, Khalil, to a fatal illness; and her new husband, Aybak, was growing increasingly unhappy with her power-sharing scheme and began to plot his independence.[49] When Shagarat al-Durr learned that he planned to take the daughter of the prince of Mosul as his second wife, she decided to have him killed, and although she was successful on that front, she also therein created the circumstances of her own downfall.

Imprisoned by the Mamluks for Aybak's murder, she neared a tragic end in the Red Tower. Though held captive, she would not allow another woman in the harem to wear the pearls given to her by al-Salih. It is alleged that, determined to prevent another from wearing the pearls, she crushed them into powder. She died soon after, purportedly killed with a pair of wooden bath slippers by the women slaves in Aybak's harem.[50]

The former sultana was buried in the cemetery of the Mamluks below the Citadel in the exquisite tomb she had commissioned during her rule. The interior of the tomb was decorated with a Byzantine-influenced glass mosaic, depicting a tree with pearls, no doubt a reference to the name given to her—the Pearl Tree. She was the first and the last Muslim woman ever to govern Egypt.

The Bahri Mamluks:
The City of the Slave Sultans

LOCATED JUST BEYOND THE CITADEL, the minaret of the mosque of Sultan Hasan—the highest in Cairo—must have been the ideal point for an observer in the final decades of the fourteenth century to contemplate the magnificent panorama of urban Cairo. A traveler in today's Cairo can imagine the awe that such views must have inspired in visitors at the time, including Ibn Khaldun, one of the most distinguished historians of the medieval Islamic world. From the vantage point of the minaret, Ibn Khaldun would see the monumental mosque of Baybars in the northern suburbs beyond the walls of Cairo. Just south from the center of al-Qahira proper was the complex of Qalawun with its minaret rising next to its madrasa and mausoleum. Looking south, Ibn Khaldun would locate the minaret of the mosque of al-Nasir rising above the walls of the Citadel. He had traveled across the world, as far east as the distant lands of Tamerlane and as far west as Andalusia, but the sight of Cairo was unmatched by any other he had seen: "What one can imagine always surpasses what one can see, because of the scope of the imagination, except Cairo because it surpasses anything one can imagine."[1]

Ibn Khaldun was a contemporary of Sultan Hasan, but he did not arrive in Egypt until the end of Bahri Mamluk rule. He witnessed Cairo during its heyday as one of the most important of the commercial centers in the Middle East that linked the trade routes between Europe and the Orient. From the height of Sultan Hasan's minaret, Ibn Khaldun could have taken in the degree of Cairo's magnificence. It was a view that prompted him to write: "He who has not seen Cairo, does not know the grandeur of Islam. It is the metropolis of the universe, the garden of the world, the ant-hill of the human species, the portico of Islam, the throne of royalty, a city embellished with castles and palaces, decorated with dervish monasteries and with schools, and lighted by the moons and stars of erudition."[2] Contemplating such unprecedented development and urban vitality, Ibn Khaldun would have reflected on the Mamluk sultans who had ruled Cairo for the past one hundred years, while surveying the spectacle of the minarets that rose above their mosques and madrasas. It was in part due to the military bravery of these Mamluks that Cairo had attained such prosperity by profiting from a prolonged period of economic and political stability.

Ibn Khaldun (1332–1406) was a philosopher and historian born in Tunis, and is regarded as one of the most prominent scholars of medieval Islam. He served in the courts of Fez, Granada, and Tunis, and eventually settled in Cairo in 1382. Upon his arrival, he was appointed an instructor at the Qamhiyah school, and he later became Egypt's chief judge.[3] Many of his writings have not survived, but his greatest work is considered to be a history of the Arab states whose introduction, *Muqaddimah,* contains the essence of his ideas. The *Muqaddimah* provides a theory of the rise and fall of urban civilizations. Indeed, Ibn Khaldun can be considered the father of urban historical sociology, as he was the first scholar to use a sociological method to interpret history. In the third chapter of his opus, he discusses the formation of states, which he believed came into existence through tribal force or solidarity, or *asabiyah,* and religion. He speaks of the natural age of a state as comparable to that of a man, arguing that a state generally did not exceed 150 years and three generations of successors. Contributing to the state's dissolution would be dissent and injustice, which he believed led to the destruction of civilization.[4]

Having dedicated a considerable part of his work to the study of political regimes, Ibn Khaldun was specifically fascinated with the Bahri Mamluk empire and its many slave-sultans (and with the first Burji Mamluk sultan, Barquq, who was his main patron). He wrote not only about the Mamluk general al-Zahir Baybars, the founder of the Bahri Mamluk dynasty, but more broadly on his campaigns to establish the new political structure that governed Egypt and other parts of the Levant for more than two centuries.

In the period roughly corresponding to the rule of the Bahri Mamluks, Cairo experienced a tremendous surge of growth and development.[5] The Mamluks first took over the city in a bloody struggle that followed the death of the last Ayyubid ruler. They did not consolidate full control over Cairo until after General Baybars's victory over the Mongols, who had succeeded in destroying the Abbasid caliphate in Baghdad. Even though Baybars was not the first Mamluk sultan, he is remembered in Islamic history for founding the new dynasty.

As a general, Baybars managed to repel attempts to invade the Levant by both the Crusaders and the Mongols. Since unifying under the rule of Genghis Khan, the Mongols had vanquished everything in their path, passing through China and Russia and reaching as far as the gates of Vienna. Led by Genghis Khan's brother, Hulagu, the Mongols invaded the Middle East in 1255, destroyed Baghdad, and set their eyes on Syria, Palestine, and Egypt as their next targets.[6] Rather than await attack on Egyptian soil, Sultan Qutuz chose to confront Hulagu's armies in Ain Jalut, north of Palestine, with the support of the Bahri Mamluks who were led by Baybars. On their way to Syria the Mongols obliterated several cities in Persia.[7] Qutuz's connection to Persia, as he was of both Turkish and Persian descent, may have factored into his decision to go to battle rather than surrender to Hulagu's ultimatum to cede control over Egypt.

Arab victory at Ain Jalut came in early fall of 1260. The Mongols were weakened by the death of their leader, Genghis Khan. Nevertheless Qutuz may not have emerged victorious had it not been for the Bahri Mamluks. Baybars's actions proved decisive in crushing the invading armies, forcing them to retreat out of Syria.[8] However, when Qutuz rewarded his generals for their feats by distributing the Syrian principalities, Baybars was not given Aleppo as he desired. This caused Baybars and the Bahri Mamluks to turn against the man whose rule they had just preserved in battle. As did the Mamluks before him, Baybars came to power through the assassination of a sitting sultan, in this case Sultan Qutuz.

Baybars ultimately remained in power for seventeen years (1260–1277). Like Salah al-Din, his rule was based on strongman tactics and military prowess.[9] Likewise he sponsored numerous religious institutions and was

responsible for the construction of military and civil buildings throughout Egypt and Syria.[10] He attempted to legitimize his rule by transferring
the collapsed Abbasid caliphate to Cairo, and by hosting the caliph as a
nonruling religious figure.[11] He established diplomatic links with Constantinople and several states in Italy as well.[12] Nevertheless, his first priority
was always to hold the Mongol invaders in check, and because he understood the necessity of a united front in Syria, he expanded his control over
dissident principalities in that area.

During Baybars's reign, Cairo developed largely toward the north. Some
scholars consider the construction of the al-Zahir mosque in a northern
suburb there to be an attempt to create the core of a new Mamluk capital.
But the effort eventually succeeded only in converting some agricultural
land into residences for the rich and, in later centuries, into a cemetery.[13]
Notwithstanding, the monumental al-Zahir mosque (1266–1269) was the
first Friday mosque erected since the Fatimid-era mosque of al-Hakim.
Baybars paid great attention to the building, supervising its planning and
construction. Many of its materials were taken from Crusader structures
in Jaffa, and Baybars directly organized its procurement.[14] The layout
consists of a courtyard, or *sahn*, surrounded by arcades, or *riwaqs*. The
prayer hall, which is made up of three aisles at its center, leads toward a
domed sanctuary facing the mihrab. The mosque is accessible by a main
axial gate and two smaller ancillary ones. Above the vaulted entrance of
the mosque is the founder's inscription. In general, however, the decoration is characteristically restrained, consisting only of crenellations
atop the walls, and carvings and medallions on the gates.[15] Following his
predecessors, Baybars also founded a madrasa on a site next to al-Salihiya in Bayn al-Qasrayn.[16] However, unlike previous rulers, he dedicated
it exclusively to God, and did not include a mausoleum for his burial.

Baybars was succeeded by two of his sons, though their rule did not
last more than a few years. They were deposed by Qalawun, another
powerful Mamluk whose star was on the rise. Like Baybars, Qalawun was
a Kipchack Turk intent on establishing a dynasty by ensuring the succession of his sons to the throne. When he came to power as Sultan al-Mansur
Qalawun, he ushered in a period of stability that lasted a century. During

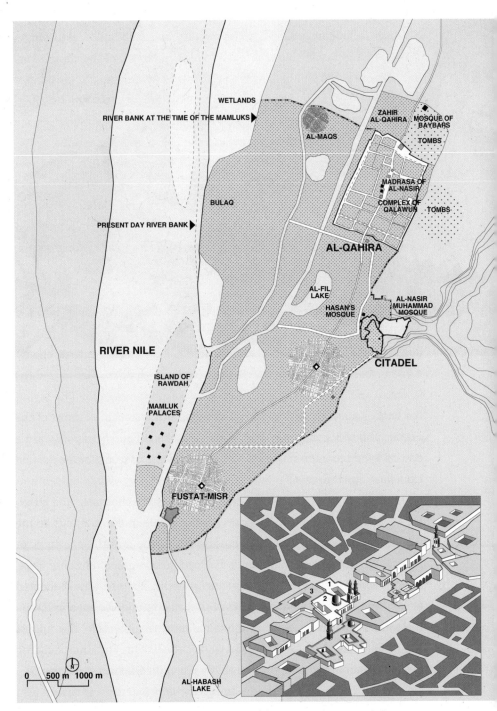

Figure 6.1   Map of Cairo area during the Bahri Mamluk period. (Key: 1. Madrasa al-Nasirya; 2. Madrasa al-Zahirya; 3. Bimaristan Qalawun.)

Figure 6.2   The Mosque of Sultan al-Zahir Baybars. ▬▬▬▬▬▬▬▬

his reign, Qalawun not only kept invading armies such as those of the Franks and Mongols at bay, but he also established alliances with Castile and Sicily, diplomatic relations with the emperor of Constantinople, and trade links with Genoa.[17]

The building complex where Qalawun's mosque, madrasa, and hospital are located introduced an entirely new architectural typology to the city. It combined religious and educational functions with a *maristan*, or a hospital serving the community. Facing the mosque of al-Salih, Qalawun's complex was erected in thirteen months, a speed unprecedented at the time, especially for projects of that magnitude. An inscription on the entrance dates the work to sometime between July 1284 and August 1285.[18] Qalawun's choice of methods to accomplish his ambitious building project was considered controversial by many. In addition to dismantling several structures in the Citadel to reuse their materials, Qalawun also sped up work on his complex by devoting all builders in Cairo to the project and using the labor of hundreds of Mongol prisoners of war. Moreover,

Figure 6.3 The funerary complex of al-Mansur Qalawun.

according to historians, the complex was built on illegally occupied land, as Qalawun evicted the residents of the Qutbiyya palace to clear land for the hospital. For these reasons, religious scholars have questioned its status as a spiritual institution.[19] According to *waqf* documents, Qalawun endowed his complex with mostly urban estates, which included markets, shops, and bathhouses, or *hamams,* built nearby, and other estates located abroad.[20]

The complex was unprecedented not only due to its size—at 20.2 meters high and 35.1 meters long—but also the novelty of its functions and decoration. The complex had a social and charitable mission and welcomed all Muslims regardless of gender or social standing. Its façade is divided into panels containing pointed-arch recesses with three levels of windows. Historians have claimed this design to be evidence of a western European stylistic influence.[21] The triple window composition, containing two arched openings crowned by a circular opening, is a configuration typically found in Romanesque churches.

The master plan of the complex is also one of the earliest examples of urban design in Cairo. The framed perspectives that resulted from the location of its minaret and madrasa demonstrate concern for the overall position of the complex's elements. In particular, a conscious decision was made to place the mausoleum on the north side of the complex, separated from the madrasa by a long corridor, with the hospital located in the back. The minaret, too, was not situated at the entrance, nor was it connected to the madrasa, as was common in other buildings of the time. Rather, it was placed on the north, connected to the mausoleum, to serve as a landmark for processions approaching from that direction. This specific configuration would later become characteristic of Mamluk funerary architecture. The minaret design is also notable for its rectangular base beginning at roof level and its three-story shaft. The horseshoe arches located on the first and second stories are of Andalusian influence. Its last level, built by Qalawun's son, is circular, constructed of masonry, and decorated with stucco ornaments.[22]

Qalawun's madrasa was dedicated to the study of Islamic law as well as the study of medicine.[23] The layout consisted of a courtyard formed by four *iwans* (with the largest of the four located on the qibla side), marked at the corners by three-storied living quarters. The prayer hall projected onto the street, receiving bright natural light on one side, while a two-story wall enclosed the courtyard. The wall consisted of three arches, with the central arch being slightly larger than the others. The same composition was repeated at the upper level, crowned by a circular clerestory window. Dual entrances were located on either side of the arched façade of the central nave. Two recessed spaces, or *suffa,* flanked the iwan. The courtyard was paved with marble, and archaeological research has uncovered the remains of an octagonal central fountain.[24]

The mausoleum could be reached from a small, arcaded courtyard, which also once held a central decorative fountain. Its eastern and western arcades carry three small masonry domes supported by spherical pendentives with the northern portion of the dome vaulted. A stucco-decorated arch marks the main entrance, which stands taller than the other porticoes. The main hall of the mausoleum is rectangular, with its top marked by a dome supported by an octagonal base.[25] In addition to being a burial place, this main hall had a ceremonial function. During Qalawun's lifetime, as well as after his death, a group of select eunuchs, the *namus al-mulk*, would perform rites and royal ceremonies there.[26] The mausoleum was also used for teaching Islamic law. Its interior was decorated with marble mosaic panels, which may have been inspired by similar Roman and Byzantine mosaics. Its mihrab, ornamented with mosaics and flanked by columns of marble, had horseshoe arches and was of unprecedented size. Over time the mausoleum became the chosen place for the inauguration of amirs, a ceremony that had previously been held in the adjacent al-Salih dome.[27]

It is believed that Qalawun's decision to include a hospital in his complex owed much to the fact that he had once been cured at Nur al-Din's hospital in Damascus. Built in 1284, Qalawun's hospital was a philanthropic foundation, open to all regardless of social and economic position.[28] Divided into two sections, one for men and the other for women, the hospital is described as being lavishly decorated and having a cruciform plan with four halls surrounding a courtyard.[29] Ibn Battuta, a Moroccan traveler and scholar who spent time in Egypt in 1326 as a pilgrim in a caravan bound for Mecca, expressed his admiration for Qalawun's complex—in particular, for the beauty of the structure housing the hospital: "As for the maristan," he wrote, "no description is adequate to its beauties."[30]

Benefiting from a generous endowment that Ibn Battuta estimated to be one thousand dinars per day, the hospital treated as many as four thousand patients daily. It was organized by the type of treatment offered—infectious diseases, surgery, or ophthalmology. According to the waqf deed, priority was to be given to the patients found to be most in need and those who were the most impoverished.[31] The low-income patients were housed at the hospital until their treatment was deemed complete, and at discharge they were given clothing and money. During treatment each patient received meals and medicine prepared at the hospital, and each was provided with a wooden bed with linens as well as a pot. Not only were medical services accessible to all at no cost, funerary costs could also be covered if needed. As part of the charitable work of the Cairo elites, the hospital was a testimony to the enlightened intellectual community that developed in the city during the thirteenth and early fourteenth centuries. According to Ibn Battuta, the amirs of Cairo competed "with one another in charitable works and the founding of mosques and religious houses."[32]

The Qalawun dynasty was partly based on heredity. But this model was eclipsed by the typical system of Mamluk succession, characterized by frequent violent power struggles, in which the most powerful and calculating would ascend to the sultan's throne. The story of the Mamluk period, which lasts the course of several hundred years, cannot be told without reference to the remarkable life journey made by members of this military elite. That journey began outside the Islamic world, in the slave markets around the Black Sea. Here, young boys were purchased and sent to Egypt to serve the sultan and other powerful men. During their upbringing, these youths were converted to Islam and underwent rigorous military training. After their emancipation, they continued to serve their masters. But often these same Mamluks later became powerful men, such as amirs, or rose to important positions in the military.

Emanuel Piloti, a Venetian merchant who traveled to Egypt frequently and who was received at the court of Sultan al-Nasir Faraj, left a detailed account of the training methods of the Mamluks. Piloti, who owned warehouses in Cairo and Alexandria and who had traveled across the Levant for forty years, witnessed the rise and fall of five Circassian sultans.[33] He describes how Mamluk boys were divided into groups of twenty-five and entrusted to the care of eunuchs upon their arrival in Egypt. First they received the teachings of the Quran. When they had advanced in age and in training, they were taught Islamic theology. After these lessons, they were considered ready to receive military training. The completion of their education was marked by a ceremony in which they were brought before the sultan and examined by their religious masters. Piloti witnessed this certification ceremony, and describes how after a period of scrutiny, the sultan would identify those students who had proved to have exceptional skills by drawing them together in the center of the examination site. The next day the recruits were presented with new titles, salaries, and other benefits to be bestowed on them at the start of their service.[34]

The principal means for a freed Mamluk amir to consolidate his power was to purchase his own Mamluk slaves and bring them into his household. A wide system of taxation on farm output also made it possible for Mamluks to gather considerable economic power. This operated on the basis of *iltizams,* or licenses, which were granted to elites by the government. The holders of such grants, the *multazims,* could extract several times the value of the iltizams in either tax or agricultural production from an increasingly burdened peasantry. Most of this revenue was concentrated in the hands of Mamluks.[35]

The story of the Mamluk amir Taz illustrates well the ways in which a Mamluk slave could rise to power.[36] Purchased in his early youth by Sultan al-Nasir Muhammad, Taz later earned the favor of the sultan and was awarded his freedom and the title *saki,* "the cupbearer." Over time he became the amir of a thousand Mamluks, and one of the most important amirs in Egypt.[37] Through such efforts, a Mamluk might not only become part of the political elite, but could even ascend to the throne. It should be noted that only first-generation Mamluks who arrived to Egypt as slaves and were brought up receiving training in military households could gain access to the aristocratic circles or the throne. Very rarely would their sons participate in struggles for political power.

Although the Mamluk system did not formally mean hereditary succession to the throne, most Mamluk rulers sought to ensure the accession of their sons. Qalawun was one of the most successful at consolidating his power within his family, as he was succeeded by his son, al-Ashraf Khalil, who continued forward with his father's military projects. After Khalil was assassinated during a struggle with rival Mamluks, his half-brother, al-Malik al-Nasir Muhammad, emerged victorious, redeeming the throne for the Qalawun family. During al-Nasir's lengthy reign (1298–1340), Cairo entered one of its most prosperous periods. Al-Nasir was a strong ruler, harsh on his amirs and merciless with his political opponents. He stayed in power for almost a half century, a record unsurpassed by any other Mamluk.

Al-Nasir came to the throne when he was only eight, and the first years of his rule were marked by political turbulence, during which he was twice dethroned by opponents. The first time came after only a year, when he was supplanted by the viceroy Kitbugha, a Mamluk sultan of Mongol origin. Kitbugha was in turn deposed by Lajin, the sultan who undertook the restoration of the mosque of Ibn Tulun. Al-Nasir came to power for a second time at the age of fourteen after Lajin was deposed and assassinated. During this period, al-Nasir's rule was nominal, as a group of older amirs held all decision-making authority. Eventually al-Nasir was forced to abdicate and was replaced by the amir Baybars al-Jashankir, who had the support of the Burji Mamluks. But al-Nasir returned to the throne for a third time at the age of twenty-five—this time with the support of Syria, and with the intent of removing from his court all of the amirs who had previously curtailed his power.

The last thirty years of al-Nasir's rule brought a period of peace and stability. Contacts with lands beyond Egypt were made through trade rather than military confrontation. During this time the Mongol threat had subsided and merchants from Europe traveled to Cairo, as it was then the center of trade with the Orient. Al-Nasir also turned his attention away from military defense and toward internal governance. In particular he focused on fiscal reform. Over 40 percent of the empire's revenue came from fiefdoms al-Nasir had distributed to his amirs, which included Mecca, Damascus, and Allepo.[38] He employed this wealth for many vital public projects.

During al-Nasir's reign, Cairo's built environment underwent great change. Ibn Battuta, who arrived at this time, describes the city's spectacular development:

> I arrived at length at Cairo, mother of cities and seat of Pharaoh the tyrant, mistress of broad regions and fruitful lands, boundless in multitude of buildings, peerless in beauty and splendour, the meeting-place of comer and goer, the halting-place of feeble and mighty, whose throngs surge as the waves of the sea, and can scarce be contained in her for all her size and capacity. It is said that in Cairo there are twelve thousand water-carriers who transport water on camels, and thirty thou-

sand hirers of mules and donkeys, and that on the Nile there
are thirty-six thousand boats belonging to the Sultan and his
subjects which sail upstream to Upper Egypt and downstream
to Alexandria and Damietta, laden with goods and profitable
merchandise of all kinds.[39]

Both al-Qahira proper, the walled city, and Zahir al-Qahira, the section
outside the walls, developed rapidly. Development in the north was
outpaced by growth to the west and south. By the end of al-Nasir's reign,
the area to the south stretching between Bab Zuwayla, the Citadel, and the
mosque of Ibn Tulun had become the most populous district of the city.
Development in the western suburbs was encouraged by the construction
of the Khalij al-Nasiri canal, and the area between the canal and al-Qahira
developed rapidly.[40] Even the area west of the canal stretching from Bab
al-Nasr to the Muqattam Hills was open for development. During this
time, the banks of the Nile shifted westward, exposing new land. The old
al-Maqs port was filled in and a new harbor named Bulaq emerged to take
its place.[41]

Important buildings from this era include a madrasa first funded in 1295
by the viceroy Kitbugha, who terminated al-Nasir's first reign. The madrasa
was later completed by al-Nasir, as indicated by an inscription bearing his
name on the façade.[42] Located on the *qassbah* and sandwiched between the
Qalawun complex and the madrasa of Sultan Barquq, which was built a few
decades later, the madrasa's most distinctive element is its marble pointed-
arch portal, which was formerly part of a Gothic church in Acre, brought to
Egypt by Kitbugha following a campaign against the Crusaders in 1291.[43]
The portal made a strong impression on the Egyptian historian Maqrizi,
who praised it for its beauty and craftsmanship. Bearing the word Allah
inscribed on a rosette at the apex of the arch, the portal must have symbolized the military victory of the Mamluks against the Crusaders.

The madrasa is based on a cruciform plan with four vaulted iwans of
various sizes surrounding a sahn with a central fountain. The ten-meter
mihrab in the iwan is decorated with elaborate stuccowork, attributed to
Persian craftsmen from Tabriz.[44] A central corridor separates the madrasa

Figure 6.4   Madrasa and mausoleum of Sultan al-Nasir Muhammad.

from the mausoleum. Another remarkable feature is its three-tiered minaret, decorated with elaborate stucco ornaments thought to be the work of Andalusian craftsmen.

Another building funded by al-Nasir is the congregational mosque in the Citadel (1318–1335), a hypostyle structure with two minarets.[45] The two stone minarets, possibly the work of Tabriz craftsmen, each consist of three shafts articulated by two balconies, with the top shaft decorated with faience. The exterior of the mosque is sparsely decorated, without the arabesques, keel-arched windows, or other forms of ornamentation typical of the religious structures of Cairo at the time. Its plain exterior is defined only by the three portals, one of which, facing south, served as al-Nasir's private entrance.

Al-Nasir's passion for building gave Cairo one of the most outstanding built heritages in the world. The city was probably more than twice the size of London or Paris during his reign. But this period of growth was short-lived, as al-Nasir died in 1340 at the age of fifty-eight, and his successors were weak. In the six years that followed, five of his sons were murdered or deposed in struggles over the throne. After the clashes

Figure 6.5 The Mosque of Sultan al-Nasir Muhammad at the Citadel. ■■■■■

subsided, the next ruler of any continuity was al-Nasir's son Hasan, who was only twelve when he came to the throne. But his accession in 1347 coincided with the arrival of the plague in Egypt.

When the plague struck Egypt, the country was in no position to withstand the pandemic.[46] Cairo alone lost at least half of its population.[47] Maqrizi writes of deserted streets, empty houses, abandoned belongings, and inheritances that changed hands as many as five times a day.[48] The depopulation caused by the epidemic left Egypt in deep crisis, with particularly severe economic consequences. There were not enough laborers to work the land, leading to an increase in the cost of labor and a decrease in tax revenues. Thousands of Mamluks also died, leaving the ranks of the military considerably diminished. The misfortunes of the fourteenth century did not stop with the first outbreak of the disease. The plague returned to Cairo in 1374–1375 and again between 1379 and 1381. Natural calamities, such as the Nile flood of 1354 and a famine in 1375, also contributed to the prolonged decline in the city's population. [49]

In an ironic twist of fate, the sultan's treasury grew considerably during this period. All the belongings of families killed by the plague were confiscated and became property of the state. The land revenue of

Figure 6.6 The Mosque of Sultan Hasan. Exterior view (left). View of the iwan (right).

1376 recorded an increase of nine million dinars, which helps explain the number of monuments that were funded between 1350 and 1380. [50] Sultan Hasan may have decided that the proper way to make use of this wealth was to build a magnificent religious edifice dedicated to those killed in the epidemic. Maqrizi writes that the Hasan mosque was one of the most expensive monuments ever built in Cairo, at a total cost of twenty million dihrams (a large amount for its time).[51]

Hasan founded his mosque in 1356 on a site near the Citadel, and its construction lasted five years. Its scale gives no hint of a state weakened by calamities. Indeed, its construction proved a heavy burden on the treasury. The mosque is believed to have been the only Cairo mosque designed to have four minarets at the time. Two of these were built at the corners of the mosque's principal façade.[52] Two others supposedly stood above its entrance, but they collapsed in 1361, causing great loss of life.[53]

Upon their completion, Sultan Hasan's complex, which included a mosque, madrasa, and tomb, covered an area of almost ten thousand square meters. Its limestone walls stood forty meters high, and the minarets rose to eighty-five meters. As many as five hundred students could be accommodated in its residential quarters, in addition to the numerous men who served there in such roles as prayer-callers, professors, calligraphers, and physicians. The mosque was lavishly detailed, although its center was a simple cubic space. The imposing doorway of the main entrance was topped with a half-dome decorated with stalactite stone carvings.[54] Although the mosque was never fully completed, it remains one of the best-preserved medieval mosques in Cairo due to its durable construction. Work on the mosque ceased when Sultan Hasan was murdered at the age of twenty-six by his generals, whose influence he had tried to restrict.

During their centuries in power, the Bahri Mamluks were among the few rulers in Egypt to never assimilate into the population. Rawdah Island symbolized their power and isolated them as a class, allowing them to maintain a certain distance from ordinary people. Meanwhile, co-residence had almost become a necessity for the organization of the lower social orders. During Mamluk times, craftsmen and ethnic communities lived in segregated areas. As new areas were settled, these quarters came to be called by the names of the ethnic, religious, or occupational groups that resided in them.[55] The division of the city into administrative quarters was advanced under Mamluk rule and further formalized in the layout of the streets, which reflected the social composition of the society.

During the rule of al-Nasir, the major commercial zone, the qassbah, running from Bab Zuwayla to Bab al-Futuh, bustled with activity. There were twelve thousand shops and an abundance of itinerant vendors.[56] Inside al-Qahira proper, most of the thirty-five major suqs dating from Fatimid times were still very active. A large number of new markets also developed outside the walled city by the end of the Bahri Mamluks' rule. *Wekalas*, or urban caravanserais, were for the most part located around the al-Hakim mosque at the city's edge, while the farmers' markets were kept outside the city walls.[57] Other industries, such as tanners, dyers, and blacksmiths, were located in areas that would not disturb the rest of the population—the student in the madrasa, the worshiper in the mosque, or the shopper in the bazaar.[58]

During this time, guilds for commerce and trade were heavily regulated.[59] The *muhtasib* no longer acted simply as a market supervisor; he now had a moral and legal function, and was assisted by inspectors, or *arifs*, who served as the mediators and enforcers of city and state policy. The muhtasib was also responsible for seeing that building occupants respected the right-of-way and did not protrude onto the street, which was considered public property. The placement of building materials and construction activity were carefully watched and regulated as well.[60]

In general the streets of Cairo were governed by strict ordinances, which were concerned not only with construction and development, but also public safety, cleaning, and the maintenance of moral order. The city was administered by judges who oversaw matters of civil law, while police monitored public order, supervised firefighting, and patrolled the streets at night. The sovereign also wrote directives concerning public order, as seen in a document issued by Qalawun during a period of war. These edicts not only imposed strict curfews and restrictions on the movement of women in the streets, but also ordered police patrols both inside and outside the city gates at night. Places considered to be of ill repute were patrolled, and no one was allowed to frequent them. Men and women, moreover, were forbidden from congregating in cemeteries on Friday nights.[61] Maqrizi notes that the gates of Cairo were closed every night, and that guards were posted at each gate during evening prayer.

The waqf system reached its greatest development in Mamluk times. The sultans maintained it as a means of preserving the buildings inside the walled city.[62] Waqf funds were used to provide social services and supported cultural institutions, including schools and hospitals. Mamluk documents show the creation of a number of technical positions associated with the waqf system.[63] These included the *mo'alem,* who supervised the construction of buildings; the *shahedi al-imara,* who enforced building codes and specifications; and the *al-mur'khem,* who maintained and beautified the buildings.

Prior to the Black Death in 1348, Cairo was once again a great and prosperous city that had redeveloped and spread in all directions.[64] As residents moved outward and settled peripheral areas, they erected buildings and formed new streets. A considerable number of streets outside the walled city were laid during the rule of the Bahri Mamluks. Among these were the streets of Zahir al-Qahira and the streets connecting al-Qahira with its southern suburb, Fustat-Misr, and its western suburb, Bulaq. A hierarchy of streets developed as a result of strict laws regulating the different kinds of activities that could take place in them.[65] Different types of traffic were equally regulated.[66]

Inside the walled old city, the pattern set by the Ayyubids of building in the Bayn al-Qasrayn continued under the Bahri Mamluks. Three madrasas—al-Nasirya, al-Zahirya, and al-Munsourya—were built there between existing Ayyubid-era madrasas.[67] But the Bahri Mamluk additions did not alter the visual profile of this area as it had been developed during Ayyubid times. Rather, new functions were added to Bayn al-Qasrayn, and these formed a separate internal district with a number of new landmarks.

The Fatimid palaces on the main qassbah, begun during the Ayyubid period, also underwent transformations under the Mamluks. In 1262 Baybars issued an official document requiring the approval of the Abbasid caliph to make parts of the palaces the property of the public treasury. Lots were subsequently resold and redeveloped individually, replacing the palaces with structures of various functions, from religious edifices to bazaars and living quarters. The Mamluk amir Baktash bought part of the Eastern Fatimid Palace, and built stables and living quarters on it. By the time of Maqrizi, only a few of the great Fatimid palaces remained, as most had been reduced to rubble.[68] Eleven Fatimid mosques also appear to have been torn down during this period.

By the end of the Bahri Mamluks' rule, however, the main spine of the qassbah still retained its three-district structure, with each district possessing its own internal landmarks. The space in front of al-Azhar had become a religious and educational node after the Mamluks returned the *khutbah* to its mosque. The space around Bab al-Nasr became a major wholesale commercial center after the construction of several wekalas in the area around it. When new buildings were erected, they were often located close to existing agglomerations of earlier structures. Both the Qalawun complex and the al-Nasirya madrasa represented attempts to maintain and strengthen the existing structure of the qassbah.

Inside the walled old city the Mamluks built exclusively along the major arteries, but beyond its walls they sought to build anywhere they could. Because they considered Zahir al-Qahira to be their capital, they constructed most of their buildings there.[69] Under the Bahri Mamluks, Zahir al-Qahira had its greatest period of development. Of thirty-one major Bahri Mamluk structures, only ten were constructed inside the walled city; the majority were located in Zahir al-Qahira.

The Bahri Mamluks were careful to position new buildings near already existing ones. Judging from the homogeneous urban complexes that were constructed under their tenure, one can safely say that they were concerned with providing fine architectural additions without disturbing the identity and the character of existing buildings. Of the fourteen major madrasas and mosques built in the time of the Bahri Mamluks inside Cairo, twelve had staggered exterior façades, usually with one side aligned to the street. In contrast, those located outside of the city proper had very uniform plans and plain exterior façades.[70]

The similarity of the minarets and domes built at this time provides a visual effect that defined the city's skyline. Most Bahri Mamluk minarets are of medium height (less than sixty meters tall) and composed of three segments. The first is square in shape; the second, and tallest, is octagonal; and the third has the form of a cylindrical cap.[71] The square base of the minarets usually followed the orientation of the qibla. That is, the base had two sides parallel and two sides perpendicular to the qibla. Minarets were usually positioned on the corner of a building, adjacent to the street or above its main entrance. Bahri Mamluk domes were wide, relatively low, and usually located deep inside a mosque, where they were often unseen by passing pedestrians. Street-level entrances, which evolved as separate and significant architectural elements during Bahri Mamluk times, were either recessed or aligned with the exterior.

Depopulation due to the plague and other natural calamities were not the only crises the city had to face toward the end of the fourteenth century. The Mongols under Timur (known in the west as Tamerlane) launched another attack on Egypt in 1382. In desperation, the Bahri Mamluks turned to the talented Circassian general Barquq for help. Barquq would eventually become the first Circassian sultan of Egypt and the founder of the Burji Mamluk dynasty, which would rule until the Ottoman conquest. The Circassians were referred to as Burji Mamluks because they lived in the Burj, or the Citadel of Salah al-Din in the Muqattam Hills. But the shift to Circassian rule represented more than a simple change in dynasty; it was a social revolution of profound significance. While it facilitated the flourishing of medieval Cairo, it also contained the seeds of its own eventual decline.[72]

Ibn Khaldun arrived in Cairo in 1384 at the end of the Bahri Mamluk rule and at the start of the takeover by the Burji Mamluks. Sultan Barquq, who presided over this transition, and who would later send Ibn Khaldun to serve as his ambassador to the Mongol court, welcomed Ibn Khaldun to Cairo, offering him protection and a generous salary.[73] Upon his arrival, the sultan also appointed Ibn Khaldun as a professor at the Qamhiyah school, a Maliki institution located in the vicinity of the mosque of 'Amr. But soon after, when the serving Maliki chief judge passed a wrongful judgment and fell of out favor with the sultan, Ibn Khaldun was summoned once again. This time Sultan Barquq gave him the robe of honor, and the title *Wali al-Din,* or guardian of religion, and appointed him *qadi,* or chief judge, which was considered one of the four highest posts in the Egyptian state.

Ibn Khaldun's court was housed at the Salihiya madrasa, which was founded by the Ayyubids and was the most powerful college in Egypt at the time. The madrasa housed all four schools of law, with Ibn Khaldun at the Malikite school.[74] His appointment, however, was marked by disputes and unrest. No sooner had he taken over his duties than intrigue and antagonism began to loom over him. Local officials regarded Ibn Khaldun's rapid advance to a much-coveted public post as unusual and unfair. The fact that he was determined to eradicate the corruption reigning in Egyptian courts at the time also contributed to severe opposition and criticism, and he lost the support of many dignitaries.

The difficulties posed by his new appointment were soon eclipsed by a much greater calamity. Once he decided to settle in Egypt, Ibn Khaldun asked for his family to join him. Hoping to persuade Ibn Khaldun to return to his country of origin, the sultan of Tunisia prevented his family from leaving. Sultan Barquq intervened and Ibn Khaldun's family was allowed to board a boat headed to Egypt. But it would all end in a tragic accident. Ibn Khaldun described how a storm led to the loss of his wife and children at sea and how this led him to request a release from his duties only a year after his appointment in 1385.[75] Although he lived an affluent and stable life in Egypt, Ibn Khaldun became a recluse after the loss of his family: "Misfortune and despair were great and I was inclined to lead a hermit's life."[76]

Ibn Khaldun is said to have been the mentor of another important historian of Egypt, Taqi al-Din al-Maqrizi. Although Maqrizi studied under many scholars and shaikhs, Ibn Khaldun was one of the most prominent figures among them. Maqrizi was a regular member of Ibn Khaldun's circle while the latter was teaching in Cairo. The influence of Ibn Khaldun's interpretation of history is evident in many of Maqrizi's written works, particularly his treatise on the calamity of the early fifteenth century.[77] Maqrizi wrote portions of Ibn Khaldun's biography in two of his books: *Durar al-'Uqud al-Farida,* a comprehensive biography; and *Al-Suluk,* in which he tells the story of Ibn Khaldun's life in Egypt and Syria. It is believed that during his stay in Cairo, Ibn Khaldun lived near al-Salihiya, where he was teaching. Some of his contemporaries recount seeing him walking home, in the company of several of his assistant judges, in the district of Bayn al-Qasrayn.

Living in a century marked by societal shifts, regime changes, and colliding civilizations, and having traveled across the world, Ibn Khaldun was afforded a unique perspective on history. Standing in the courtyard of the Sultan Hasan madrasa, which is considered by many the heart of Islamic Cairo, Ibn Khaldun must have pondered the essence of history itself. His description of Cairo was panoramic in its reach, and his attempts to explain the structural order of the social and political world, as exemplified by cities like Cairo, came to constitute one of the greatest theories of history, the *Muqaddimah.* Here Ibn Khaldun brought together history, philosophy, and sociology to reflect on the cyclical changes that occur within nations and states, and the forces at work in the formation of political regimes: "When the universe is being turned upside-down, we must ask ourselves whether it is changing its nature, whether there is to be a new creation and a new order in the world. Therefore today we need a historian who can declare the state of the world, of its countries and peoples."[78] The Cairo of the Bahri Mamluks was indeed on his mind as he wrote these words.

Governing from the Tower:
The Burji Mamluks

THE HISTORY OF CITIES has always been the history of individuals, events, and places and the interactions among them. Few places in Cairo speak to the history of the city throughout its millennial development as does Bab Zuwayla, the southern gate of the old Fatimid city. Bab Zuwayla and its adjacent mosque are a good place to begin the story of the Circassian Burji Mamluks in Cairo. The Burji Mamluks, or Mamluks of the Tower, who had succeeded their Bahri counterparts, were so named because of their residence in the Citadel, where the protagonists of our story, al-Zahir Barquq, al-Mu'ayyad Shaiykh, Qaytbay, and Qansuh al-Ghuri, all lived.[1] Bab Zuwayla is likely the vantage point from which the great historian of Cairo, Taqi al-Din al-Maqrizi, would have witnessed the unfolding of major events in the life of the city, ranging from celebrations to funerals to the occasional execution.

The minarets built by the Burji Mamluks were some of the tallest that Cairo had ever seen. In particular, the magnificent twin minarets rising atop Bab Zuwayla must have offered Maqrizi a unique view of the development of the Burji Mamluk city. Looking southeast toward the Citadel, he would have witnessed the expansion of Cairo and the unprecedented density of building in the heart of the city. Looking north, he would have seen the magnificent dome and minaret of Barquq's funerary complex, completed only a few decades before he wrote his voluminous compendium, *Al-Mawa'ez wa al-I'tibar bi-Dhikr al-Khitat wa al-Athar*. The *Khitat*, as it became known, was both a history of Cairo and a documentation of its physical layout, including descriptions of its major buildings and primary locales as they existed at the time.

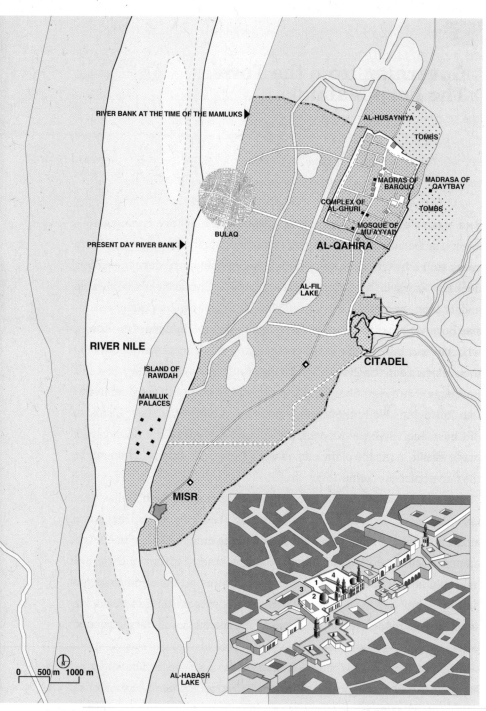

Figure 7.1   Map of Cairo area during the Burji Mamluk period. (Key: 1. Madrasa al-Nasirya; 2. Madrasa al-Zahirya; 3. Bimaristan Qalawun; 4. Madrasa al-Munsourya.) ▬

The towers atop Bab Zuwayla were an addition made in the fifteenth century by the Burji Mamluk sultan al-Mu'ayyad Shaiykh. Maqrizi wrote that al-Mu'ayyad vowed to build a mosque on the nearby site of the thirteenth-century Shama'il prison, where he had been incarcerated before becoming the sovereign. During the Burji Mamluk period, Bab Zuwayla was the gate through which the Mamluk sultans entered the city from the Citadel. It was the official site of public executions and the location where the bodies of criminals, war captives, and political prisoners were put on display.[2]

Maqrizi was not only an eyewitness to the demolition of the old prison and the building of al-Mu'ayyad's mosque and madrasa, he was later a professor of Islamic studies at the madrasa.[3] It has been suggested that the name Bab Zuwayla was changed to the more popular Bawabat al-Mitwali around this time. The change likely reflected the fact that the surrounding neighborhoods no longer accommodated military forces associated with the Zuwayla tribe, who had come to Egypt with the Fatimids. Instead the area had become a place of worship, where the people of Cairo honored a saintly preacher by the name of Mitwali.[4]

Maqrizi was one of the most prominent Egyptian historians to author a *khitat,* a genre of historical-topographical writings on cities. Cairo has been fortunate to have had several such works authored by well-regarded writers. But Maqrizi was in a special position to write such monographs, having served for some time as Cairo's *muhtasib*, or market supervisor. The second volume of his khitat provides detailed descriptions of the city's religious, institutional, governmental, and commercial structures as well as many of its other important landmarks. Despite some charges of inaccuracy, historians of Cairo owe a great debt to Maqrizi's *Khitat*, as it remains one of the most comprehensive accounts of the Mamluk city and its life, preserving the names, locations, histories, and dates of places that have since disappeared, in a manner that makes Maqrizi the guardian of Cairo's Mamluk heritage.

Maqrizi, born in 1364, grew up in the core of the old Fatimid city near its main corridor, or *qassbah,* in a small quarter, or *hara,* named Harat Berguan. The hara was connected to the market al-Jamaliya, named after amir al-Juyush, who had built the second Fatimid city wall.[5] It is

Figure 7.2   Bab Zuwayla, also known as Bab al-Mitwalli.

believed that Maqrizi lived in the home of his maternal grandfather, who was one of the most renowned learned men in Cairo, a Hanafi *faqih* who had written several books on philology and grammar.[6] Many of Maqrizi's family members also appear to have held important juridical positions. His father, who died when Maqrizi was fourteen, held a position in the judiciary and the vice-regency. But it was under his grandfather's guardianship and influence that Maqrizi received his education and developed as a young scholar, studying under noted shaiykhs in Cairo, Mecca, and Damascus. When Ibn Khaldun began teaching in Cairo in 1382, Maqrizi joined his circle and subsequently began attending his lectures. Maqrizi's writings were greatly influenced by Ibn Khaldun's work and theory of history. Maqrizi spoke of his mentor with utmost reverence, and considered him "our master, the great scholar and professor, the chief of justice."[7]

Maqrizi's lineage is not very well known. In the prefaces of his works, he refrains from providing an extensive genealogy of his forefathers, as was a common practice at the time.[8] Some of his ancestors may have been Fatimid, which he neither acknowledged nor disclosed, as such a public declaration of his Fatimid and Ismaili origins could have jeopardized his career as a scholar, or *'alim,* in the Shafi'i school, or *madhab,* as well as his public standing. Biographers hostile to him, such as al-Sakhawi, inferred from his writings that Maqrizi had Fatimid roots, based on what they characterized as his overly positive depictions of the Fatimids in his *Khitat.*[9]

According to one biographer, Maqrizi had adopted the Sunni Shafi'i madhab around 1384, after renouncing the Hanbali and Hanafi madhabs of his education.[10] As a Shafi'i scholar, Maqrizi lived during a period when historical writings proliferated and several schools of historiography divided historians and their disciples into rival factions. Several of Maqrizi's biographers knew him personally and, depending on their relationship to him, shed different perspectives on his life and work. Some stressed his value as a scholar, his importance as a historian, and his religious and moral virtues; another small group of critics called into question his methods as a historian; and a few even accused him of plagiarism.[11] But nonetheless it is from Maqrizi that we get the feel for life during the Burji Mamluk dynasty. Living at the time of Sultan Mu'ayyad, Maqrizi could fully observe the fall of the Bahri Mamluks and the rise of al-Zahir Barquq, the Circassian who became the first Burji Mamluk sultan.

Although Maqrizi's description of Cairo during the Burji Mamluks' reign indicates that their hold on power was tenuous, the city remained a wondrous achievement, exceeding anything Europe had yet produced, according to the European travelers who visited at the time.[12] We learn from Maqrizi that Cairo's western section, Khalij al-Nasiri, between the walled city and the canal from the Nile, was filled with palaces and gardens. We discover that its eastern section served as the official cemetery of the Burji Mamluks, and a few scattered madrasas and *khanqahs* were also built there. The northern suburb al-Husayniya, as he describes it, was never fully able to recover from the desolation induced by the plague, and in the south, Fustat-Misr continued its steady deterioration.[13] The development of Bulaq to the west, as the major port on the Nile and later as a heavily populated district, also took place during the Burji Mamluk period.

The Mamluk ruling elite emphasized their role as champions of Islam, and the pious foundations and religious institutions they sponsored became defining aspects of this period. Such religious institutions were usually foundations established by Mamluk princes, based on the *waqf* system. This means of philanthropic endowment was developed within Islam to underwrite major construction projects and maintain important religious institutions, often utilizing private enterprise as its source of revenue.

Even though waqf institutions were introduced during earlier periods, the system achieved its greatest influence during Mamluk times. It developed a certain flexibility over time, as the successors had the authority to modify or enlarge the terms of a trust. As such, waqf funds supported a variety of purposes, including religious, educational, and health services, as well as infrastructure projects, all of which served diverse social groups. In a nonhereditary ruling system, the waqf system was a way for princely founders to play a role in religious life and society. And because waqf structures bore patrons' names for posterity, the system allowed them to claim their places in history. Indeed, the waqf system made legends of Mamluk figures. Sponsorship of institutions housed in major monuments was not only a gesture of religious devotion and charity, it also had a pragmatic motivation, as its patrons could accrue benefits, including a portion of the institutions' revenues. As such, many Mamluk waqfs were a combination of philanthropic endowments and family trusts.[14]

In some cases the establishment of religious institutions also entailed provisions for public leisure and entertainment. This component may have emerged from the influence of Sufi spirituality, which sought to integrate acts of piety with those of pleasure in daily life. In his writings, Maqrizi termed these provisions *muftarajat*, or allowable pleasures, and *muntazahat*, or promenades. In particular, Maqrizi refers to several mosques located amid gardens or landscaped grounds. Such scenic locations enabled the mosques also to serve as venues for public festivals and ceremonies.[15]

When the Circassian Mamluks took control of Egypt, there was little change in their form of government. The Citadel, al-Burj, once again became the symbol of elite power. During this time certain areas of the city also came to be favored by the wealthy because of their salubriousness. However, no one class dominated a given district of the city.[16]

Al-Zahir Barquq was the first sultan to return to the tradition of residing in the Citadel. The founder of the Burji Mamluk dynasty, he rose to power by first serving as the commander-in-chief of the army during the tenure of the last two young sultans of the Qalawun dynasty. In a manner common during the Mamluk era, Barquq briefly took over the throne in 1382 after he deposed Sultan Hajji. But a year later, he, too, was deposed after suffering a military defeat in Syria.[17] His second period of rule, starting in 1390, marked the beginning of a new dynasty.

The Circassians were a regiment of Mamluks originally purchased as slave-children in the Caucasus. Ethnically different from the Turkish Bahri Mamluks, they were initially entrusted to guard Sultan Qalawun's palace. The barracks where they trained were located in the Citadel in the Muqattam Hills.[18] There they were put through strict military training and given religious instruction before becoming army men. Eventually the competitive succession system made the Circassian Burji Mamluk period a time of turmoil, power struggles, and instability, as different Mamluk factions, formed under different households, engaged in continuous political rivalries.

From the descriptions of European travelers written during the rule of Barquq, we learn that Cairo was a city full of activity. Leonardo Frescobaldi, who visited Egypt on his way to Jerusalem, wrote of the city:

> Cairo and Babylon is a very big city, more than eighteen miles long and eight miles wide. The river Nile runs beside the city and has a good port. When we were in Cairo there were so many ships that putting together all the ships I ever saw in the ports of Genoa, Venice and Ancona, leaving out ships of two decks, they would not make a third of all that were there. ... In the piazza of the Sultan near the castle where he dwells, there is a great number of jewelers, who have many precious stones, as emerald, ruby ... and stones of every kind.[19]

Frescobaldi was an Italian nobleman who came from a prominent Florentine family. He was deeply religious, had trained in the military, and participated in numerous battles. His pilgrimage to Jerusalem took him to Cairo in October 1384 as a member of a contingent of Italians. Upon their arrival, Cairo was in celebration: "The Sultan was returning from the chase that lasted several days, and they had a thousand pavilions, and a richer thing had never been seen before."[20] Frescobaldi wrote that Barquq had already ruled for two years by the time he and his fellow pilgrims arrived. He believed the Circassian ruler was formerly a Christian from Greece who came to Egypt as a slave-child. Barquq later renounced the faith of his upbringing and became the ruler of Egypt by deposing the preceding sultan. According to Frescobaldi, Barquq also replaced the caliph when he refused to recognize Barquq's authority. And to undertake major reforms in Cairo, Barquq also replaced all the *qadis* in Egypt.[21]

We learn from Maqrizi that during the reign of Barquq, Cairo achieved a remarkable recovery from the plagues that had devastated its population a decade earlier.[22] But the rebuilding was concentrated in the central portion of the walled city, while the areas outside remained abandoned or only sparsely populated.[23] The recovery included construction of Barquq's funerary complex in the Bayn al-Qasrayn area—exceptional for its time in that it combined a madrasa that taught the four madhab, with a khan-qah, or a monastery dedicated to the Sufi rite, and a tomb. The inclusion of a khanqah points to Barquq's attachment to the Sufi orders. A nota-ble aspect of Mamluk religious patronage was the rise of Sufism, which reflected an affinity for Sufi shaiykhs of Turkish and Iranian origin. Under the Burji Mamluks, Sufi rites were gradually integrated into both religious teachings and the configurations of the madrasas. The khanqah, a build-ing type brought to Egypt by Salah al-Din, was at first a distinct religious institution. But during the late Mamluk period the khanqah, the madrasa, and the mosque were often merged into a single, multifunctional building, in which Sufi services were provided alongside more orthodox ones.[24]

Located on the site of the Fatimid western palace, adjacent to the madrasa of al-Nasir Muhammad and the Qalawun complex, Barquq's complex bears inscriptions that date its completion to 1386.[25] This institution was a waqf foundation, as were many others of its kind. It consists of a cruciform-plan madrasa and an adjacent mausoleum, built in a manner similar to the prevailing Bahri Mamluk style. Like other madrasas of this kind, it contains an extended prayer hall in the main *iwan*. The tripartite layout, with a central nave flanked by two smaller aisles marked by triple archways, replicates the layout of the neighboring madrasa of Qalawun. Although the main nave covers a wide area, it has a flat roof supported by large timbers, a singular example of this construc-tion type in Mamluk architecture. The ceilings of the adjacent iwans are of vaulted stone construction, similar to Sultan Hasan's madrasa. A courtyard leads to the entrance of the mausoleum, whose interior is covered in polychrome marble panels, with a tall dado displaying rows of marble rosettes believed to be fragments of ancient columns. Behind the madrasa are the student living quarters as well as the stables. During its time, the complex must have possessed one of the most elaborate, ornate interiors in all of Cairo.[26]

At eighteen meters in height, the main façade of the complex towers above its adjacent buildings. It extends forty-three meters in width along one street. An entrance portal projects outward, dividing the façade in two. Six shallow recesses further partition the main façade, with two levels

Figure 7.3   The madrasa and funerary complex of Sultan al-Zahir Barquq.

of grilled openings piercing each recess and round openings with wooden grills punctuating the projecting sections. The main façade is topped with crenellations; below this is a *tiraz,* or calligraphic, inscription running the entire length of the wall.[27] The octagonal stone minaret stands approximately fifty-three meters high and is divided into three shafts. Its middle section is inlaid in marble and carved in a pattern of intersecting circles. The dome of the mausoleum was originally constructed of wood and covered in lead, but was later rebuilt in bricks.[28] Although the mausoleum later became the burial place for several members of his family, Sultan Barquq was not himself interred there. He chose instead to be buried along with the Sufi shaiykhs that he admired and followed. This wish was fulfilled by his son Faraj ibn Barquq, who had him buried in a khanqah in the Eastern Cemetery.

After his father's death, Faraj (who ruled from 1399 to 1412, with a short interlude in 1405) encountered a great deal of political turbulence. Coming to the throne as a child, his reign was disrupted by political problems in Syria and economic problems in Egypt, including famine and a return of the plague. He was eventually assassinated, and the Abbasid caliph al-Musta'in assumed power for a short time. A symbolic religious figure, al-Musta'in was a descendant of the Abbasid caliphs who had been brought to Cairo by Baybars following the downfall of the caliphate in Baghdad. Al-Musta'in was in turn deposed by another important sponsor of Cairo's built heritage, Sultan al-Mu'ayyad Shaiykh.[29] Barquq had purchased al-Mu'ayyad as a young Mamluk, and Faraj later appointed him governor of Tripoli. Al-Mu'ayyad came to the throne in a way typical of Mamluk power dynamics. He first helped to depose Faraj—the son of his main patron, Barquq. Then six months later he removed Caliph al-Musta'in from power and seized the throne for himself.[30]

Al-Mu'ayyad was an active patron of architecture and was responsible for several important buildings in Cairo, the most significant of which was his funerary complex, built between 1415 and 1420. As we have seen, al-Mu'ayyad's mosque was erected on the site of the prison, adjoining Bab Zuwayla, in which he had once been held.[31] When he came to power, al-Mu'ayyad demolished this prison and built in its place a complex consisting of a Friday mosque, a khanqah-madrasa, and a mausoleum. Therein he fulfilled the promise he made to himself while in captivity to build a religious institution of great significance.

The most distinctive feature of this complex is its twin minarets, built on top of the nearby Bab Zuwayla.[32] Their placement above the Fatimid-era gate posed structural difficulties; construction took a long time, and one of the minarets had to be demolished and rebuilt. A third three-storied minaret was built over the west portal of the complex, but it collapsed and was rebuilt in 1427, only to collapse again centuries later.[33] To allow for easy access from the mosque to the minarets on top of Bab Zuwayla, al-Mu'ayyad's architects carved out the core of the gate to create a concealed secondary door. They then transformed the hollowed vaulted space into a library. They also constructed a residential complex on the top platform of the gate.[34]

The mosque has three entranceways. The principal portal was constructed with alternating black and white stripes of masonry, known as *ablaq*. The trilobed vault of the portal is edged with molding, and its semicircular crown tops the *muqarnas* on the upper part of the façade. The portal is composed of a pair of bronze doors, which had been taken from Sultan Hasan's mosque in the southern district.[35] The initial layout provided rental space for merchants below the mosque's elevated façade.[36] The mosque follows a hypostyle plan, with two domed mausoleums to the north and south of the prayer hall.[37] The hall is three aisles deep and decorated with polychrome marble paneling and a gilded ceiling. Similarly, the niche of the mihrab wall is decorated with marble mosaic and crowned with a hood. Two granite columns with capitals containing Mamluk details flank the mihrab, while the rest of the columns in the prayer hall have Corinthian capitals.[38]

After the death of Sultan al-Mu'ayyad, the development of Cairo continued only sluggishly until Sultan Barsbay came to power in 1422. Barsbay renewed trading activities and established Egypt's monopoly of the east–west spice trade, a move that ensured Cairo's prosperity until the end of the Mamluk era. Cairo owed its commercial prosperity during the Burji Mamluk period to merchants and traders—particularly the *karimis,* major

Figure 7.4 The minarets of al-Mu'ayyad Mosque above Bab Zuwayla.

Figure 7.5 The funerary complex of Sultan al-Mu'ayyad.

handlers of the Indian trade who used Cairo as an entrepôt between the East and West.

In his writings, Maqrizi divides the population of Egypt into seven social classes: officers and high public officials; wealthy merchants and the upper classes; the lower middle class, composed of tradesmen, dealers, and farmers; members of the religious classes, comprising students and teachers, judges, and notaries; artisans and skilled workers; beggars; and the poor.[39] Despite this classification, these social groups were fluid. Indeed, the sense one gets from Maqrizi's writings is that immutable boundaries or definite hierarchies did not exactly exist. A family could include members of various trades, such as merchants, teachers, or artisans. Meanwhile, the philanthropic nature of teaching institutions in Cairo allowed for men of all social backgrounds to receive an education and become teachers of Islam. And those who did not advance in administrative positions had the option to become craftsmen or traders.[40]

The one absolutely entrenched social group was the Mamluks. The authority of this foreign-born elite was not limited to political and military realms, but extended to religious, artistic, and architectural domains. On the one hand, despite their humble roots, their militaristic upbringing made them intrepid rulers who were successful in repelling external threats. Among these men were exceptional governors, administrators, and jurists who contributed to making Egypt a dominant force in the Mediterranean. On the other hand, the hubris of this militaristic regime disturbed the domestic life and public peace of everyday Cairo. Under the iron grip of the Mamluks, who ruled Egypt as if it were their personal fiefdom, the population of Cairo experienced its share of oppression and brutality. The violence was not strictly confined to vicious disagreements among Mamluk factions; it also spilled onto the streets. Mamluk officers often used sheer force against the population as a way to assert their power. According to Maqrizi, "Some Mamluks were responsible for much disorder. They attacked the inhabitants, slaughtered them, pillaged their wealth, and carried off their wives."[41]

The end of the Bahri Mamluk period nevertheless brought a gradual change from a regime based on militarized foreign campaigns to one characterized by forged trade links and political alliances. Burji Mamluk control, starting with Barquq's reign, also brought about the loosening of the strict Mamluk system of military training and religious education. Mamluk individuals were allowed to live outside the Citadel and build residences in Cairo's diverse quarters. They also began to mix with the local population and adopt the culture of Egyptian society.[42] Just as there were no definitive social hierarchies in Cairo, there was no pronounced spatial segregation of social classes. With no quarters associated exclusively with the aristocracy, Burji Mamluk palaces spread throughout Cairo and its suburbs. These palaces were not tucked away but integrated into the fabric of the city next to mosques and ordinary residential structures alike.[43] During the Burji years, the Mamluks gradually lost the strict military culture that bound them together as an elite social group and separated them from the larger population. Maqrizi, who became a strong critic of the Burji Mamluk regime, noted this cultural decline and determined that the Mamluks were no longer fit to lead the country.[44]

Among the most powerful and prestigious groups in Cairo in the Mamluk period were the merchants, a class composed of brokers, foreign traders, wholesalers, and dealers of luxury goods. They played a crucial role in the distribution of commodities between urban areas and the rest of the country and mediated exchanges between Egypt and Asia. The merchants dealt directly with the Mamluk state and became inextricably linked with the regime in power, for which they often acted as bankers and advisors in monetary policy. The Mamluks were not only their clients but also their business partners, as some amirs invested capital in spice-trade expeditions or subsidized cotton exchanges with Venice. However, the most important activity involving the merchant class was money lending. Many merchant associations participated in this enterprise, but lending was principally under the control of the spice traders, the karimis, whose large fortunes and solid organization enabled them to make large loans. The karimis lent capital to those in the highest political ranks—to the sultan and his amirs. But such arrangements were often nothing more than extortion, forced upon the traders by a regime that regarded them as a reservoir of capital.[45] While vital to the functions of the state, the merchants were entirely dependent on the state's diplomatic protection and its postal services. Given this interdependent relationship, the Mamluk regime gave high priority to protecting the merchants and promoting trade.

Although the full extent of merchant fortunes were rarely recorded, for fear of confiscation, the wealth of the merchant class was believed to be comparable to that of the Mamluk amirs, and certainly evidenced in the size of their landholdings and their palatial residences. Merchants owned urban property that included markets, apartment buildings, shops, bathhouses, and caravanserais. And their social prestige was further secured by their ownership of slaves. Many were involved in the slave trade with Crimea and Caucasia that had been crucial to the very formation of the Mamluk regime.

The importance of the karimis, however, was greatly reduced in later years of Mamluk rule when merchant functions were assumed by the state, and when merchants came under the direct tutelage of the sultan. Following the period of instability in the first two decades of the fifteenth century, the Mamluks began to monopolize formerly private sectors of the economy and exact more tax revenue from the population. At this time trade became a government activity, with merchants serving as direct agents of the sultan.[46]

During the Mamluk era, great public works projects were carried out by the sultan and the amirs. But smaller works such as street lighting, street sweeping, and water provision were the responsibility of shopkeepers. In general the streets of Cairo developed in an irregular manner, with regulations enforced only when violations gravely interfered with traffic or, more broadly, undermined the public good. However, during the Burji Mamluk period several decrees were issued that specifically addressed the maintenance and regulation of streets and public spaces. Among these were a series of planning measures undertaken to beautify the city. By the end of the fifteenth century a document titled "An Exposition of the Rules Concerning the Streets of Cairo" regulated building in much of the city.[47] At this time the uneven and narrow streets of Cairo were often obstructed by building extensions that blocked light and traffic. However, in 1457 Sultan Inal began a project in the area of the Two Palaces consisting of public baths and an apartment complex. During the process he ordered the qassbah, Cairo's main corridor, to be widened. This entailed demolishing non-uniform buildings and readjusting the setback of many others. Another decree issued by Sultan Inal banned construction on roads running along the shores of Bulaq, where protruding structures frequently obstructed public access to the Nile. Such measures were often met with criticism by the sultan's council, but they garnered the approval of several chroniclers of the time, such as Ibn Taghribirdi, given these measures' aim to improve public safety.[48]

A similar planning initiative taken by Yashbak, a secretary of state in the fifteenth century, was met with great public dissent and criticized by chroniclers such as Ibn Iyas. Yashbak ordered the widening of Cairo's arteries and secondary streets. His decree specified that all buildings violating right-of-way should be demolished, and between 1477 and 1478 many houses were torn down. Although the decree applied mainly to the city proper, the historian Ibn Iyas wrote of three apartment complexes, or *rabs,* that were demolished in a quarter south of Bab Zuwayla. Yashbak also issued city beautification measures and initiated the restoration of mosque façades and the refinishing of storefronts.[49]

Throughout the Mamluk era, the city official responsible for supervising the activities of the market and the maintenance of public morality was the muhtasib. As mentioned, Maqrizi was one of the most well-recognized holders of this position.[50] The office was connected to the *hisba,* an Islamic concept tied to the Quranic dictum to "order what is good and forbid what is evil." Indeed, the term muhtasib originates from *ihtasba,* meaning "to seek God's favor by acting righteously." But the term is also linked to the Greek *agoranomos,* or "market inspector."[51] In general, then, the muhtasib was responsible for enforcing the observance of the hisba in the Muslim population. But aside from its religious and moral dimensions, the hisba evolved during Mamluk times to include the regulation of markets.

Sources refer to the appointments of muhtasibs as early as the beginning of the Abbasid period. Ibn Khaldun writes that the function of the muhtasib was to ensure "that people act in accord with the public interest in the town." In other words, the political authority of the muhtasib and the nature of his activities were quite vast. This partly explains why the muhtasib was involved in setting the price of food items in times of short-age. Regulating food prices became one of his primary responsibilities— even though he held a broader religious position that necessitated faith, a sense of justice, and legal expertise, among other qualities.[52]

During Maqrizi's times the duties of the muhtasib were further elabo-rated as the institution became involved with the collection of tax reve-nue, and the office became increasingly controversial and beset by high turnover rates. Although many appointees were religious figures, such as Maqrizi and his rival Badr al-Din al-'Ayni, it was not unusual for muhta-sibs to come from outside religious institutions. Maqrizi, who insisted that the position required higher professional and moral standards, later wrote critically of several appointees, accusing them of being "devoid of learn-ing" and "famous for abominable deeds of stupidity, shamelessness, and evil conduct."[53]

One of the last rulers of Mamluk Egypt, Sultan al-Ashraf Qaytbay (1468–1496), was a great patron of art and architecture. Qaytbay was a Circassian who had been purchased by Sultan Barsbay. He served under several sultans before he was offered the post of commander in chief by Sultan Timurbugha. Qaytbay's rule was marked by external mili-tary threats from the Ottoman Turks and plagued by internal rebellions. Egypt's economy was weak at the time, due to the severing of political and trade relations with the Ottomans and, to a certain extent, the large expenditures made on building construction.[54] Despite this, Qaytbay's reign lasted almost twenty-nine years, during which he improved trade links with Europe and made significant additions to the built heritage of Cairo. Qaytbay came to the throne at a late age and concluded his reign when he was in his eighties and in poor health. Because the political climate of his court was strained by conflict, he did not want his young son to succeed him, given the possibility that he might become a puppet ruler. Nevertheless, at the end of his reign in 1496, when Qaytbay was deposed by his amirs, his fourteen-year-old son was enthroned in his stead. The day after his son's succession, Qaytbay died.[55]

One of the most important structures built by Qaytbay was a funerary complex in the Eastern Cemetery. Waqf documents identify it as a Friday mosque with a Sufi service, but inscriptions on the structure call it a madrasa. Based on the engravings on the portal and other structures in the complex, historians have established that ground was first broken in 1470. The portal inscription is dated 1472–1473, and the mausoleum, 1474.[56]

The funerary complex was designed to be entered from the northeast by way of a monumental staircase leading through a groin-vaulted trilobed portal built of terra-cotta and white stone and crowned with a hood of muqarnas. To its right stands a minaret and a *sabil-kuttab*. The sabil-kuttab has rectangular grilled windows and an arched loggia above its front façade. The three-shafted minaret features finely carved balconies separating each shaft. Its octagonal bottom has alternating openings and keel-arched niches flanked by colonnettes; the second shaft is decorated with a stellar pattern of stone relief; and its top section is supported by eight columns and crowned by a bulging pinnacle.

The southern façade of the madrasa is divided by three niches of different size, pierced by rectangular grilled windows at its base and pointed arches on its second level. The rectangular volume of the mausoleum projects out of one corner of this façade. The transition area and the cylindrical portion of its dome are of equal proportions. The decoration on the dome also reverses the normal star typology[57]—instead of a star pattern radiating from the base to the top, it features a central star that starts at the pinnacle of the dome and extends downward in radial fashion to its base.[58] The madrasa's interior follows a cruciform plan, and the central portion of its gilded and painted ceiling is pierced by an octagonal skylight that is set higher than the iwan roofs. Two iwans, differing in size, face each other across its center, framed by horseshoe archways decorated with ablaq masonry. In the qibla iwan, the qibla wall has four grilled openings, with the mihrab at its center.

The complex of Qaytbay is considered exceptional due to its fine decorative finishes. Its plan was representative of the inventiveness and flexibility of Mamluk religious architecture and its capacity to incorporate multiple uses in a single structure. Indeed, it is one of the most elegant buildings of its era.

Figure 7.6 The funerary complex of Sultan al-Ashraf Qaytbay. ▬▬▬▬▬

The sabil-kuttab is a relatively small structure that contains a public fountain and school. As a building typology, it emerged during the Bahri Mamluk period but proliferated during Qaytbay's reign. Such charitable institutions, sponsored through waqf endowments, typically had two levels. A fountain, or *sabil,* located on the lower level, provided a public source of drinking water, while a Quranic school on the upper level provided primary education for residents of nearby neighborhoods. The two constituted one homogeneous architectural unit, where the upper level opened to the outside through windows and balconies, while light and air entered the lower level through grilled windows. Bringing essential services to Cairo's quarters, such foundations were scattered throughout the city, providing a measure of visual unity throughout. The structures were either freestanding or attached to mosques and secular buildings, as was the sabil-kuttab of Sultan Qaytbay. This structure was located behind the al-Azhar mosque and next to a *wekala,* or caravanserai.[59] The style of major buildings built by the elite class during the height of the Mamluk era differed from those built by earlier rulers. But they, too, helped transform the image of the city.

After Qaytbay was deposed, Mamluk factions continued to fight for power. After a few years of rule by Qaytbay's son, followed by the short-term rule of a few others, Sultan al-Ashraf Qansuh al-Ghuri acceded to the throne in 1501. The last effective Mamluk ruler, al-Ghuri was the forty-sixth Mamluk sultan and the twentieth of the Burji rulers, whose tenure lasted a long fifteen years.[60] He was a Circassian purchased by Qaytbay and was named "al-Ghuri" after the barracks where he received his training as a young man. After participating in military campaigns against the Ottomans, he was appointed governor of Tarsus, then chamberlain of Aleppo.[61] He took over the throne of Egypt after the country's economy had been considerably weakened, though his rule heralded a period of stability.[62] Like his predecessor, Qaytbay, al-Ghuri came to the throne late in life, at the age of sixty-two. In an effort to fill the country's treasury, he imposed new taxes, and although his reforms did not improve the economy, they brought in enough revenue to allow him to engage in extensive building and infrastructure projects.

Al-Ghuri's most important projects were the madrasa, khanqah, and wekala in the area now named after him, al-Ghuriya. The mosque to the west and the funerary dome to the east face each other across the qassbah in the heart of Cairo, forming an urban composition that has appeared in the drawings and photographs of many travelers over the years. Although the sultan dedicated substantial funds to the eastern structure, assuming he would be buried in it, he died while participating in a military campaign against the Ottomans in Syria, and his body was never found.[63] His adopted son, Tumanbay, whose rule was short-lived, succeeded him.

The dome and minaret in this complex belong to different buildings, separated by the qassbah, but they should be nonetheless conceived of as a cohesive composition, particularly when approached from the south. The two structures are visually tied together by the lapis-blue ceramic tiles that cover both the brick dome and the upper portion of the minaret.[64] In order to build his funerary complex in such a prominent location, al-Ghuri took the controversial step of first expropriating and clearing several buildings, including a madrasa, a market, and other residential and commercial structures. On the western side of the complex, an inscription dates the completion of its mosque and minaret to 1503. The eastern structure is dated 1504.[65] Both structures contain shops below the complex. Later a wooden roof was added to cover the street between the two buildings.[66]

The funerary complex has several notable features. These include a sabil-kuttab that projects into the street and a staircase that leads through its trilobed portal into a vestibule lit by a lantern. As noted, the mausoleum is crowned by a large dome covered in blue tiles.[67] However, like Barquq before him, al-Ghuri was not buried in his mausoleum, although several of his family members rest there.[68] The mausoleum is adjacent to a khanqah, which consists of a prayer hall without residential quarters. This configuration is rather unusual for the Sufi rite, since the Sufi sessions had to take place in separate structures.

The façade of the complex is divided by recesses with grilled openings at ground level and double-arched loggias above. The transition from the base to the dome embodies a further architectural innovation, featuring a pair of triangles at each corner, in contrast to the configuration of multi-tiered triangles encountered in other domes of the Mamluk period. The construction of the complex's interior is equally innovative in the case of the twelve-and-a-half-meter diameter of the dome, which is supported by tall pendentives contiguous with its supporting walls.

The main façade of the mosque is flat rather than segmented by windowed recesses. One enters the mosque through a portal decorated with black-and-white marble paneling crowned with muqarnas. The imposing rectangular minaret is located at one corner of the mosque. It was a novelty when it was built, because it was the first minaret in Cairo to have a rectangular shaft with four bulbous finials.[69] Some scholars believe that this configuration was of Syrian influence, brought to Cairo by Syrian masons.[70] The whole of the structure's upper portion is also covered in blue tile, attached to its underlying masonry with nails. The madrasa contains two large iwans, the larger of the iwans attached to two smaller iwans with raised floors on each side. The plan of the madrasa is similar to that of the *qa'a,* open to the sky and originally covered with a net.

Figure 7.7   The Mosque and funerary complex of Sultan al-Ashraf Qansuh al-Ghuri. As portrayed in the nineteenth century by David Roberts in the *Bazaar of the Silk Mercers* (left). Present day (right).

Figure 7.8   The madrasa and khanqah of al-Ghuri viewed from al-Azhar overpass. ▬▬

In his description of Cairo, Maqrizi elaborates on the suqs and caravanserais concentrated along the qassbah where commercial activity
was most intense. The markets were categorized according to trading
specialty, such as spices, cloth, or luxury goods. In Maqrizi's day the
epicenter of the city's market activity lay between the Quarter of the
Goldsmiths to the north and the Market of the Biscuit Merchants to the
south, an area that contained twenty-one suqs and eighteen caravanserais. According to Maqrizi, more than half of Cairo's suqs and almost all
its caravanserais were located between Bab Zuwayla and Bab al-Futuh.[71]

While market areas consisted mostly of single-floor stores lined up
along the street, the caravanserais were usually multi-level structures.
The caravanserai is a building type that took on various names over time.
It appeared in Syria during Saladin's time under the name *funduq*—a term
of Greek origin. The Persian term *khan,* meaning a way station or outpost

along a trade route, was also in use during the thirteenth and fourteenth centuries. The term wekala, short for *dar al-wekala*—meaning "depot hall," perhaps in reference to the customs point for imported goods—was widely used in Egypt. The Greek term *qaysariyya* was also in use in Egypt and originally meant a covered market for trading luxury items. Wekalas were arranged around a central courtyard and accessed through a covered portal. The ground level contained shops, and the upper levels provided living quarters for itinerant traders.[72]

One of the most important wekalas of Cairo during Burji Mamluk times was built by Sultan al-Ghuri in 1504 or 1505. Located in the vicinity of his madrasa and khanqah, this multi-level structure is accessed through a trilobed portal topped by a groin-vaulted hood and muqarnas squinches.[73] Inside, a central courtyard is enclosed in an arched portico at ground level, behind which are storage spaces and accommodations for merchants. Octagonal ablaq piers support the arches, and above them are a gallery and a rab, an apartment complex for merchants. The structure features *mashrabiya* and iron-grilled windows, while the upper registers of the façade are also constructed of ablaq masonry. Each apartment was designed as a triplex unit with sleeping spaces above the service and reception areas on the lower levels. Because there were no kitchens in the complex, guests relied on outside services for food.[74]

As we have seen, the Burji Mamluks inherited from the Bahri Mamluks a declining city, a city that had suffered a series of disasters ranging from famine to the Black Death. As Cairo shrank in population and activity, many of the great buildings left by the Bahri Mamluks fell into ruins. When construction activities were later renewed, new buildings were concentrated inside the walled city. To accommodate these new buildings, patrons and their architects had to find ways to build around numerous older monuments, some of which were in disrepair, but others of which were in reasonable shape. The tailored placement of newer structures in relation to existing buildings and the treatment of their exterior façades has had a major effect on the subsequent pattern of Cairo's streets. Builders here seemed to have realized how difficult it was to work around an array of surviving structures of different styles; nevertheless, these newer

Figure 7.9 The wekala of al-Ghuri.

design strategies reveal both an awareness of the problems at hand and active efforts to resolve them.

Most of the building regulations that developed in the time of the Bahri Mamluks were, with minor additions, still in effect at the time of the Burji Mamluks. But new initiatives were also established. For example, Sultan Qaytbay ordered all merchants on the qassbah to renew the façades of their shops—a measure that caused the economic ruin of many families and was perceived as tyrannical by the population. And in 1503, Sultan al-Ghuri issued a decree lowering the level of all major streets in the city (which had risen significantly over the years as a result of efforts to level them).[75] Such decrees by the Burji Mamluk sultans suggest that they thought of themselves not only as the sultans of Egypt but also as arbiters of the city's form and appearance.

By the end of their rule, the Burji Mamluks brought great changes to the center of the city. Most importantly, the visual focus of the qassbah shifted from the Bayn al-Qasrayn area to al-Ghuriya. The addition of other monuments along this main corridor also enriched its visual structure. The hierarchy of spaces that exists along the qassbah today was likely established in Burji Mamluk times. Meanwhile the Citadel, southeast of the city, regained its status as the seat of government and a symbol of power. Descriptions by Maqrizi, however, suggest that it remained isolated, although it towered over the city as a reminder of the rulers who governed from there.[76] As the site of new commercial or administrative development, the al-Jamaliya area saw considerable change during the rule of the Burji Mamluks. Amid commercial buildings constructed there were the wekala of al-Ashraf Qaytbay around the inner court of Bab al-Nasr and the wekala of Bazara'a nearby. The area's major administrative building was the *maq'ad* of Mamay, close to Bayn al-Qasrayn, which functioned as the residence of the qadi.

Under the Burji Mamluks, construction inside the walled city included fourteen major structures, primarily clustered near preexisting buildings. Characteristically, however, nine out of the ten main madrasas and mosques built there had principal façades that were neither parallel to the centerline of the street nor perpendicular to the qibla. The Burji Mamluks produced some of the city's most elaborate, irregular building plans in an effort to adhere to a street pattern that they had inherited from earlier times. The exterior walls of these buildings typically had many openings, and their textured façades were composed of alternating rows of black and white, or red and white, ablaq masonry.[77]

Another distinctive attribute of Burji Mamluk architecture is the height of their minarets: eight of the ten minarets built during this era were more than eighty meters tall. Like those of the Bahri Mamluks, a typical Burji Mamluk minaret had three segments, with each segment achieving additional height and attaining proportions of greater elegance. The plan of each segment became varied, given the range of minaret treatments introduced to the city during this time. Such an array of minarets contributed to an impression of Cairo as both rich and enduring. One of the most intriguing variations in Mamluk-era minaret design involved their positioning. Minarets with square bases usually followed the direction of the qibla, even when a mosque's exterior wall did not; this practice resulted in a diverse range of angular relations between building footprints and the street.

Domes also became much higher and narrower in Burji Mamluk times. Most were richly decorated, and some had cylindrical drums. As used by the Burji Mamluks, domes played a significant role in providing structure to the overall image of the city as well as its major thoroughfares. Their height and visibility created distinctive vistas when seen from various angles within the surrounding urban fabric.

The protruding entrance, an architectural element introduced during the time of the Bahri Mamluks, was also used extensively by the Burji Mamluks. Most of the principal Burji Mamluk buildings had protruding entrances with staircases. The stairs usually followed the direction of pedestrian movement, so that they could be ascended or descended parallel to the street.[78]

Another significant attribute of the structures built during the Burji Mamluk period was their location between existing layers of the city fabric. Most of the new structures were positioned in respect to older architecture and helped balance the composition of seemingly competing elements. At the same time these buildings produced a distinctively new architecture. To accomplish such a balance, Burji Mamluk builders introduced original exterior façade treatments and novel ways of arranging minarets and domes.[79] More often than not, builders did not follow any prescribed rules. For example, a builder of a Burji Mamluk mosque would not automatically position a minaret above a building's entrance or at one of its corners, as his predecessors would have done. Instead, he would have carefully examined every possible location and chosen the one that would create the most attractive configuration from various angles without disturbing the views of existing minarets. The overall goal was to create a composition in harmony with the elements of surrounding structures.[80]

Burji Mamluk builders sought to establish proportionalities between the size of minarets and the height of domes. Thus, as minarets were made taller, the domes that accompanied them increased in height and size, with the distance between minaret and dome reduced. It became common practice later on to place domes and minarets so close together that the space between them appeared to dissolve.[81] The variety of architectural relations and visual similarities introduced by the Burji Mamluk builders became their major contribution to Cairo's skyline. These achievements enhanced the image of Cairo, differentiating it from other cities of the Arab Muslim world.

During the Mamluk period, Cairo's main qassbah gradually became a royal funerary and religious district, although most of the monuments there did not contain the bodies of their founders. This empty symbolism can be read as a physical manifestation of Mamluk political rivalries and of the instabilities that characterized their rule. In addition to marking his presence in the heart of Cairo with the construction of a religious structure, each Burji Mamluk patron attempted to tie his name to monuments of the past. Sultans Aqbugha, Qaytbay, and al-Ghuri all added minarets to the al-Azhar mosque; Qaytbay restored the mosque of 'Amr; and al-Mu'ayyad created one of the most important landmarks of Cairo by building minarets atop of the Fatimid Bab Zuwayla.[82]

Bab Zuwayla marked the endpoint of the Mamluk regime. In 1516 the Ottoman sultan Selim, who had just defeated the Persians, moved his troops into Syria and massed them on the border with Egypt. Although Selim's offensive was ostensibly directed at Persia, Sultan al-Ghuri sent Egypt's troops to northern Syria and confronted the Ottomans in the battle of Marj Dabiq.[83] Mamluk forces were overpowered, and al-Ghuri died of a seizure on the battlefield. His successor, al-Ashraf Tumanbay, was the last Mamluk sultan at the helm of Egypt, and he reluctantly accepted the throne. Soon afterward the Ottoman forces advanced into Egypt, and the Mamluks were defeated again in 1517 at Raydaniya. Tumanbay was sent an ultimatum by Selim, who asked to be recognized as the sultan of Egypt, offering Tumanbay the title of viceroy. When Tumanbay refused, Selim made his final advance on Cairo, bringing Egypt under Ottoman rule that same year.[84] After a final attempt to repel the Ottoman troops outside the city, Tumanbay escaped only to be betrayed and handed over to the Ottomans at Giza.

Tumanbay's tragic end was witnessed by Cairo's crowds in the spring of 1517 at Bab Zuwayla. By the order of Sultan Selim, Tumanbay was executed by hanging. Accompanied by a procession of Ottoman soldiers, Tumanbay crossed Cairo in chains, riding on the back of a camel and wearing a long cape and a skullcap. Arriving at the place of his execution and contemplating his impending death, he stood up and recited the Fatiha verse from the Quran three times, after which he asked his executioner to perform his duty.[85] It took three attempts to complete the execution, as the rope repeatedly broke.[86] At his death, he was bareheaded and dressed in rags, his feet bound, and mourned by Cairo's crowds.[87]

Bab Zuwayla was not only a place where history was made, it was also a place where history was written. Working nearby, Maqrizi recorded in his historical masterpiece, *Khitat*, a topographic and architectural description of the fabric of Cairo at the time. As a teacher for many years at the al-Mu'ayyad mosque, he must have been able to observe activities in the city from the minarets built atop the adjoining Bab Zuwayla.

During the rule of al-Mu'ayyad, Maqrizi began to retreat from political and public life. The murder of his patron and good friend Fath Allah contributed to this reclusion. At the end of al-Mu'ayyad reign, Maqrizi found himself disillusioned, out of favor, and deeply saddened by the deaths of his concubine and his daughter.[88] Unsuccessful in his attempts to gain the favor of the new sultan, he resigned himself to his faith and spent the remainder of his life studying and writing his *Khitat*. Maqrizi died in 1442 of an unknown illness. He was given a simple burial in the Sufi Baybarsiyah cemetery in northern Cairo, the resting place of his mentor, Ibn Khaldun.[89]

For Maqrizi, Cairo served as, in his words, "the place of my birth, the playground of my mates, the nexus of my society and clan, the home to my family and public, the bosom where I acquired my wings, and the niche I seek and yearn to."[90] The stated goal of his monograph was to record all of Cairo's streets and landmarks prior to what he imagined to be their impending destruction.[91] This sense of imminent loss, and his disenchantment with the ruling regime at the time, likely made him fervently determined to put into words the details of the urban and material culture of his city, an enormous task for which all historians of Cairo will always be indebted.

A Provincial Capital
under Ottoman Rule

THERE ARE FEW PLACES in Cairo that clearly stand out as uniquely Ottoman in character. Although the city was under Ottoman rule for nearly three hundred years, there are even fewer figures who can be relied upon to tell the story of Ottoman Cairo. Indeed, during this period, which started in 1517 and lasted until the arrival of Napoleon in 1798, 110 viceroys ruled Egypt, each with an average tenure of only three years.[1] But every age has its own specificities, requiring us to narrate it according to its terms, not ours. Diverting from our usual form, therefore, this will be a story told without significant figures and unanchored in specific places.

When the Ottomans finally defeated the Circassian Mamluks in 1517, the center of power in the Middle East shifted from Cairo to Istanbul. The alleged corruption of the Mamluk rulers—in particular their abuse of the Islamic *waqf* system—was one of the principal reasons cited by the Ottoman sultan Selim (who ruled from 1512 to 1520) for his invasion of Egypt. Much controversy surrounded the ways in which the Mamluk elite exploited waqf endowments at the time. Based on statements made by Sultan al-Ghuri's chief *qadi*, Selim and the new Ottoman administration learned how illegal appropriations of land had been made through the practice of *istibdal*. To rectify such alleged abuses, Selim ordered a cadastral survey of all land in Cairo as well as an investigation of waqf documents and military land grants immediately following his victory. Although the Mamluks opposed these measures and refused to share land records, Selim promulgated the Qanunama, a law designed not only to outlaw istibdal, but also to protect the waqf endowments of former Mamluk rulers.[2]

For the three centuries following its fall to the Ottomans, Cairo was reduced to the status of a provincial capital, and as a result it entered a period of stagnation. At first the administration instated by Sultan Selim did not bring significant change to Egypt's government. In particular, Selim did not establish a powerful governing apparatus as he had in Syria, where he had implemented rigorous reforms. In this respect Egypt was the exception to the typical manner in which the Ottoman Empire administered its colonies and possessions. To establish his rule in Cairo, Selim originally appointed Turkish officials from his retinue. But when they proved ineffective, he appointed the Mamluk amir Khair Bey as his viceroy.

Among the difficulties faced by the new regime were revolts by the Mamluk amirs. Selim reasoned that because Khair Bey was a Mamluk, he could smooth out the political transition. Khair Bey, purchased at a young age by Qaytbay, served as governor of Aleppo during al-Ghuri's reign. But during the Ottoman attack on Egypt, he forged an alliance with Selim by betraying his comrades in the battle of Marj Dabiq, the same battle in which al-Ghuri was killed. His appointment may thus have been a reward for his collaboration with the invading force. Once named viceroy by Selim, he adopted Ottoman garb.

The new Ottoman administration officially ended the Mamluk dynasty, but this did not mean the end of the Mamluks as a ruling elite. Some Mamluks who resisted the Ottomans were marginalized or punished; but others who cooperated were rewarded, and some were even able to thrive anew. This was the beginning of the "neo-Mamluk" era.[3] For years to follow, the practice of purchasing young Mamluk slave-soldiers, particularly Circassians, continued among Egypt's military households, although the new Mamluks did not enjoy the same privileges as earlier generations in terms of their ability to rise in the political hierarchy. As in earlier times, the Mamluks also maintained political and economic power through the exaction of *iltizams*, or tax farms.

Khair Bey ruled Egypt from Cairo for five years, and was the first Ottoman viceroy to fund construction of a new mosque there. This handsome structure, often featured in sketches and photographs by nineteenth-century travelers, possesses a small, albeit elegant, dome and minaret that were well placed and well proportioned in relation to each other, thus projecting a sophisticated image. Though its architecture is typical of the late Mamluk era, this mosque was not intended to serve a congregation. Rather, according to the waqf deed, it was to have been a madrasa for the teaching of *hadith*. Nevertheless, after Khair Bey's death it became a Friday mosque.[4]

The mosque's ornate minaret, which was likely built later, is also designed in a Mamluk style.[5] Decorated with carved stucco ornaments, it is topped with a bulbous crown. Rising from a square base, its two shafts, one octagonal and the other cylindrical, are separated by balconies. The lower, octagonal shaft includes keel-arched recesses and is pierced with openings; the upper cylinder is decorated with stucco arabesques and is perforated by arched openings. The masonry dome, with its intertwined, carved arabesques, creates a striking perspective when approached from the south.[6] Inside, the prayer hall was designed with three cross-vaulted bays, connected by arches. The vaults are of red and white ablaq masonry, and the entire space is lit by an octagonal lantern in the central bay. The architects of Khair Bey's monument designed its jagged exterior walls to run parallel to the street, as was the case with many other monuments of the preceding Mamluk period.[7] However, the direction of the qibla was not fully resolved and remained at odds with the orientation of the mausoleum.

The adjacent palace of amir Alin Aq, dating from the thirteenth century, became the residence of Khair Bey, who renovated and occupied it, reviving the tradition in early Islam for governors to live in a central part of the city next to a Friday mosque.[8]

Egypt remained stable until Khair Bey's death in 1522. Soon after, however, it was shaken by two revolts, which signaled to the Ottomans the need for a stricter form of government. The first revolt was led by two Mamluk amirs; the second was provoked by the Ottoman viceroy Ahmed Pasha. Discontent with being appointed viceroy in Egypt instead of grand vizier of the empire, the latter proclaimed himself sultan of Egypt in 1524. His revolt was eventually crushed, and a new viceroy, Ibrahim Pasha, was sent from Istanbul. A former grand vizier, Ibrahim Pasha began his

Figure 8.1   The funerary madrasa of Amir Khair Bey.

administration in 1525 by instating a strict new administrative code, accompanied by a reorganization of the economy. The viceroy led the *diwan,* or court council, an important institution from the former Mamluk regime. Other administrative urban functions were left to organizations such as the professional guilds and the waqfs. Significantly, however, the Mamluks were allowed to retain their authority as *multazims*, which allowed them to control much of the wealth generated in the countryside.[9]

During the early Ottoman period, Egypt's governing apparatus was organized around three power centers. The most decisive was the governor, followed by the judiciary and the janissary militia. Given the sizable tax revenue exacted from its economic activities, Egypt was of great importance to the Ottomans—hence the great control accorded to its governor. As a representative of the sultan, the governor had supreme military and civil authority. He was responsible for protecting the public good, maintaining order, and collecting taxes.

The post of governor, or viceroy, in Egypt was a ministerial position and the appointee received the title *pasha.* Several pashas of Egypt later held important functions in the Ottoman Empire, such as that of grand vizier. The pashas resided in the Citadel, the former quarters of the Mamluk sultans. During the Ottoman period, a number of Egyptian Mamluks were appointed pashas elsewhere in the empire. At home, prominent Mamluks often also held the title *bey* or *amir* based on their status or lineage. But other than the first pasha, Khair Bey, no Mamluk was appointed pasha of Egypt during the three centuries of Ottoman rule.[10]

However powerful a pasha might be, his control over the country was limited by other sources of authority—the treasurer; the qadi; and the janissary militia, led by the *agha.* The dignitaries of the high council also served as advisors to the pasha and had the power to oppose his decisions. This structure of governance bred political tension and instability, and resulted in a high turnover of rulers.[11] The judges of Cairo extended their authority to all matters of civil law, religion and morals, commercial activity, and urban planning. They also had great political influence, given their participation on various committees that advised the governor. Their purpose was not only to administer Islamic law, but also to enforce

orders from the sultan in Istanbul. Another powerful force was the janissary militia, an arm of the Ottoman army that had conquered Egypt, part
of which remained there to support the new administration. With the help
of the Mamluks, and under their supervision, this militia demanded revenue from tax farms to augment their meager salaries. At times as many as
sixteen thousand men were in this militia. Their numbers allowed them to
exert great influence in the diwan and over the local population.[12]

Egypt thrived economically under the Ottomans for some time,
although a great deal of its resources were appropriated by Istanbul.
Commercial development was accompanied by population growth; and
even if Cairo had become a provincial city, it retained some of its glory, as
its fabric remained unchanged despite the Ottoman presence. Long gone,
however, was the era of rulers consumed with leaving their mark on the
religious and social fabric of the city through the construction of elaborate monuments. All but two of the 110 Ottoman viceroys served very
short terms; the brevity of their terms was intended to prevent them from
consolidating power or building important religious institutions. The two
viceroys who ruled the longest did so only because they were engaged in
military campaigns and in resolving internal conflicts. Overall, serving
as a viceroy in Cairo was often an intermediate position in the career of
an ambitious Ottoman noble.[13] As a result, the viceroys did not have the
same desire for legitimation nor the same inclination toward philanthropy
as the Mamluk sultans. They also lacked the resources that had been
available to the sultans, as most of Egypt's resources were diverted to
Istanbul.

For all of these reasons, the first monument of any significance built in
the tradition of the Ottomans did not appear in Cairo until half a century
later, in 1517, built by Sinan Pasha.[14] A governor of Albanian descent,
Sinan twice ruled Egypt (1567–1568 and 1571–1572) under Sultan Selim
II. Recruited as a servant when he was very young, Sinan Pasha eventually rose to become a cupbearer for Suleyman the Magnificent and later
an Ottoman grand vizier. He also became a wealthy patron of the arts and
architecture. In Cairo he built his mosque in Bulaq, an area that was extensively developed during the Ottoman period. The fact that Bulaq was a

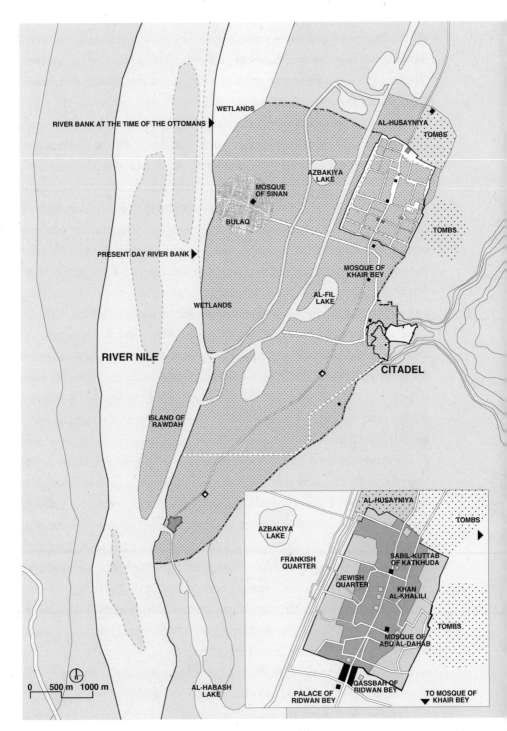

Figure 8.2   Map of Cairo area during the Ottoman period.

relatively new area of the city allowed for such a large-scale project, which would have been near impossible in the dense fabric along the *qassbah*. The mosque was part of a complex that included a *sabil-kuttab*, three *wekalas*, a residence, and a *hamam*, or bath house.[15]

Built in the Ottoman style, the mosque of Sinan is a freestanding structure surrounded by landscaped grounds and based on the basilica plan typical of the Byzantine-influenced mosques of Istanbul. Covered by a vast dome, the structure is surrounded on three sides by a domed arcade opening to the street. Three entrances lead into the central domed area; one from each side except that of the qibla wall. Decorative windows inset with colored glass express Ottoman influence. Eight of these were located in the transition segment, and sixteen more were set in the dome above an access gallery.[16] But typical Mamluk architectural details, such as *muqarnas*, or squinches, at the mihrab wall, are also evident.

As the Mamluks sought to regain power during the early decades of Ottoman rule, they jockeyed with the viceroys appointed by the sultan for the support of the Ottoman garrison. But these soldiers also often revolted in pursuit of their own interests. It was not until the arrival of Ibrahim Pasha, who became viceroy in 1604, that new rules were designed to keep the soldiers in line. However, Ibrahim Pasha was eventually killed in his residence by a group of soldiers, an incident that signaled to the imperial authority that there was a need for even greater controls.[17] It was only with the aid of several Mamluks that the new viceroy, Muhammad Pasha, managed to suppress such rebellions. But this moment also brought the full, although unofficial, return of Mamluk rule to Egypt, as it corresponded to the rise of the Beylicate, a group of Mamluk beys who had retained power under Ottoman rule.

In succeeding years, although they were not a formal part of the government, the members of the Beylicate had influence over many strategic administrative offices in Cairo. They effectively controlled the military as well as the fiscal and administrative functions of the state. The beys also constituted a strong military force, as Mamluk households continued to cultivate soldiers, even though the factionalism of the Circassian era still prevailed.

Figure 8.3   The Mosque of Sinan Pasha.

As a parallel organization of the state, the Beylicate gained so much influence that it was finally formalized and the twenty-four members of the Beylicate in effect came to run the state. Although its rise reduced the viceroy to a nominal role, the Beylicate still fully cooperated in the collection of tribute tax as required by Istanbul. In return the Ottoman viceroys often abided by the rules of the Beylicate. But if conflicts arose, as when the viceroy Musa Pasha killed a member of the Beylicate, the Beylicate could depose the viceroy. In such instances it became standard for the Ottoman sultan to defer to the will of the Beylicate. This typically made relationships between the viceroys and the Beylicate tense, if not overtly hostile. The viceroys, however, could also wield political power by taking advantage of frictions between dominant Mamluk families. Thus, in the mid-seventeenth century the viceroys were able to regain considerable influence by playing Mamluk factions against each other, and they even forced several Mamluk amirs into exile. This strength of viceregal authority lasted only until the beginning of the eighteenth century, when the Beylicate managed to reclaim its authority.

The exception to these conditions was Ridwan Bey, who came to power in 1631 and ruled Egypt like a monarch. An influential Mamluk amir, Ridwan Bey ruled for more than two decades, until 1656, and left behind an important built legacy in Cairo. According to waqf documents, his development south of Bab Zuwayla was constructed between 1629 and 1647, and covered about one hectare. Among other structures, it included the suq of the shoemakers, a wekala, two convents, several residences, a mill, and a water fountain. Built along the main street that linked Bab Zuwayla to Saliba, the complex reoriented the entire quarter by enlarging its main street and correcting the irregular alignments of existing constructions.[18] The market stretched along the main qassbah, 150 meters in length, 6 meters in width, and was covered by a 50-meter-long wooden roof lit by skylights. Buildings along it had double-height dwelling units on their upper levels, which cantilevered over the stone façades of the shops at ground level. The eastern portion of Ridwan Bey's street followed this mixed-use configuration of commercial units at ground level and dwellings above, but it also included a small convent,

Figure 8.4 The wekala and bazaar of Ridwan Bey.

or *zawiya,* at street level and a residential complex with a separate entry point.[19] Next to the Tentmakers Bazaar, which occupied part of the qass-bah, Ridwan Bey built a sumptuous palace for himself. This was planned around a courtyard and included two large, tall interior halls, or *qa'as,* and a second-floor loggia with a sitting area known as a *maq'ad.*[20] The maq'ad had three arches resting on marble columns under a wooden canopy. A trilobed portal allowed access to the upper floors.[21]

In 1711, conflict broke out between the seven corps forming the Otto-man military force in Egypt. Rival Mamluk households became involved, and by the end of the violence the Mamluks emerged victorious, leaving the viceroy without effective political or military backing. Weakened by internal political troubles, a sharp economic decline, rebelling soldiers, and military threats from the Hapsburg and Russian empires, the Otto-man Empire also began to lose its grip on Egypt. This enabled the Beyli-cate to again regain de facto control of all of Egypt. By this time many Mamluk households were once again very affluent, owning hundreds of slaves and soldiers, maintaining extensive land holdings, and resid-ing in luxurious houses or palaces.[22] The political influence of the beys and amirs was maintained by patronage relationships that tied them to the administration. But their power was primarily ensured by military strength. Thus, while the viceroy retained formal power, the beys were able to control the real center of power, or the *riasa,* or headship, a term later adopted in modern Egypt to refer to the presidency.

The most notable leader to control the riasa was Ali Bey al-Kabir, who ruled as a strongman from 1760 to 1772. Ali Bey made significant changes in the administration of Egypt, centralizing its government, increasing his political power, and dismantling the politically autonomous Ottoman janissary militia around 1770.[23] A rival faction attempted to remove him from power in 1766, but their opposition ultimately proved unsuccessful. After a year Ali Bey returned to power and not only eliminated those who had opposed him, but deposed the two viceroys appointed by Istanbul.

This was not the only way Ali Bey challenged the Ottoman sultan, however. Responding to a call for help from the Hashemite rulers in Hijaz, Ali Bey not only restored the ruler in Mecca but also appointed a trusted

Mamluk official, instead of an Ottoman, as governor in Jeddah. These actions signaled his intent not simply to consolidate power but also to legitimize his political position by becoming a guardian of Islam's holiest places. Ali Bey then proceeded to conduct military expeditions, eventually gaining control of Syria and Palestine, but he failed to hold power there for long. Within a year of taking Damascus, his troops began a retreat to Cairo. And in 1772 Ali Bey was removed from power by rival Mamluk forces. He was killed a year later when he made a last attempt to recoup power with a small military force.[24]

Ali Bey was succeeded by Muhammad Bey Abu al-Dahab (1760–1773). Abu al-Dahab was originally a Mamluk slave owned by Ali Bey, and it is believed that he gained his name, meaning "Father of Gold," at the moment of his investiture, when he generously distributed gold to his supporters. Abu al-Dahab is best known today for a mosque he built next to the mosque of al-Azhar. The structure, completed in 1774, was part of a larger religious complex, which included a madrasa, library, and *sabil*. Its lower level was lined with commercial spaces, which generated revenue for the upkeep of the madrasa.[25] As if making an identity statement, the minaret of Abu al-Dahab's complex is built in the Mamluk style, unlike the slender, conical-top minarets that came about as a result of contemporary Ottoman influence on the city. The plan of the mosque, however, is similar to that of the Ottoman-influenced mosque of Sinan. It had a central space, covered by a dome supported by squinch arches, and an exterior arcade also overlaid with domes. The ablution fountain was placed behind a *mashrabiya* screen and separated from the main structure. According to Mamluk practice, Abu al-Dahab's body was buried in the mausoleum he built adjacent to the mosque.[26]

After the death of Ali Bey and Abu al-Dahab, Egypt entered yet another period of decline. The struggle for power among the Mamluk factions brought about grave political instability, which affected the economy. In the last half of the eighteenth century, natural disasters, new plague epidemics, and demographic decline further depressed Egypt's economy. Social cleavages also increased significantly, as did government brutality and tensions between the populace and those in power.

Figure 8.5   The Mosque of Abu al-Dahab.

Architecturally, although late-Mamluk influence continued to persist, Ottoman traditions gradually began making imprints on Cairo, as many Ottoman-style mosques and sabil-kuttabs were constructed. Toward the end of the Ottoman period, as many as seventy-seven mosques and forty-one sabil-kuttabs had been built in Cairo alone, although most were built by powerful Mamluks and not by Ottoman viceroys.[27]

Mamluk traditions continued in the social life of Cairo, but Ottoman customs blended in as well. One important change was the introduction of coffee. Initially frowned upon by the Egyptian authorities, the new drink was adopted quickly in Cairo, as it had been in Istanbul. Outlawed by the *ulama* in the sixteenth century, coffee was received with enthusiasm by Sufis, who were generally resistant to institutional prohibitions. The new drink also brought its own building type, the *qahwa*. In Egyptian Arabic, qahwa simply means "coffee" or "coffeehouse." Soon coffeehouses became so popular that the men of Cairo frequented them nearly as often as the mosques. Toward the end of the Ottoman times, there were as many as 1,350 coffeehouses in Cairo—about one for every 200 of the city's residents.[28] One could find coffeehouses in almost every neighborhood, and their patrons, usually all male, visited them daily. The shops not only became social spaces where Cairo's residents gathered for conversation, but also places for vernacular performances, such as the telling of stories and recitations of poetry. The merchants of Cairo reaped such great profits from coffee that the city quickly became the principal node in the international coffee trade.[29]

One of the most powerful Mamluks of the Ottoman period was amir 'Abd al-Rahman Katkhuda, a senior officer of the Qazdughli regiment. His title *katkhuda* meant he was the lieutenant of the janissaries. Although he was not appointed by Istanbul, he was the most powerful Mamluk amir of his time, having more authority than the Ottoman viceroy. He held several administrative appointments between 1757 and 1773, before finally being deposed as katkhuda. 'Abd al-Rahman was a dedicated patron of the arts and architecture, and restored and built numerous structures in Cairo. However, his most notable contribution was a sabil-kuttab bearing his name, which he built in 1744 before his official appointments began. It was sited explicitly for maximum visibility on a narrow triangular lot, creating a fork in the main qassbah of Cairo. Inscribed atop the entrance of his sabil-kuttab is a poem celebrating his achievements:

> The declarer of happiness called
> When the twilight of jealousy set,
> From the time I built this *sabeel*
> Its water in abundance flowed.
> And the voices of the people called
> Abdul Rahman's name deserved heaven's reward.

Although Mamluk architectural influences remain evident in the voussoirs of its arched windows, as well as in the mosaic decoration and stalactites crowning the first level, this sabil-kuttab was one of the first

Figure 8.6 The sabil-kuttab of 'Abd al-Rahman Katkhuda.

structures to articulate a specifically Ottoman architectural style in the city. For example, the joggling stone masonry of the façade and the figurative carvings in the spandrel area are distinctive Ottoman elements.[30]

As Cairo was reduced in status to a provincial capital under Ottoman control, its economy stagnated. As the sea trade developed around the Cape of Good Hope, on the southernmost tip of the continent, Cairo also lost its position in the older East–West trade routes.[31] It is debatable whether Cairo's recurring deterioration during this period can be fundamentally blamed on its Ottoman overlords, but the fact remains that Cairo's prominence waned considerably over the three centuries of Ottoman rule. Nevertheless, Cairo continued to expand and, as with other growing cities, the internal organization of the urban fabric shifted during this time. In particular the qassbah, formerly the city's major spine, gradually lost its importance. The center of the city moved westward toward Bulaq, and specialty markets started to appear west of the Khalij al-Masri canal.[32]

Scholars concerned with the social structure of Ottoman Cairo have described the development of sharp class differences during this time. The elite, who had previously favored residing around the Citadel, moved to the new western district of al-Azbakiya. Cairo proper, abandoned by the upper classes, was left to deteriorate.[33] Although the departure of these more-affluent residents affected the built environment, the heterogeneous groups that formed the city's lower classes soon provided older residential quarters with a new social structure. During this time a typical quarter, the *hara*, had its own main street, the *zuqaq*, out of which branched a number of smaller dead-end streets, known as *a'tfa*. A hara often had its own gate, guarded by a *bawab*, or doorkeeper, and nonresidents needed permission to enter. Each hara also had its own shaiykh who acted as an administrator in dealings with city officials.[34] The shaiykh was often chosen by the hara's residents, and his appointment had to be confirmed by the governing authorities. It is erroneous (but common in some histories of Cairo) to think that the haras at the time of the Mamluks resembled fortresses. In fact, permanent defenses, such as heavy doors and gates, were erected only in times of crisis, and it was not until late Mamluk and early Ottoman times that these gates became physical and symbolic components of hara streets.[35]

During the seventeenth and eighteenth centuries Cairo had a heterogeneous population, with a great number of foreign communities. At the end of Ottoman rule the city's population was estimated to be a quarter of a million people, of which twenty-five thousand were local Jews and Coptic Christians, and another twenty-five thousand were foreign Muslims.[36] This diversity derived from Cairo's former status as a major international trade center. But it also owed much to the city's location on the hajj pilgrimage route. Encouraged and enabled by Ottoman rule, a sizable community of Turks established itself in the heart of the city in the area of Khan al-Khalili. This was a largely closed and homogeneous group, which reached about ten thousand individuals.[37]

In the daily life of the city, large mosques served as meeting places in addition to being religious and educational institutions. Men gathered there not only to pray, but also to lounge, chat, or even eat. The few large open spaces, or *maydans*, of Cairo, near the major mosques and the junctions of these thoroughfares, created spaces for markets.[38] In the context of Egypt's general economic decline, local commerce was sufficient to keep markets active and relatively stable. The suqs were open structures lined with small shops, and were generally divided into areas occupied by specific trades and artisan associations, such as cloth merchants or coppersmiths. Most of Cairo's suqs were provisional, but some were planned developments, such as on the qassbah of Ridwan Bey.

The merchants of Cairo lived close to the qassbah. Given the density and high cost of land in the central district, large residences there were the exclusive domains of the elite. These multi-level houses were typically organized around a courtyard, onto which opened wood-lattice mashrabiya windows and loggias. The layout of each house was divided into public, private, and service quarters. Large qa'as provided reception areas for guests and family events. Usually located on the second floor, these rooms had polychrome marble floors and often featured a water fountain in a sunken area in the center of the room. The house of 'Abd al-Rahman al-Harawi is one of the most remarkable extant examples of such an Ottoman courtyard residence. It was built in 1731 and has two large qa'as on the first level and another on the upper level.[39]

Bayt al-Sihaymi is another remarkable residence built during this time. Located near the qassbah, it was originally built by a shaiykh named al-Tablawi, who had served at the al-Azhar mosque. Although the house owed its name to its last owner, shaiykh Muhammad al-Sihaymi, its form was the result of additions made by several owners.[40] Entered through a passage that led to a central courtyard, it was divided into reception and living spaces organized around the courtyard, with garden, storage, and service areas located in the rear of the building. The living spaces were in turn divided between *haramlik*, private areas and women's quarters, and *salamlik,* men's quarters and public areas for the reception of guests.

In general the outdoor area in the rear of the house belonged to the women while the courtyard belonged to the men. The courtyard contained a *tahtabush*, a seating area on the ground floor where the head of the household would receive guests during the day. There was also a maq'ad, a second-story loggia where the owner would entertain guests in the evening. The most formal reception area, however, was the qa'a, which contained a central fountain. This space was used for dancing and music performances; in an atrium adjacent to the qa'a, the Quran was recited at social gatherings.[41] The women's private quarters, along with the bathrooms (only wealthy residences had bathrooms), were located upstairs. The women's quarters featured fine mashrabiya screens, which filtered sunlight, allowed ventilation, and ensured privacy while allowing the women to observe the activities taking place in the maq'ad. A feature characteristic of homes of that period was the flexible use of living spaces. Such spaces were not dedicated to specific uses; their uses changed based on weather and other seasonal considerations.

Apartment buildings, called *rab,* were another common residential typology in the central district. These were occupied by middle-class merchants and artisans, and were managed either by private investors or by waqf administrators under agreements whereby the rental income would fund religious foundations. Most of the residents had low to moderate incomes and either bought or rented their apartments.[42] These were located in multistory structures with shops on the ground level, and they could be either independent complexes or part of a wekala, laid out around a courtyard. The units were generally two or three stories tall with rooftop terraces and individual interior stairways.

During Ottoman times, the ruling elites lived separately from the local population. Generally they chose sites outside of Cairo to build luxurious homes ensconced in lush landscapes. For example, Muhammad Ali Bey al-Alfi, who wanted to stay away from the crowded streets of Cairo, built his principal residence in 1798 at the lake of Azbakiya, which allowed him to escape the heat and congestion of the city.[43] His palace would later be used for several important functions.

Despite this trend we can assume that the city proper remained a secure and desirable area throughout the three hundred years of Ottoman rule, because even though members of the elite built their residences to the west of the walled city, they continued to build religious and administrative buildings in al-Qahira, often on the sites of ruined monuments. For example, the mosque of Shaiykh Muttahar was built over the ruins of the Ayyubid madrasa of al-Sifufiya. The mosque of al-Fakahani, a Fatimid-era ruin, was likewise renewed and used again during Ottoman times. Most notable for their overall impact, however, were the many sabil-kuttabs built along the major streets of the city. The characteristic architecture of these structures contributed to a unified image of the Ottoman city. The zawiya, or small prayer place, was also introduced during this period and played a social role comparable to that of the street-level sabil.

Ottoman-inspired mosques generally had large openings and very elegant exterior walls. When built inside the dense, central city, they were identifiable by the small spaces fronting them. By contrast, those outside the urban area were generally larger, with symmetrical plans, fronted by wide, axial open spaces. Ottoman domes were notably voluminous and

Figure 8.7 Courtyard view of Bayt al-Sihaymi.

low, with a number of openings, and many incorporated exterior architectural elements such as piers. Entrances were either recessed or lined flush with the façade, with minarets placed just above them. Some Ottoman mosques were built on platforms with staircases descending in various directions.

Ottoman minarets were tall and slender, and featured steep, sharply inclined conical tops. Unlike Mamluk-style minarets—which were still built during the Ottoman period—these thin minarets, resembling sharpened pencils, did not rise above the level of a mosque's roof.[44] And unlike earlier Mamluk minarets, with their multisegmented shafts, Ottoman minarets were predominantly composed of only one or two elegantly proportioned segments. Yet because Ottoman minarets were nearly identical in form and size, they had visual unity at street level. The overall form of Cairo proper was not substantially changed during Ottoman times, but these distinctive pencil-top minarets may have helped orient and direct pedestrians, contributing to the city's distinctive skyline.

During the period of Ottoman rule, the waqf system also remained unchanged. It maintained its two complementary historical functions: to serve the financial interests of the powerful who endowed it, and to provide the community with philanthropic institutions and financed projects in the service of diverse social functions.[45] Building regulations also remained unaltered. With little or no sense of the public domain, most inhabitants did not hesitate to occupy public thoroughfares with stalls, shops, and other ad hoc constructions. Not surprisingly, travelers' accounts continually emphasized the narrowness and crookedness of Cairo's streets, and increasingly, during the Ottoman period, deplored the city's decline. Until the beginning of the sixteenth century, travelers' descriptions were mindful of the city's grandeur. But by the end of the seventeenth century, many visitors were concerned with its changes and the deterioration wrought by time.[46] They frequently complained that a visit to the city was an unpleasant experience.[47]

Several Europeans documented the built environment of Cairo in the eighteenth century. One of the most detailed and important accounts was a map made by the German traveler Carsten Niebuhr. Bound for Cairo in 1761 with a royal Danish scientific expedition, of which he was the only survivor, Niebuhr published an engraved plan of the city in 1774 titled "Ichonographic Plan of the City of Cairo and Its Suburbs Bulaq, Masr al-Atika, or Fustat and Giza."[48] The map shows the districts and cemeteries of Cairo and captures surrounding geographical features such as hills and bodies of water. More importantly, Niebuhr was the first to make a comprehensive record of Cairo's irregular street patterns and identify the main buildings, landmarks, city gates, and bridges. His plan is notable not only for its accuracy but also for the remarkable fact that he was able to undertake the surveys and the measurements almost single-handedly. He also authored one of the earliest descriptions of Cairo's haras, or quarters. According to Niebuhr, the haras provided communal residence space for the poorer segments of the population who worked in the suqs in the central district.[49]

When Jean Thevenot, a French traveler, visited Cairo in 1686, he remarked, "There is no one handsome street in Cairo, but only a great many little ones that wind round about; as is well known, the houses of Cairo are built without any plan for the town. Each one takes all the space that he wants for his building without considering whether he blocks the street or not."[50] He notes that the spaces inside Bab al-Futuh and Bab al-Nasr and in front of al-Azhar were all built up at that time.

The last two rulers of the Ottoman period were Murad Bey and Ibrahim Bey, who joined forces to control the riasa at the end of eighteenth century. While Istanbul's authority over Egypt was decreasing, the joint power of these two Mamluk beys increased. With no internal threat to their alliance, they raised taxes without sending the proceeds to Istanbul. The Ottomans retaliated in 1786 by sending Ghazi Hasan Pasha with a military expedition to depose the two Mamluk beys and reestablish control of Egypt. Although Hasan Pasha initially defeated the Mamluks and forced them to retreat to Upper Egypt, he eventually had to give up this campaign when he was instructed to deal with military crises elsewhere. The two beys then regained control of Egypt in 1787, establishing themselves as the last Mamluks to hold power before the ultimate elimination of the Mamluks as a privileged class by Muhammad Ali. Ismail Bey died in 1791, but the Mamluks remained in power until the arrival of Napoleon.

A Changing City: From
Napoleon to Muhammad Ali

THE ELEGANT MOSQUE of Muhammad Ali dominates the skyline of Cairo from every angle. Built atop the highest point of the Citadel of Salah al-Din, it towers over the city, giving it a distinctive identity while hinting of connections to other places and times. To anyone familiar with Ottoman mosques—with their domes of varying sizes and slender, conical-topped minarets—the link to Istanbul is unmistakable. Indeed, to a casual observer the architecture of Muhammad Ali's mosque may seem to mimic that of the famous Suleyman mosque in Istanbul. Muhammad Ali, a renegade Albanian soldier, was initially an agent of the Ottoman Empire. He would later declare Egypt's independence and establish the modern Egyptian state. Why would he, after his break from the Ottomans, employ such a loaded symbol to proclaim the identity of a new state? The answer to this question is complex, and it starts not with his mosque but with the site on which it stands.

The Citadel of Salah al-Din was almost seven centuries old when Muhammad Ali started to build his mosque there. From this elevated stronghold, rulers from Ayyubid, Mamluk, and Ottoman times had governed all of Egypt. For centuries it was also a site that fascinated visitors and residents of the city alike. One can imagine what a French soldier in Napoleon Bonaparte's 1798 invasion force would have seen, or what a British visitor like Edward William Lane would have experienced when he first arrived in the city in 1825. For many of these Europeans, the Pyramids of Giza, the landmarks of the ancient kings standing on the other side of the Nile, were the main objects of fascination and curiosity. But the other living landmark that attracted them was the Citadel complex,

Fig 9.1 **The skyline of Cairo with the Mosque of Muhammad Ali.**

whose towering presence had dominated the city since the life of Salah al-Din.

Before the mosque of Muhammad Ali was erected, the area had been frequented by Napoleon and his army for military purposes. It is likely that it also had been visited by the scholar and historian 'Abd al-Rahman al-Jabarti (1753–1825), who chronicled Napoleon's occupation of Egypt. The mosque would have provided an exceptional vantage point from which al-Jabarti could have watched Napoleon's troops enter Cairo in the spring of 1798. For al-Jabarti and his generation, the Citadel was a place associated with the changing governments and shifting alliances of their time.

One can imagine an encounter between al-Jabarti and Lane on the future site of the mosque of Muhammad Ali. From the highest piece of ground in the Citadel, they would have enjoyed a similar panoramic view of the city below; but in all probability they would have interpreted this landscape differently. Looking southwest, they would have seen the Pyramids of Giza, which captured Lane's imagination as a symbol of the great Egyptian civilization of antiquity—a fascination that al-Jabarti, like most of his Egyptian contemporaries, may not have shared. Looking south, they would have seen the expansion of Cairo, which by then included the old city of Fustat, known to Cairenes as Misr al-Qadimah. Looking north, they would have seen al-Qahira, the city in which they both lived, with its Fatimid core and Mamluk minarets. And looking beyond the horizon, they would have seen the burgeoning district of Bulaq and the nearby Azbakiya Lake, home to many new commercial activities and elite residences.

The story of Cairo at the end of the eighteenth century lies at the intersection of the lives of al-Jabarti and Lane, two individuals who may never have met but who emerged through their writings as major commentators on the period. Al-Jabarti witnessed the arrival of Napoleon in Cairo, while Lane wrote extensively about the city during the rule of Muhammad Ali, the founder of modern Egypt.

The scholar al-Jabarti came from an upper-class family known for its alliances to various social groups. Through marriage, the trade in Mamluk slaves, and other commercial activities, his family had come to include members of the military, scholars, and traders on the Red Sea. At age eleven, al-Jabarti knew the Quran by heart and showed great promise as a future learned man. As a youth he lived in the area of Bayn al-Qasrayn. He benefited from his family's considerable wealth, which allowed him to pursue both a career in letters and a life of comfort.[1]

Edward William Lane, the son of a clergyman, was also drawn to life as a writer. He would eventually produce one of the most extensive and detailed ethnographies of nineteenth-century Cairo—one that came under great criticism a century later. Lane excelled in mathematics during his student years and initially intended to further his studies at Cambridge. But he abandoned this path in favor of learning the craft of engraving in London. There he became fascinated with Egypt's ancient history, possibly influenced by the exhibitions organized in the city during that period. In particular he became interested in hieroglyphics and the work of Champollion.[2] Lane decided to go to Egypt in 1825 to study Arabic and capture its sights in lithographs. He remained there for twenty-four years, adopting an Egyptian lifestyle, wearing native garb, and studying Cairo and its social life. Lane eventually dedicated himself to writing about Egypt. In 1828 he started his *Manners and Customs of the Modern Egyptians,* in 1830 he worked on a translation of *1001 Arabian Nights,* and in 1842 he began his *Arabic-English Lexicon.*[3]

The nineteenth century was a period in which Egypt succumbed once again to European colonization and in the process became an attractive destination for travelers. Early on, its aura of danger and mystery made it of interest primarily to European nobility, adventurers, artists, and traders. This changed toward the end of the century, when Egypt became a common destination for European travelers. For Europeans, the grand tour of ancient civilizations—an itinerary of cities in Egypt, Italy, and Greece—was not merely a luxury but also a necessary course in the cultivation of the elite.

But our story of the European public's discovery of ancient Egypt must start with the Cairo that Napoleon Bonaparte occupied in the summer of 1798. Although the idea of a French colony in Egypt had been a looming possibility since the time of the Crusades, Napoleon sought to legitimize his military invasion in the spring of 1798 by invoking the greater good of the Egyptian people. Aboard the ship *L'Orient,* en route to Egypt, he wrote the following message to the people of Egypt: "For too long, this pack of slaves purchased in the Caucasus and Georgia has tyrannized the better part of the world. ... If Egypt is theirs to farm, then let them show the lease God gave them for it. A curse on the Mamluks and happiness to the people of Egypt."[4] Napoleon issued the proclamation soon after landing in Alexandria on July 1. Calling himself a servant of Allah and the Ottoman sultan, he declared that his purpose was to liberate Egyptians from oppression and from the abuse of power by the Mamluks, who had ruled Egypt for more than five centuries. But his real motivations and political aims were varied and complex. They ranged from economic interests to imperial expansion, from overpowering his political rivals at home to challenging British influence in the Orient as represented by the East India Company.[5]

Given the state of the Ottoman Empire at the time, Napoleon saw Egypt as the easy conquest of an almost defenseless territory. While extending the dominion of the French empire over three continents may have been his political aim, he was also a visionary who dreamed of personally spreading the principles of the Enlightenment and the French Revolution to the Orient. In his memoirs he would later write: "I saw myself founding a religion, marching into Asia, riding an elephant, a turban on my head and in my hand the new Koran that I would have composed to suit my needs."[6] Napoleon's propaganda leaflet, translated into Arabic, created much excitement and commentary when it reached the people of Cairo. Al-Jabarti, who devoted much of his scholarship to understanding the French, would later deliver a scathing critique of the manifesto, ridiculing its stylistic and grammatical inadequacies.[7] Nonetheless, the final statement of his proclamation made it clear that any resistance on the part of Egyptians would be met with harsh reprisals, and that any village or town that opposed French military rule would be burned to the ground.

As a resident of Cairo, al-Jabarti experienced the French invasion firsthand and described in great detail the turmoil in the city's streets after it became known that a French fleet had arrived in Alexandria. Cairo's streets were soon deserted, although the authorities attempted to give an impression of normalcy by ordering cafés to stay open and residents to hang lamps in front of their homes and businesses. Meanwhile, the Mamluk beys attempted to mobilize the city in anticipation of the arrival of the French army. While most of these residents, who were unarmed, were sent to Bulaq, a motley army of Mamluks crossed the Nile to confront Napoleon head-on. These Mamluk forces were described by al-Jabarti as "at odds with each other, envious, fearful for their lives and their comforts, immersed in ignorance and self-delusion, arrogant and haughty in their attire."[8] According to al-Jabarti, Cairenes were shocked by the arrival of the French. The two Mamluk amirs in charge, Murad Bey and Ibrahim Bey, sent for help from Istanbul straightaway. Murad Bey then took charge of mobilizing Mamluk forces against Napoleon, while Ibrahim Bey oversaw the construction of a naval blockade to stop the French fleet from approaching Cairo through the Nile.[9]

On July 21, 1798, as the French troops approached Cairo, Murad Bey confronted them at Imbaba in what became known as the Battle of the Pyramids.[10] With twenty-five thousand men, the French army was almost double the size of the Mamluk force. The Mamluk army, moreover, was ill equipped to withstand the French, overrun by its firepower. After battle, the Mamluk beys fled the city in an effort to save their own lives, leaving Cairo's residents to the guidance and support of the shaiykhs of its great mosques, particularly al-Azhar.

Most of the city's able-bodied men had been sent to fight with the Mamluks or defend the city in Bulaq, so the population left behind in the city proper consisted mainly of the elderly, women, and children. Cairo's streets became filthy after daily upkeep and business life came to a halt. A week later, French troops entered the city without resistance, allowing for their occupation to begin peacefully. With this conquest in hand, the Ottoman sultan promptly declared war on France. Although it was Napoleon who had defeated the powerful Mamluk beys, the sultan wished that his armies could have deposed them much earlier and taken control of Egypt for himself.[11]

For his residence Napoleon chose the palace of a wealthy Mamluk, Alfi Bey, in the area by Azbakiya Lake. He immediately set out to reform Egypt's administration, in part by introducing new political structures. He began by creating a grand *diwan*, made up of representatives from all regions of the country. He constituted new civic organizations, for which he recruited Egyptians with influence and status. Believing that the religious *ulama*, or learned men, were crucial to mobilizing the population toward modernization, he also spent time cultivating his relations with them.

Following the takeover of Cairo, Napoleon wasted little time trying to win over his new subjects. Occasionally he participated in local events and made public appearances designed to convey to the Cairenes his role as a benevolent ruler. Napoleon had a complex understanding not only of Egypt's history, but also of local politics. He was fully aware that the physical occupation of Egypt was only the beginning of his mission. He followed the advice of Count of Volney, the French philosopher and

Orientalist, who had written that a conqueror of Egypt had to engage in three wars: the first with the British, the second with the Ottomans, and the third against the local Muslim clergy. Napoleon knew that if the Egyptians, especially the educated Muslims, saw no difference between his troops and the Crusaders that came to Egypt centuries ago, French rule would not take hold.[12]

With this in mind, in the latter part of 1798 Napoleon attended the annual celebration of Wafaa al-Nil, a unique Egyptian ceremony observed since ancient Egyptian times, meant to express gratitude to the Nile as a source of life. He ordered his troops to line up for the event, and allowed Cairenes to board and explore the French ships and see their wares. Later that year Napoleon resuscitated the Muslim practice of celebrating Prophet Muhammad's birthday. At an event to mark the occasion, attended by French military officers along with leading Muslim clerics, French troops paraded alongside Egyptians in celebration of the Prophet. Napoleon, who had invariably ordered his troops to show utmost respect for the religious traditions of the native population whenever possible, attended the event wearing traditional Egyptian garb. This made him almost indistinguishable from the other shaiykhs of Cairo present by his side. The festivity programs included recitations of the Quran by local Egyptians, along with fireworks and massive banquets that the general public was invited to attend.[13] The leading cleric, Shaiykh Khalil al-Bakri, put together a feast for Napoleon and his officers where a hundred al-Azhar clerics dined alongside French officers. But while the clerics were seated on carpets around low tables, the French sat at tables; the cultural divide was made even more conspicuous by the silverware, plates, and rare bottles of wine that they were offered.[14]

When Bonaparte attempted to convince the imams to deliver the Friday sermon in his name, an act reserved for Muslim rulers such as the Ottoman sultan Selim, it was with the intent of incorporating the world of Islam into his rule, hoping that the locals would come to eventually accept the foreign Christian presence on their soil. Egyptians, however, were already showing signs of discontent and unrest. Later, during his exile in Saint Helena, Napoleon would write, as if he were an independent observer,

"The position of the French was uncertain. They were only tolerated by the believers, who crushed by the rapidity with which events unfolded, had bowed before force."[15] But his strategy did not end with trying to appease only the imams. He soon proposed to prominent Egyptian men a form of government in which they would hold office and rule by *sharia*—Islamic law. This was not merely Napoleon's attempt to live up to his initial promise of instituting representative government and civil liberty in Egypt. It was a tactical and necessary move on the part of a self-appointed ruler in a precarious position. Isolated from France by the British blockade, and faced with the prospect of local revolt, he decided to invoke the sanctity of the Quran and involve the clerics as the most effective forms of defense.[16]

The arrival of the French had brought the Egyptians face-to-face with the Europeans for the first time in many centuries and ushered in an era of European colonization that lasted for almost one and a half centuries. In its wake, it exposed Egyptian society to the ideas of modernity and industrialization, which had been strikingly absent in Ottoman Egypt. Not only did French military superiority inspire a desire among some Egyptians to learn from the West, but it also brought technological advancements and modern engineering, which were seen by some as beneficial for the country.

During the following year the French built defensive structures and military camps all over Cairo. Most of these took advantage of existing spaces or facilities, including not only houses but also mosques. The French installations repurposed the mosque of al-Zahir Baybars, whose minaret was used as an observatory, and the palace of the Mamluk Ibrahim Bey, which was turned into a military hospital. The Nilometer, which had been maintained at the southern tip of Rawdah Island by various rulers since the time of the ancient Egyptians, was structurally fortified during the French presence. The French also built a bridge to Rawdah and later a second bridge connecting Rawdah to Giza.[17] In addition to this construction, several mosques and homes of many amirs were demolished. The site of an old bridge was filled with the accumulated debris from these demolitions. The French also leveled a series of hills to install artillery towers. At Azbakiya Lake, a large site was cleared of buildings to make way for a square. The French conducted extensive infrastructural works around the lake, filling in parts of it to level the pavement along its shore. They also built a road that ran along the Nasiri canal, and another connecting Azbakiya to the mosque of Baybars.

Along the way, the French removed existing obstructions that hindered movement, creating an extensive network of roads that connected various parts of the city.[18] Given the level of destruction in Cairo during the French occupation, it may be appropriate to view it as a colonized city. But in reality the city was seen by both its residents and its French occupiers as a big military camp. Later, as Napoleon devised administrative structures that included Egyptians, the military form of government gradually changed and Egypt began to function as a colony.

The arrival of French forces also involved the seizure of the elegant homes of a number of important Mamluks. Many were deliberately destroyed, including that of the Mamluk leader Murad Bey. But others were occupied for specific purposes. One of these included the elegant mansion of Muhammad al-Alfi, a structure that had barely been completed in early 1798. It was built in the Ottoman style and consisted of three multistory wings and a large garden. The main façade of this building overlooked Azbakiya Lake and one of the canals that branched off the Nile. Napoleon took residence in this house and designated it as his main palace. It was here that for two consecutive years he celebrated Bastille Day to commemorate the emergence of the French Republic. To make it more to his liking, he asked General Caffarelli, his chief engineer, to make changes to the structure that would allow him direct access between all levels of the compound. He also had the ground floor fully renovated and refurbished with portraits of prominent French political figures.[19]

Most of the homes in the quarter of Nasiriyya were appropriated by the scientists who arrived with the French expedition. The most important of these was the house of Hasan al-Kashif. Al-Kashif had spent a fortune building his house, and it was near completion when the French arrived.[20] Under the French, however, it became a new institute for the study of Egypt.[21] For the next two years the Institut d'Egypte served as the headquarters for the learned men who accompanied Napoleon and were

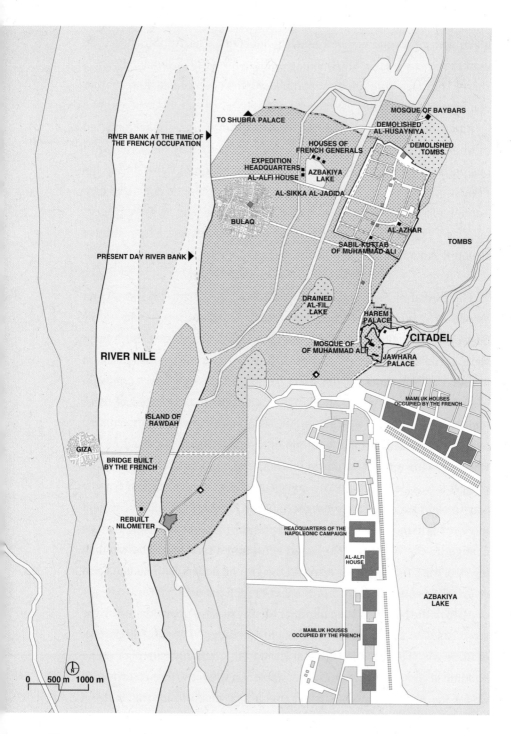

Figure 9.2   Map of Cairo at the end of Muhammad Ali's rule.

Figure 9.3   Headquarters of the French army in Azbakiya. ▬▬▬▬

engaged in documenting all aspects of the country as well as its culture. Altogether a team of nearly one hundred scientists was tasked with researching Egypt's language, customs, crafts, architecture, topography, and natural features. Their work was later compiled in the twenty-four-volume encyclopedia *Description de l'Egypte,* a comprehensive account of life in Egypt as observed by the French. The institute and its library were open to the public, who were invited to visit and peruse its collections, if not directly observe the ongoing work of the French scientists there.

Al-Jabarti, who visited this establishment, was fascinated not only by the books and scientific instruments used by the French but by their keen interest in every aspect of Egypt's history and society.[22] He marveled at the scientific experiments the French carried out in the institute's laboratories. He described in great detail the technology and scientific advances used there, including electricity, with which he was entirely unfamiliar. To many of al-Jabarti's fellow shaiykhs, such endeavors made little sense, because to them the origin and nature of the world was already known through religious texts. But for al-Jabarti these scientific discoveries were worthy of attention.[23]

Mapping was one of the primary interests of the French. Napoleon's cartographers produced the first reliable map of Cairo, which shows the development of its three major sections—central Cairo; suburban Bulaq; and Misr al-Qadimah, or old Cairo. It is apparent from this map that many of the *rahbahs*, or small spaces, that had existed since the time of the Mamluks, as had been documented by Maqrizi in the early years of the fifteenth century, were built up with new development by the time of Napoleon.

Apart from their scientific mission, the French brought to Egypt the culture of brothels, which al-Jabarti described as "places for amusement and licentiousness, including all kinds of depravities and unrestricted entertainment." Near Azbakiya Lake the French constructed several brothels and made them available to both French soldiers and Egyptian civilians. According to al-Jabarti, these establishments hired cooks, cupbearers, attendants, European female singers, and dancers, and visitors could either pay single-day entrance fees or keep rooms for an entire month.[24]

With the French occupation of the city, it was not long before the

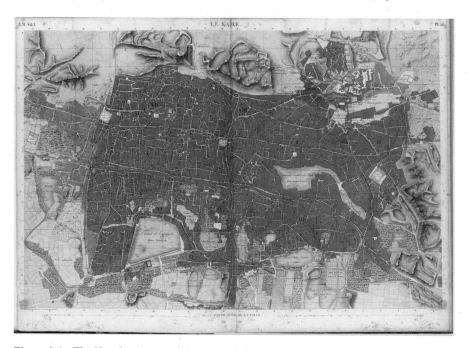

Figure 9.4 The Napoleonic expedition map of Cairo. ▬▬▬▬

population staged their first revolt. Barricading themselves in the old city, Egyptians defended its cavernous streets and enclosed the *haras*, its gated residential quarters. Responding in force, the French destroyed and dismantled the gates and transported them to Azbakiya Lake to be thrown away or used as firewood in their army camps.

In their attempt to quell such rebellions, the French sought to demolish any buildings that obstructed their movement.[25] Such techniques of surveillance and control were later widely used throughout Europe. Notably, these mechanisms were applied to the medieval core of Cairo almost fifty years prior to their implementation in French cities under the restored Bourbon monarchy. Their best-known use, of course, came after the Paris Commune uprising, as new widened streets and grand boulevards were placed throughout the dense residential quarters of central Paris according to the modernizing schemes of Baron Haussmann. As in Cairo, these demolition and reconstruction projects were aimed at facilitating the movement of troops and controlling popular revolts rather than exclusively facilitating traffic and beautifying the city. In addition to destroying major buildings, a number of mosques, and entire neighborhoods in Cairo, the French eliminated all encroachments on streets extending from stores and residences. They demolished the mosques of Katkhuda and Khair Bey in the neighborhood of al-Fil Lake and the entire quarter of Husayniyya, and barricaded a few of the city's gates, among them Bab al-Futuh.[26]

Following French moves to abate the initial resistance by Cairo residents, the city soon regained a measure of normalcy, as its cafés reopened and business activities resumed. But the apparent calm did not last for long. Local resentment grew as the French began to hold public executions as reprisals for the resistance. In October 1798 the French began by bombarding Cairo from the Citadel with heavy artillery. They not only continued to ravage the old city, tearing down barricades put in place by the city's residents, but also desecrated the al-Azhar mosque by entering it on horses, an act at complete odds with Napoleon's original statement of deference to religion. Later they altogether prevented locals from entering the mosque on Friday. Very soon French rule became so repressive that the local population began to publicly liken it to that of the brutal Mamluks, whom the French had supposedly come to remove from power. Indeed, the French surpassed the Mamluks in the amount of taxes exacted from the locals in order to fund their presence in Egypt.[27]

Isolated from France and vulnerable to Ottoman and British pressure, Napoleon eventually decided to start an offensive in Syria rather than await attack in Egypt. After seizing several Syrian cities and success- fully confronting both Ottoman and British forces, his army suffered an outbreak of plague and was forced to return to Egypt. Though Napoleon's Syrian campaign had failed, his army defeated an Ottoman force waiting for it outside Alexandria on its return to Egypt.

Sensing that Egypt would be difficult to control in light of both external military threats in the area and new turmoil at home, Napoleon sailed for France in August 1799. In his absence, he left general Jean-Baptiste Kléber in charge of the country.[28] Kléber soon found himself in such a precarious position that he had to bargain for the safe exit of his troops from the region by negotiating a treaty with the Ottomans and the Brit- ish. The British, however, would accept nothing less than French surren- der, and the agreement soon fell through. In March 1800 an Ottoman force encountered Kléber on its approach to Cairo. Although greatly outnumbered, the French managed to defeat the Ottomans—only to be confronted with another popular rebellion in Cairo, which lasted more than a month. These events came to an end when Kléber was assassi- nated by a young Syrian, Suleyman al-Halabi, in June 1800.[29]

General Jacques-François Menou took over the helm left by Kléber. But his task was no less challenging than Kléber's had been, as replenished Otto- man and British forces were fast approaching the country. Before taking over, Menou had married an Egyptian woman from a prominent Cairene family. Such marriages were not unusual; indeed, many French soldiers chose to marry local women instead of living under celibacy or frequenting brothels. For such marriages, conversion to Islam was obligatory.

Egyptians such as al-Jabarti expressed their indignation at such calcu- lated acts of conversion. But Menou saw his as a necessary political act to foster closer relations between Egyptians and their French colonizers. Menou was actually a follower of Deism, prominent in western Europe at the time. Deists did not adhere to an organized religion but instead believed that God could be determined through reason and observation of the natural world, and they rejected prophecies, miracles, and supernatural events. This may have made Menou more prone to embracing Islam. However, his conversion attracted the scorn of his comrades, who already had little respect for his military abilities.[30]

Menou was not eager to take over the French expedition after Kléber's death. Although his age and rank made him next in the line of command, his religious conversion made him unpopular with soldiers. Nevertheless in the summer of 1800, he took control of the government of Egypt.[31] However, in March 1801 the French forces under his command were defeated, and soon the three-year French occupation came to an end. General Menou was forced to negotiate with the Ottoman sultan for the surrender of Egypt and the return of the remaining French troops to France. After these arrangements were finalized, British forces also withdrew from Egypt in 1803 in accordance with the Treaty of Amiens.

Following the departure of the British and French forces, a new ruler, Khusraw Pasha, was appointed by Istanbul. Arriving with Ottoman forces, he managed to control Egyptian politics for the next two years. During this time the Mamluks made an attempt to regroup themselves in Upper Egypt. Although fewer in number, considerably weaker, and divided by rivalries, they remained a powerful group, eager to reassert their dominance. Among others vying for power was a rogue Albanian detachment that had played an important role in defeating the French and had chosen to stay in Egypt after French withdrawal. It was headed by a man whose name was to become part of Egypt's history—a young Albanian officer named Muhammad Ali. In the political struggles over the two years following French defeat, the rioting Albanians eventually were able to depose Khusraw Pasha. Through much political maneuvering, Muhammad Ali emerged as the new authority of Egypt.

Muhammad Ali was likely born in 1769, supposedly the same year as Napoleon. He was from Kavala, a Macedonian city located in today's Greece. He had a troubled childhood and was purportedly a bully as a teenager. According to his family, this may have been the reason he was recruited into the Albanian contingent sent by the Ottomans to confront Napoleon in July 1798. Muhammad Ali, who spoke Turkish and thought of himself as an Ottoman, quickly rose through the ranks of the sultan's army, and came to Egypt as the second officer in his detachment.[32] Although the Ottoman forces were defeated by the French, Muhammad Ali remained in Egypt after the commander of his unit was killed when he chose to enter a contentious political field made up of Mamluk factions struggling for power.

The collapse of the government in Egypt after the French departure in 1801, coupled with decades of consecutive weak Ottoman pashas, complicated the formation of a new Egyptian government. In an attempt to assert his authority, the viceroy Khusraw Pasha instituted new taxes. But Cairenes, who had been briefly exposed to a different and more democratic system under the French, were no longer willing to accept absolute rule by an Ottoman governor or the ad hoc tyranny of the Mamluks.[33] When Cairenes rebelled against French control, the remaining Ottoman forces under Muhammad Ali aided them. In 1804, when the city residents revolted again, against the Ottoman viceroy and the possible return of Mamluk rule, Muhammad Ali once more ordered his troops to protect them—an act that gained him the respect and admiration of the Egyptians.

Muhammad Ali soon began to consolidate power by playing the Mamluk factions against one another. But he also strategically forged an alliance with Khusraw Pasha, only to break it when it became convenient for him to do so. As might be expected, the returning Mamluks did not accept Muhammad Ali's authority; instead they mobilized around the leadership of al-Alfi Bey, whose house had been confiscated by Napoleon several years earlier. Al-Alfi's death two years later, however, created another vacuum, which allowed Muhammad Ali to further consolidate his control over Egypt. Eventually Muhammad Ali gained the support of the Cairene ulama, strengthening his political position to such an extent that he demanded to be appointed pasha. Recognizing that it was in his best interest to acquiesce to the demands of the people of Egypt, the Ottoman sultan recalled Khusraw Pasha in July 1805 and appointed Muhammad Ali as viceroy of Egypt. Although it was unusual for Istanbul to appoint to such a post a man whose political support came from outside the Otto-man establishment, Muhammad Ali had a unique advantage, given his ability to leverage local support.[34]

Upon assuming his new position, Muhammad Ali had to keep in line not only the Mamluks, but also his former Albanian military detachment. His fortunes took a positive turn in 1807 when he repelled a new British expe-dition to Egypt. This helped him reinforce his power locally. In the years that followed, the diminishing attention of the Ottoman sultan also left him to rule Egypt with relative independence. The major challenge continued to be the Mamluk factions. Although Muhammad Ali governed Mamluk-controlled Upper Egypt, he still considered them a serious internal threat. Not only did the Mamluk households have considerable economic power, which allowed them to support an alternative Mamluk armed force, but they were also vehemently opposed to Muhammad Ali's reforms.[35] Given that numerous Ottoman viceroys in Egypt had been deposed by powerful Mamluks, Muhammad Ali decided that the only way to end opposition against him was to completely eliminate the Mamluks.

In March 1811, Muhammad Ali organized a celebration at the Citadel to honor the appointment of his son Tusun as the head of an expedition in Syria. All influential men of Cairo were invited to mark the occasion, and among them were nearly five hundred leading Mamluks. When the recep-tion came to an end and the Mamluks were about to depart, Muham-mad Ali's men put up a blockade around a courtyard in the Citadel and massacred the Mamluks. Legend has it that one lone Mamluk, Amin Bey, escaped by jumping with his horse over the walls of the Citadel and disap-pearing to Upper Egypt. The massacre, however, did not end Muhammad Ali's attack on the Mamluk nobles. For the year that followed, his son Ibra-him was in charge of tracking down thousands of remaining Mamluks, which meant pursuing them to Upper Egypt and beyond. These bloody events marked the beginning of Muhammad Ali's absolute and indepen-dent rule of Egypt.[36]

When Muhammad Ali originally departed for Egypt, he left behind his wife and his sons, Tusun and Ibrahim. After he became governor, his family joined him. Initially the family lived in Azbakiya. But they soon moved to the Citadel, the seat of Muhammad Ali's government for much of his life. There he built the al-Jawhara, or Diamond, palace for himself, with an adjoining palace for his harem. After gaining full control of the country, Muhammad Ali began to survey other parts of the city where he could build additional palaces. Eventually he decided to move his main residence to a suburb of Cairo called Shubra, where he built a palace close to the Nile. Construction began in 1809, and within a year Muhammad Ali moved in.[37] The palace, set among lavish gardens, subsequently became the center for a new high society composed both of Cairenes and European expatriates who began to flock to Cairo in large numbers. Such residences built by Muhammad Ali outside the city eventually generated further development that grew into expansive suburbs.

His most beloved son, Tusun, joined him in Egypt at the age of eighteen and was appointed to command an expedition to Syria against the Wahhabis of Arabia. The venture was successful, and Tusun was able to capture Mecca. When Tusun needed reinforcement later on, Muhammad Ali came to join him. Although it was a short reunion, it strengthened

Figure 9.5 Muhammad Ali's Palace in Shubra.

the relationship between father and son in spite of the years spent apart. Muhammad Ali likely saw Tusun as his successor, given that his relationship with his other son, Ibrahim, was riddled with tension. In contrast to Ibrahim, who was a strict military leader, Tusun was known as kind and generous and was loved by the Egyptians.

Upon his return to Egypt, Tusun received a hero's welcome with a celebration prepared for him at his palace. The celebration did not last long, as Tusun fell ill with the plague during the feast. Within a day he died, and by the time his father received the news, Tusun's funeral was already under way. Tusun's body was taken to Cairo and buried in the mausoleum that Muhammad Ali built for his family. The city went into a forty-day mourning period.[38] Although he lost other children throughout his life, Muhammad Ali was most affected by Tusun's death. In Tusun's honor he built a *sabil-kuttab* on Cairo's main *qassbah* close to Bab Zuwayla. One of the few constructions that Muhammad Ali established in Cairo, the *sabil* had exquisite decorations on its circular façade, and arched windows with metal grills. The façade also bore a Kufic inscription of a Quranic verse.

Although he professed his allegiance and paid tribute to the sultan in Istanbul, Muhammad Ali was depicted by the British Orientalist Edward William Lane as an absolute sovereign. Lane has described him as an ambitious man and a just, albeit strict, ruler. He was severe insofar as he sought to maintain authority, but unlike his Mamluk predecessors he refrained from random acts of cruelty.[39]

Lane's *Manners and Customs of the Modern Egyptians* (1836) moreover describes in great detail the life of Cairo's residents during Muhammad Ali's rule. Lane studied Egyptian social relations, music, dress, and customs. In his view, Cairo was still a medieval city untouched by the wave of modernization that had swept through Europe. According to Lane, European social customs remained foreign to the Egyptians, and the only social stratum impacted by change was the elite.[40]

Lane's writings, and his role as one of the first scholars to carry out ethnographic work in Egypt, have been the subject of debate among many scholars. Although his work has provided the foundation for many subsequent scholarly writings, *Manners and Customs of the Modern Egyptians* was later criticized by some for its lack of objectivity.[41] After completing a series of travel notes based on his experience in Egypt, Lane began the book, which was commissioned by the Society for the Diffusion of Useful Knowledge in Britain with intent to develop an authoritative text on Egypt. Lane, however, was deemed duplicitous by a number of later scholars, based on his habits of living with natives, wearing traditional garb, and adopting their lifestyle when all the while recording and observing everything around him with a supposedly critical eye.[42] Nevertheless, *Manners and Customs* remains a useful source of information and is emblematic of the ways in which the Orient was invented through such efforts.

The nineteenth century was a time when many European artists and writers traveled to Egypt to explore its ancient sites. One of the earliest travelers, who produced some of the most renowned artworks depicting Egypt and Cairo from that period, was the artist David Roberts (1796–1864). Roberts was forty-two when he arrived in Egypt as a member of the Royal Academy with the specific mission of producing a body of visual work documenting Egypt's cities and archaeological sites. Purportedly the first British artist to "discover" Egypt, Roberts's intent was to fill in gaps left by the French in their *Description de L'Egypte*.[43] Prior to his arrival, Roberts had read everything he could about Egypt, including the works of Edward William Lane. The artwork that Roberts brought back to England was one of the most interesting collections produced on the region. It was also one of the last to document Egypt before the advent of photography.

About a quarter of the works in Roberts's portfolio depict Cairo's street life, its people, and its Islamic monuments. The artist rendered with great detail scenes depicting the lives and activities of Cairo's residents during the time of Muhammad Ali in his paintings of the slave market and of a coffee shop. In his diary he describes the painstaking process of gaining access to sites, and of drawing in the crowded streets in the unforgiving heat, surrounded, at times, by unwelcoming crowds.[44] Unlike other traveler-artists of his time, Roberts did not include views of Bulaq and Azbakiya. His interest was exclusively devoted to the medieval heart of Cairo and the Mamluk monuments that lined its qassbah. Among the edifices captured by Roberts in his paintings were the complexes of Qalawun and al-Ghuri, the

Figure 9.6   A view of Bab Zuwayla as portrayed by David Roberts in the nineteenth century in *Minarets and Grand Entrance of the Metwaleys at Cairo.*

Bazaar of the Coppersmiths, the mosque of al-Mu'ayyad Shaikh, and the various gates of the city. Roberts produced one of the richest visual documentations of Cairo in an era when Egypt captivated the British public.[45]

One of the few women to travel to Egypt at that time was Florence Nightingale, a twenty-nine-year-old British writer from a wealthy family. Nightingale traveled to Egypt with a group of friends as a part of a world tour, a fashionable activity among members of Victorian high society. She arrived in Egypt in 1849, at the end of Muhammad Ali's rule, when the country was in turmoil because of his illness. Traveling from Alexandria to Cairo via the Mahmudiya canal, Nightingale and her companions checked into the Hôtel de l'Europe at Azbakiya. She was impressed by Egypt's ancient sites, as well as by Cairo's medieval core, still largely intact at the time, at least according to her observations. She described Cairo as "the rose of the cities, the garden of the desert, the pearl of Moorish architecture, the fairest, really the fairest piece of earth below."[46] Yet some of her other comments on Cairo were rather unflattering: "In Cairo itself, exquisite as is the architecture, everything is undone: either it has been begun and never finished, or it is falling to decay; but you never see anything complete."[47] Nightingale caused quite an uproar in her attempts to visit mosques in Cairo, with worshipers upset at the presence of a Christian woman in their sacred space.[48]

Another Orientalist who captured Egypt's sites was Jean-Léon Gérôme (1824–1904), a French painter who made six trips to Cairo between 1856 and 1880. During these trips he took some of the earliest photographs of Egypt, collected artifacts, and drew sketches of the country and its people, material from which he later was to create nearly 250 paintings back in his studio in France.[49] Because his works were done while away from Egypt, Gérôme had to reconstruct scenes based on his sketches and photographs. For his backdrops, he occasionally employed studio objects, furnishings, and models dressed in costumes from a collection assembled by his brother-in-law, Albert Goupil, a renowned collector of Islamic art.

Gérôme's oeuvre portrays characters and scenes he considered to be representative of life in Egypt. Striving for authenticity, he paid great attention to details, and as a result his paintings have an almost photographic quality to them. His scenes, however, are based on the Egypt of his recollections, and in drawing his paintings he took great liberty to interpret Egyptian culture to suit the colors and exotic atmosphere in his paintings. This meant altering reality in favor of aesthetics, an inclination common in many Orientalist painters. There are factual errors in some of his works, like his "Prayer on the Rooftops of Cairo," where the worshipers are drawn facing north rather than toward the qibla; or "The Rose," also known as "The Love Token," which depicts the *zawiya*, a balcony dedicated to the call for prayer, as a place for romantic encounters. With the help of his brother-in-law and other art dealers who promoted his work, Gérôme became one of the most renowned and sought-after Orientalist painters of his time.[50]

Other travelers rendered Cairo not through images but in prose. Rather than embellish reality, some, including the English traveler R. R. Madden, expressed outrage at the state of the city:

> In a city containing three hundred fifty thousand inhabitants there is not one tolerable street. Splendid mosques some of which surpass, in my estimation, those of Constantinople are built in blind alleyways and filthy lanes: the public thoroughfares are hardly twelve feet wide, darkened by mats to impede the rays of sun and chocked with putrid vegetables and reeking offals from the various stalls which line the streets. The first thing that astonishes a stranger in Cairo is the squalid wretchedness of the Arabs and the external splendor of the Turks.[51]

Near the end of his reign, Muhammad Ali also came to recognize problems with the layout of streets in Cairo. Their inadequacy became particularly apparent after he imported a number of European carriages initially for use by the royal family. He found that they could not be maneuvered through the city's streets.[52] In the decade of the 1840s, he ordered that *mastabas*, areas where people would sit outside of houses and shops, be removed from all main streets, and that the mats covering the suqs be replaced with lighter materials. Finally, in 1845 he ordered a Tanzim plan, which culminated in the opening of al-Sikka al-Jadida road. In a few years

Figure 9.7   *Prayer on the Rooftops of Cairo* by Jean-Léon Gérôme. ▬▬▬▬

this thoroughfare was lined with major stores, most of which were run by the European residents of Cairo.[53] Other major public works of that period included the draining of Azbakiya Lake (a project started in 1827

but completed only at the end of the 1840s) as well as the draining of two other lakes, among them al-Fil.[54]

Muhammad Ali's regard for the city was incidental relative to his main project to control the entirety of Egypt, which he sought to turn into a monarchic state. Nevertheless, many of the building regulations were updated under his rule. According to one account, Muhammad Ali consulted the ulama on how to construct a new street in the old city. To this they replied that the width of a street should be great enough to accommodate two laden camels walking side by side.[55]

In 1812 Muhammad Ali abolished the *iltizam* tax-farming system. It had served as the primary means through which Mamluk households collected taxes from the population. He also confiscated portions of *waqf* lands and land held by Mamluk households. In this way a considerable amount of Egypt's land came under the ownership of the state. In spite of these measures, landowners continued to use the waqf system to accumulate and consolidate family wealth. But Muhammad Ali's reforms centralized the waqf administration and put mechanisms in place to prevent abuses of the system.[56] After he reformed Egypt's agricultural sector, he ordered the introduction of cotton as a crop. It would later become Egypt's main export and usher in a shift from subsistence farming to the cultivation of cash crops that became a source of foreign currency.[57]

Muhammad Ali's main goal was to transform Egypt into a modern industrial state and a great military power. Inspired by the technological advances of Europe, he brought in European experts to establish projects and create infrastructure for the advancement of industry, irrigation, military capacity, and health services. One of his first major infrastructure projects was the Mahmudiya canal, which linked the Nile with Alexandria, the only harbor in Egypt that could accommodate deep-water ships. His extensive public-works program eventually resulted in the construction of as many as thirty-two canals and forty-one dams and barrages, allowing a great expansion of agriculture by converting areas of desert into farmland.[58]

Although Muhammad Ali built few structures in Cairo, the location of his mosque, built between 1828 and 1848, made it an iconic landmark that transformed Cairo's skyline. Located above the Citadel, it became a symbol of sovereign power. And just like Salah al-Din, who had demolished Fatimid palaces to make way for his building projects, Muhammad Ali tore down several Mamluk-era buildings to clear the site for his mosque. Its size was unprecedented in Egypt at the time, and its architecture signaled the beginning of a new era in Egyptian history. Initially Muhammad Ali commissioned the French architect Pascal Coste to design it. Coste produced sketches of a mosque in the neo-Mamluk style that he considered to be representative of the Egyptian nation. But with Muhammad Ali's death, this project never came to fruition. Instead a mosque was built according to the design of an American engineer and builder by the name of Yusuf Bushnaq.[59]

As designed by Bushnaq, the mosque was based on monumental proportions, its interior large enough to accommodate some seven thousand worshippers. A great dome covers its square central sanctuary, while its minarets rise to a height of eighty-two meters. Flanking the central dome are two semi-domes, which in turn are surrounded by four smaller domes. While the massing of the mosque is simple, its eclectic decoration shows a strong European influence. The mihrab niche is deeply offset and protrudes from the exterior wall. The larger of its two mihrabs is decorated with gilded wood ornamentation.[60] The architectural language of this mosque clearly exhibits a desire to step away from a Mamluk past. A preference for Ottoman forms is indicative of Muhammad Ali's political ambitions in relation to the power center of Istanbul. Indeed, the mosque may be seen as a form of mimicry of the Ottoman imperial style. In particular, its spatial composition and massing echoes the mosques of Istanbul, which are characterized by vast central domes, surrounded by semi-domes and slender, conical-topped minarets.

Standing atop the Citadel, from which the mosque of Muhammad Ali commands Cairo today, one can never fully imagine the experiences of Napoleon and Muhammad Ali, the founders of Egypt's modern history, and those of al-Jabarti or Lane, the chroniclers of that history. But their lives and experiences in Cairo were instrumental not only in defining them as historical figures, but also in sealing the fate of the people they governed or documented. Muhammad Ali became senile close to the end of his rule, and he eventually abdicated his position in favor of his son Ibrahim Pasha in 1848. Yet the latter abruptly died after ruling for only seven months. Stricken by grief over the premature deaths of his sons Tusun and Ibrahim, Muhammad Ali died a few months later in August 1849. He was buried in his mosque before its completion. His burial place, to the right of the mosque's entrance, is marked by a white marble dome. This is an unusual arrangement, as previous rulers of Egypt have been buried in mausoleums adjoining the madrasas and mosques that they founded.

Napoleon, who had opened Egypt to the European world and remained in Cairo for about a year, had an extraordinarily eventful life following his departure from Egypt. Reflecting on his Egyptian expedition, Napoleon later stated: "The time I spent in Egypt was the most beautiful in my life, because it was the most ideal."[61] He eventually met his end in exile on the island of Saint Helena, where he died in May 1821. He never regretted having conquered Egypt.

Al-Jabarti lived for several decades following French withdrawal, but his life was also greatly affected by grief. His son, who had become close to Muhammad Ali, was murdered on a return from Shubra in 1822. This affected al-Jabarti profoundly, and he abandoned his writing and died three years later after dealing with a bout of blindness.

Lane visited Egypt several times over the years before returning permanently to England in 1849 to settle in a seaside resort. There he worked on his *Lexicon,* which he never finished. Before his death in 1876, Lane gave the responsibility for completing the work to his nephew Stanly Lane-Poole, who would later himself become an authority in his own right. But Lane-Poole was able to complete only a few more volumes based on Lane's notes, leaving the project unfinished.[62] He was able to continue Lane's legacy, however, by writing a biography of his uncle, which left out many details pertaining to Lane's personal life—including the fact that his wife was originally his slave—that would not have been well received in Victorian England.[63] Lane's work remained an important source for later scholars, serving as the basis of Orientalist imagination of the Middle East at a time when educational and research institutions specializing in this form of knowledge were emerging.

As the main characters in this story, Muhammad Ali and Napoleon helped usher in a new era in Cairo, and brought about a total transformation of Egypt's relationship with the world. Through their role as storytellers, al-Jabarti and Lane were able to capture the true spirit of that time.

Modernizing the New, Medievalizing the Old: The City of the Khedive

THE CAIRO MARRIOTT is a prominent five-star hotel on the Nile island once called Gezira, which literally means "island" in Arabic.[1] Now called Zamalek, the island is located in the center of what is now Central Cairo. Although the hotel's interior incorporates the splendor of the old Gezira palace built in 1867, two unsightly towers housing more then five hundred rooms literally bury this historic structure in between them. The palace, built by Khedive Ismail, functioned as the official gathering place for many of the foreign dignitaries who visited Egypt during the nineteenth century. Looking east from Gezira Palace back then, one could see the district of Bulaq, and behind it, the skyline formed by the hundreds of minarets of the old core of Cairo. Looking southeast one could see the Citadel of Salah al-Din crowned by the Muhammad Ali mosque; and looking south one saw green fields that stretched along the Nile and into Giza where the Pyramids had stood grand for several millennia.

There is no better place from which to introduce the characters of our story and narrate the history of khedival and royal Cairo—a period that spanned nearly a century, from the government of Khedive Ismail to that of King Farouk—than from its opulent palaces, which have survived in the modern-day city as tourist hotels. The story could have equally begun with the Mena House Oberoi Hotel, which Ismail built at the foot of the Pyramids for his guests; or at the park fronting the Azbakiya district that occupied the site of the legendary Shepheard Hotel, though the hotel was later demolished. But the Gezira Palace remains unparalleled in its significance as a site from which to begin our story of khedival Cairo, as it served as a stage for many historic encounters between actors who changed the face of Egypt.

To impress his visitors, Ismail dedicated most of his time and much of Egypt's wealth to the planning and beautification of Cairo. But one aspect of this grander project in which he truly spared no effort was the palace of Gezira. Ismail had it built specifically to host Princess Eugénie, the spouse of Napoleon III, who was his most honored guest at the inaugural celebrations for the Suez Canal. It is here that Ismail likely may have met such guests as Ferdinand de Lesseps, who is credited with obtaining the permission to build the canal and begin its construction. Gezira Palace is also where Ali Mubarak, Ismail's right-hand man and master planner of the efforts to rebuild Cairo, may have also met his European counterparts who came to consult on the city's new developments. These might have included Jean-Pierre Barillet-Deschamps, the landscape architect who participated in planning the Exposition Universelle in 1867, and who was later commissioned to design the gardens south of the palace.[2]

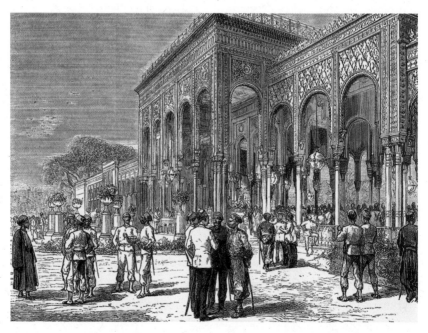

Figure 10.1   The Gezira Palace of Khedive Ismail as illustrated in the nineteenth century by the British journal *The Graphic* (left). The palace today as the Cairo Marriott (right). ━━━━━━

With the accession to power of Ismail, who ruled between 1863 and 1879, Egypt entered a new and accelerated phase of the modernization campaign launched by Muhammad Ali. Ismail came to power during a time of growth: the population was on the rise after centuries of decline; the economy was flourishing due to an unprecedented cotton boom; and the excavation of the long-anticipated Suez Canal was well under way.[3] But Egypt's infrastructural development was only part of Ismail's ambitious plans, as his rule marked an era of significant transformation for Cairo. Although Ismail is remembered as a ruler dedicated to giving Egypt a stronger political position on the world stage, his upbringing and formative years were spent immersed in foreign culture abroad. The signs of modernity he saw emerging in European cities during this time deeply influenced his desire to make Egypt part of Europe and to transform Cairo into a symbol of Egypt's modernization.

Ismail was born in Cairo in 1830 to Ibrahim, the famed military campaigner and son of Muhammad Ali. He was sent to live in Austria as a child, where he received medical attention for a condition affecting his eyesight. He later moved to France for his education in engineering and military sciences at the Saint Cyr academy in Paris. In France Ismail was exposed to the ongoing transformation of European cities and developed a passion for planning and building. Yet even though Ismail received a European education and spoke several European languages, he also demonstrated considerable pride in his native land, taking a great interest in Egypt's ancient and Islamic heritage and dedicating himself to bringing the Egyptian people into a new era of political emancipation.[4]

Prior to Ismail's rise to power, Egypt was ruled by two successors to Muhammad Ali. Both made only minor changes to Cairo's built environment, but their policies had long-term consequences for Egypt. After Muhammad Ali's death, the country was ruled formally for a year by Ibrahim, Muhammad Ali's eldest son. Following Ibrahim's sudden death, the administration of Egypt fell to Abbas I Pasha, son of Tusun and grandson of Muhammad Ali. Abbas, who died young at the age of forty, ruled from 1848 to 1854. Compared to the period of rapid modernization under Muhammad Ali, Abbas's rule brought Egypt's development to a standstill. Taking an antimodernization stance, he pursued conservative policies, closing the country to trade and travelers and halting industrialization. But his policies did not leave urban Cairo and Egypt completely unchanged. Abbas founded a small military outpost for foreign mercenaries bearing his name, Abbasiyya, on the edge of the desert, in the vicinity of the older settlement of Heliopolis. Through a policy of land grants, and the founding of institutions such as a school, hospital, and palace, Abbas encouraged development of the area, turning northeast Cairo into a well-populated district.

Despite his aim to isolate Egypt and undo his grandfather's modernization projects, Abbas is also credited with introducing to Egypt one of the emblems of modernity: the railway. Toward the end of his rule, Muhammad Ali was approached by the British with a proposal to connect the Mediterranean to the Red Sea by train, a project that would ease the passage to India.[5] Abbas was not interested in fostering such development or facilitating British investment in Egypt, but eventually he gave in to pressure and in 1851 signed an agreement with a British company to connect Alexandria and Suez by railway. In an act that appears nationalistic by today's standards, however, Abbas successfully promoted his isolationist agenda by stipulating that only Egyptian labor and capital be used to build the railway. Furthermore, in order to minimize foreign influence, Abbas replaced the initially proposed direct connection from Alexandria to Suez with two separate routes: the first, leading from Alexandria to Cairo, was completed in 1854; the second, from Cairo to Suez, was finished in 1858, after his death. The two routes made Cairo a railway hub and brought a new force of modernization to the city. The Cairo railway station was built on the site of the port of al-Maqs in 1856, near where the Bab al-Hadid, the medieval Iron Gate, used to stand.[6] Eventually the Cairo station would become a node that not only connected Cairo to the rest of the world but also interconnected different parts of the city.

Another important landmark from Abbas's time was the Shepheard Hotel. The hotel was founded by Samuel Shepheard, a British sailor who landed in Egypt in 1842 after having taken part in a mutiny. He began his career in the hotel industry by working in various British establishments

Figure 10.2 Cairo Railway Station, also known as Bab al-Hadid.

in Cairo. After a few years he had amassed enough fortune to be introduced to Abbas, whom he assiduously cultivated through a shared interest in hunting. Abbas eventually offered Shepheard a land grant in Cairo, on which Shepheard began to plan his own hotel. The land offered by Abbas was on the defunct shore of Lake Azbakiya, and included the structure that had once been the Mamluk al-Alfi's house, which had served as Napoleon's headquarters during his brief time in Cairo. During the rule of Muhammad Ali, the house had been turned into a college of foreign languages. Abbas had closed the school before giving the land and the building to Shepheard. As Egypt's most prominent hotel, Shepheard's would accommodate foreign visitors to the city well after Shepheard's return to England in 1860 and would remain open for almost a century.[7]

The second notable ruler to succeed Muhammad Ali was Sa'id, Muhammad Ali's youngest son. Although his contributions to the built environment were minor, his rule from 1854 to 1863 brought another turning point for Egypt: the signing of an agreement in 1854 between

Sa'id and Ferdinand de Lesseps, approving plans for the construction of the Suez Canal. More amenable to change and to the opening of Egypt to Europe than his predecessor, Sa'id was one of the first of Muhammad Ali's sons to receive a French education. In fact, de Lesseps, the son of the French consul in Cairo, had been one of Sa'id's instructors in France. At Sa'id's invitation, de Lesseps brought to Egypt the plans for building the canal prepared by the Société d'Études du Canal de Suez. De Lesseps was successful in obtaining Sa'id's approval for the canal, although final ratification of the agreement to build and operate it did not come until after Sa'id's death.

Sa'id's agreement changed Egypt's future forever, as it made Egypt a strategic location in world maritime transport. To begin work, however, de Lesseps also needed the consent of the Ottoman sultan in the face of British opposition. Eventually de Lesseps was able to facilitate Egypt's access to funds from various banks to finance the project, and he was able to oversee the beginning phases of excavation. Work continued after the end of Sa'id's rule in 1863, and the canal was finally opened during Ismail's rule in August 1869.[8]

Despite being at the center of such a massive endeavor, Sa'id made few changes to Cairo's built environment. As its population expanded, the city continued to grow, particularly along the new railroad line leading to Suez. However, the development of Abbasiyya stalled, as the troops quartered there were moved south of Bulaq to the newly built Qasr al-Nil military barracks.[9] Although some of the policies of Abbas and Sa'id helped lay the groundwork for it, Egypt's modernization did not truly take off until Ismail began planning the infrastructure on which the modern city of Cairo would be built.

An opponent of Abbas's isolationist regime in his youth, Ismail became involved in government during the rule of his uncle Sa'id. He held various positions, including that of regent in 1861 during his uncle's period of absence from the country. Upon taking full control of the country, Ismail's first objective was to organize the institutional and policy framework for modernization, and in 1864 he founded the Ministry of Public Works. In 1865 he founded the Cairo Water Company. Initial plans, to construct a freshwater supply network designed to draw water from the mouth of the Khalij through a pumping station, ran into financial and engineering difficulties, causing major delays and the revocation of a contract with the French firm M. Cordier. Undeterred, Ismail soon began a larger public works program that included the development of a freshwater canal called Isma'iliya, a project completed by 1866, for which he employed a French engineer by the name of Brocard.[10] Gas was also brought to Cairo in 1865 through the Lebon Company, prompting the installation of streetlights in the city's new districts and later in older parts of Cairo. Eventually this network of utilities ran from the old city outward, bringing with it significant development.

Ismail's plans did not stop there. Given his French education and exposure to the West, his vision for Cairo was influenced by his admiration of modern urban planning in France. But it was his visit to Paris during the Exposition Universelle, organized by Baron Haussmann in 1867, that provided Ismail with a comprehensive model for the transformation and beautification of the city. For the French, the Paris exposition was meant to epitomize the advances made by European planning and colonization, and it coincided with the peak of Haussmann's efforts to transform the city. For Ismail, Napoleon III's invitation to take part in the exposition was an opportunity not only to demonstrate Egypt's place on the world stage but also to make a political impression upon other rulers. Thus, one of his objectives was to have himself elevated by the Ottoman sultan—the nominal caliph of all Muslims—to the title *khedive*. While in Paris, Ismail and his court were received and entertained by Haussmann, who, it is said, gave him and his entourage tours of the newly transformed parts of the city.[11] After this trip, Haussmann and Ismail maintained a friendship along with a working relationship, as shown in their correspondence on matters concerning the replanning of Cairo.[12]

It was perhaps on one of these tours that Ismail met Pierre Grand, a civil engineer whom he later hired to work on Cairo's street networks.[13] And while there is no evidence that Ismail was similarly introduced to Barillet-Deschamps, the landscape architect who designed the Champs de Mars and Bois de Boulogne, it is possible that they, too, met, as Barillet-

Deschamps was later invited to Egypt to design the Azbakiya gardens for Ismail after much of the lake had been filled in.

During his stay in Paris, Ismail also unwittingly became the object of the public's curiosity and an item in the very exhibition he had been invited to visit. The Egyptian pavilion consisted of three principal buildings: a replica of the temple of Philae, representing the architecture of ancient Egypt; a palace; and a caravanserai. While in Paris, Ismail was housed in the very heart of this pavilion in the palace built to emulate the Mamluk architectural style of old Cairo. It was there that he received visitors and hosted receptions, thus becoming part of the spectacle that put an imaginary Egypt on display for a European audience fascinated by the Orient.[14] Indeed, Ismail and the Ottoman sultan, Abdulaziz, who also traveled with his court to the exhibition, became the main attractions for most of the visitors, namely the Parisians, at the fair.

As guests of Emperor Napoleon III and Empress Eugénie, Ismail and Abdulaziz were honored at a sumptuous reception organized for them at the Palais d'Industrie. Between twenty and thirty thousand spectators gathered to see the two Muslim rulers that day, and the popular press was enthralled by the ceremony. But many Europeans, who were expecting an encounter only with the exotic elements of the Orient, were disappointed with Ismail's impeccable French, spoken with no accent, and his European garb. This was not the image the crowds gathered that day—accustomed with the Orientalist representations of painters—had expected from the ruler of Egypt.[15]

Ismail's trip to the Paris exhibition was not solely intended to strengthen cultural and political relations between France and Egypt, or to showcase Egypt's modernization. His principal objective, which he seemed to have succeeded in accomplishing, was to obtain funds for the reconstruction of the Egyptian capital. The inauguration of the Suez Canal was scheduled to take place in the next two years, and Ismail had very little time to transform Cairo into a showpiece that would compare with, or even rival, the kind of modern city he witnessed in Paris. His plan was to transform the built fabric of Cairo in the shortest amount of time possible so that it could serve as the backdrop for a large celebration to which he would invite all the leading monarchs of Europe. But how could such a massive transformation be undertaken in the heart of Cairo, with its narrow streets and densely crowded neighborhoods? Because the renewal of the old city fabric was unfeasible, Ismail decided to focus attention on the western portion of the city. His visitors could be housed there and kept away from the medieval core to the east, which Ismail considered unsightly.

Ismail decided to entrust Cairo's revitalization to Ali Mubarak, an Egyptian engineer. Born in 1823 in a village in the Nile Delta to a traditional, rural family of shaiykhs, Mubarak was raised in a modest household of good social standing but little wealth. He received Quranic schooling at the wish of his father, but at the age of eleven he decided to enroll in a primary school. Even at a young age Mubarak understood that only with a formal secular education could he make a mark in a rapidly changing Egyptian society.[16] And later, his exceptional performance as a student of military and civil engineering in the Muhandiskhanah, the School of Engineering, resulted in his selection to the educational mission sent to France by Muhammad Ali. During this trip Mubarak made important contacts with some of the other students in the mission—and he also met the future ruler of Egypt, Ismail, who was to greatly influence his career.

Upon his return to Egypt, Mubarak began by working for the government under Abbas. He served various official functions until Abbas elevated him to the rank of colonel, gave him the title of bey, and offered him three hundred acres of land.[17] But after Abbas's death, Sa'id reformed the administration and demoted most of those appointed under Abbas, a measure that put Mubarak's career on hold. Mubarak was sent to work abroad as a military engineer and did not occupy a significant government position for the entire duration of Sa'id's rule. It is likely that during this period Mubarak resumed working on his book *'Alamuddin,* which he may have begun during his time in France. This four-volume novel telling the story of a shaiykh traveling in Europe is considered by some to contain autobiographical elements.[18]

Mubarak's career started in earnest only after Ismail's accession. Ismail had known Mubarak as a colleague during their time together on the educational mission, and when Ismail assumed the position of khedive, he appointed Mubarak to a government post and put him in charge of the Qanater barrage on the Nile. Later Mubarak was given the title *pasha* and appointed minister of public works and of *al-Awqaf,* or endowments, and eventually also minister of education. In addition to his multiple appointments, Mubarak was to write a remarkable twenty-volume historical and topographic description of Cairo, *Al-Khitat al-Tawfiqiya al-Jadida,* along with books on engineering and educational reform.[19]

As minister of public works, Mubarak was tasked with transforming Cairo into "the Paris of the Nile." More specifically, Ismail put him in charge of three major projects: developing Cairo to the west in a quarter called Isma'iliya; rebuilding the district of Azbakiya; and creating a master plan for the entire city that would unify its medieval core with its surrounding expansions according to the model Haussmann had established in Paris. Mubarak began by drafting a policy to reorganize and reform the municipal administration of the city, dividing it into four new districts, each headed by a department of urban planning. He paid particular attention to the suburbs, because they would be the stage for most of the upcoming expansion and development. A key element of this reform was the unification of Cairo with its hinterlands, including Old Cairo and Bulaq, which until then had been discrete entities. Building and planning codes were also developed, and their enforcement was assigned to a new, centralized bureaucracy. Mubarak's administration also introduced municipal policies and began generating a new map of Cairo, which was needed to plan the Haussmannesque thoroughfares that were to traverse the city. These wide, axial boulevards connecting important nodes would constitute a significant change in the character of the city, altering its former fabric of narrow, labyrinthine streets.

The development of the Isma'iliya quarter was also entrusted to Mubarak, who began to plan for its wide streets and public utilities around 1867. At the time the area was largely underdeveloped, and building new streets there proved to be relatively easy, as demolitions were unnecessary, unlike in the old core of al-Qahira. By the time of the opening of the Suez Canal, all public works in Isma'iliya were completed. The settling of the area, however, took longer. Despite the generous land grants offered by Ismail to anyone willing to build a structure costing more than two thousand Egyptian pounds, development remained slow.[20] Indeed, only a few hundred homes had been built in Isma'iliya by the time the British arrived several decades later.

Mubarak was also put in charge of planning and rebuilding of the Azbakiya district, the area slated for the most spectacular and eventually speculative changes. The old Mamluk palaces that lined the shores of the lake were demolished to make way for new roads and public buildings whose eclectic façades recalled those on Paris's boulevards. Among these buildings were the Théâtre National de la Comédie and the Opera House, which was modeled after La Scala in Milan and built in five months so as to be ready for performances scheduled for the Suez Canal celebrations.[21] The correspondence between Ismail and Baron Haussmann includes one request from Ismail asking for recommendations for French landscape architects to work in Cairo, demonstrating the importance accorded by the khedive in employing the finest European experts for his projects.[22]

Around this time Barillet-Deschamps was commissioned to plan the garden that would replace the existing Azbakiya square, at the corner of the former lake. Inaugurated by Ismail in 1872, the garden was modeled after Parc Monceau in Paris, and it included a variety of attractions, such as shops, galleries, European cafés hosting orchestras playing European music, and some Arab-style coffee shops.[23] The garden was designed in the picturesque English style, with asymmetrically placed ponds and grottos that also included some elements typical of French gardens, such as expansive vistas. Existing mosques and residential buildings in the area that were not designated for demolition were washed and repainted. Although the gardens were unfinished when the European dignitaries arrived for the Suez Canal inauguration, Ismail was still able to accommodate his guests in the newly rebuilt Azbakiya quarter. Among these guests were the Prince and Princess of Wales, whom Ismail received in February 1869 and who stayed at a palace in Azbakiya built specifically to accommodate them.[24]

Another project that had yet to be completed was the iron swing-bridge at Qasr al-Nil, which was scheduled to be ready before the arrival

Figure 10.3 Qasr al-Nil bridge. ━━━━━━━━━

of Princess Eugénie. The bridge was built by the French firm Fives-Lille
to connect the eastern part of Cairo to the island of Gezira. By then the
island had established boundaries, protected from Nile floods by Muhammad Ali's dam projects upstream. With the bridge still under construction, however, the princess instead crossed the Nile by means of a floating
bridge to reach the luxurious Gezira Palace, built to serve as her residence
during her short visit.[25]

The decoration of the interior of Gezira Palace brought together the
style of the Princess's own quarters at the Tuileries Palace with motifs
typical of Islamic palaces, such as *mashrabiya* screens and banded marble.
These luxurious fixtures and interior furnishings were imported from
France. Ismail put a German architect, Julius Franz, in charge of the

construction of the palace, while Barillet-Deschamps planned the garden to its south. Another ongoing project was the improved access route between Cairo and the Pyramids at Giza. The existing road had often flooded when the Nile was high and during occasional rains. An elevated road leading to the Pyramids was completed with remarkable speed, just in time for the arrival of Ismail's European guests. It, too, was landscaped by Barillet-Deschamps.[26]

This extensive planning and building activity culminated in the celebrations marking the inauguration of the Suez Canal in 1869. For several months Egypt received European visitors, ranging from royalty and government officials to journalists and planning professionals. Ironically, while Ismail's objective was to showcase a modern and Europeanized Egypt, these visitors came with the hopes of seeing the Egypt portrayed in the Exposition Universelle in Paris in 1867. That is, they wished to see scenes and places reminiscent of the stories of *One Thousand and One Arabian Nights* that had animated the popular European Orientalist imagination.

In the end, the khedive spared no expense to entertain his guests even after the festivities came to an end. As part of the Suez Canal celebrations, Ismail had planned to open the Opera House with a performance of *Aïda,* the Egyptian-themed work for which he had commissioned the Italian composer Giuseppe Verdi. However, Verdi was unable to complete the work in time. Instead his *Rigoletto* was performed for the opening. *Aïda* eventually premiered at the Opera House in Cairo after the canal festivities came to an end, and was met with acclaim. The Egyptologist Auguste Mariette contributed not only to writing its script, but also to the design of its stage set and props. Ismail spent lavishly on mounting the opera, and the extravagant production involved three thousand performers. Ethiopian slaves were brought on stage, and original Egyptian artifacts and statues representing ancient gods were borrowed from Mariette's own collection.[27] Verdi, however, did not attend the opening in Cairo. He objected to the fact that the premiere was open only to nobility and dignitaries and not to the general public. He held his own premiere in Milan a few months later.

After the festivities had ended and most of the guests had left, the pace of building slowed considerably. Unfinished public works and landscaping projects slowly progressed toward completion. Until his death in 1874, Barillet-Deschamps continued to work on landscape projects in Cairo, as well as in the area on the western bank of the Nile that led from Imbaba to Giza.[28]

Another significant building project coordinated later on during Ismail's rule was the reconstruction of the Abdin Palace. Ismail ordered the replacement of the old palace with a grand structure with a classical façade and a layout modeled after the horseshoe plans of French palaces. Facing the palace was a grand square, Maydan Abdin, also modeled after the open spaces that surrounded European royal palaces. Ismail considered this an appropriate modern setting to symbolize the state's power, and consequently moved the seat of his government there from the Citadel. Completed in 1874, the Abdin Palace was the last symbol of modernity Ismail added to the fabric of Cairo. Later it would provide a stage for events marking the end of Egypt's independence—and, almost a century later, its reemergence as a modern sovereign nation-state.

As minister of public works under Ismail, Ali Mubarak continued some

Figure 10.4   Abdin Palace in Cairo at the end of the nineteenth century. ▬

of the infrastructural projects started in previous years, including a two-kilometer-long boulevard to connect Azbakiya with the mosque of Sultan Hasan. According to Mubarak, in order to clear the land for this colossal project, entire neighborhoods had to be demolished, including hundreds of dwellings, several mosques, bathhouses, and commercial structures. The wide boulevard that cut through the medieval heart of the city was later named after Muhammad Ali, and it was built, landscaped, and equipped with gas lighting at record speed.[29] It not only became the centerpiece of urbanization under Ismail but also paid homage to Muhammad Ali and his vision of modernization. Indeed, if Muhammad Ali is the founder of modern Egypt, as it is commonly recognized, then Ismail is the founder of modern Cairo.

But there is another coda to this great era of building. The debts incurred in constructing all these symbols of modernity and European luxury brought great financial difficulties to an overleveraged Egyptian state. On the one hand, the revenues of the state diminished in the face of an economic downturn and from the exactions of tribute paid to Istanbul in return for Egypt's autonomy. On the other hand, Ismail found himself unable to repay the money he had originally borrowed from European banks to finance his efforts. This ultimately pushed Egypt into bankruptcy, and in the end Ismail was forced to sell his shares in the Suez Canal to the British in 1875. Additional pressure came from European powers who began to take control of Egypt's state institutions. When Ismail attempted to resist these forces in 1879, he was promptly deposed, and his son Tawfiq (1879–1892) was installed in his stead.

In 1880 Egypt also began to see the first signs of political unrest in a rebellion that broke out in Cairo, led by an army colonel named Ahmed Urabi. Urabi was a nationalist whose oratorical skills and peasant origins—what became known as *fellahin* among the Egyptian elite—gave him wide support among Egyptians. Urabi and a group of Egyptian army officers formed a party called *al-Hizb al-Watani*—or the patriotic faction—which opposed the control of Egypt by foreign forces and the Turko-Circassian aristocracy of the khedival family.[30] Egypt at that time was run by outsiders, as Khedive Tawfiq had little authority over a country under

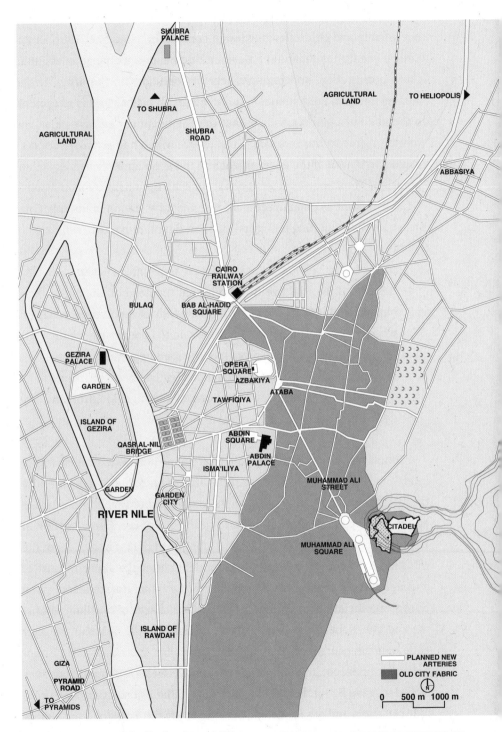

Figure 10.5   Map of khedival and royal Cairo.

receivership and controlled by foreign consuls. In September 1881, Urabi brought his troops to Abdin Palace and demanded a change of regime, a new constitution, and improvement of conditions in the army. Urabi later became a major national figure in Egyptian history for his statement to the khedive in Abdin square that day: "You cannot enslave us as we were born free to our mothers." The revolt, which had popular support, resulted in the fall of the government and the appointment of an Egyptian Council of Ministers—and for the first time, an Egyptian prime minister.

Colonel Urabi's coup attracted a great deal of attention in Europe. One British journal, agitating for intervention in Egypt, remarked:

> In the native opinion, he has achieved unqualified success. He has forced the Khedive to keep him at the head of affairs; he has wrested internal power from the hands of the Europeans, whose fleets, his followers say, are afraid to take vengeance for the insults, which his soldiers have heaped upon them. Moreover, he is now not only countenanced by the Sultan of Turkey … but has even been awarded one of the highest Ottoman decorations.[31]

Political instability continued into September 1882, when British forces intervened, occupied Alexandria, and marched onto Cairo on the premise that Egypt was likely to default on its loans. Urabi's revolt was crushed at Tal al-Kabir, an event that ushered in the era of British occupation of Egypt.[32] Urabi was captured and tried along with the other leaders of the rebellion by a court assembled and modeled after the French Court of Justice. In front of the court, composed of Egyptian notables and many European officials, Urabi pleaded guilty to the charge of rebelling against the khedive. Rebellion was punishable by death in the Ottoman military code, but the court ruled instead that Urabi should be sent into perpetual exile.[33] Because the only other alternative was execution, Urabi was forced to leave Egypt. He spent a few years in the British-controlled province of Ceylon, today's Sri Lanka, but eventually returned to Egypt, where he remained until his death a few years later. Urabi's revolt was the first instance of anticolonial nationalist mobilization in Egypt and the first step toward the larger project of modern independent nation-building.

Mubarak, who did not support Urabi, played no role in the revolt. Rather, he supported Khedive Tawfiq, whose position he considered as better for Egypt than the excessive demands of the revolutionary officers.[34] Mubarak continued to hold posts in the government even after the demise of Ismail, and in 1879, during the rule of Tawfiq, he was reappointed minister of public works. During this period he dedicated himself to writing his *khitat*, which, much like the work of the historian al-Maqrizi, documents in great detail the topographic characteristics of Cairo and its monuments. But while Mubarak's written work focused on preserving in words the historic built fabric of Cairo, his work as an administrator and public-works practitioner centered on transforming and removing much of that fabric in reality. As a European-influenced reformer with beliefs firmly anchored in progress and modernization, Mubarak was not interested in retaining elements of medieval Cairo that he saw as obsolete and in need of change, in spite of his religious convictions to the contrary. And in neither of the two domains to which he had made contributions— historical documentation and planning practice—did Mubarak address the social inequalities that lay behind the dramatic urban renewal projects he oversaw. This phase of modernization would turn Cairo into a divided city, whose impoverished eastern half stood in stark contrast to its new western half, the home of the local elite and foreign expatriates. However, Mubarak, who was loyal to his country, believed that advancing modernization and change could only benefit Egypt, and he saw such inequalities as necessary to progress. He considered Egyptians to be a people who needed to be told what to do if they were to develop an understanding of the common good and accept change. This was a trope that is equally present in his novel *'Alamuddin,* which he published after the British occupied Egypt and he was removed from office.[35]

While his comprehensive history of Cairo shies away from such critical commentary on the social and cultural habits of Egyptians, his novel liberated him from this restraint and allowed him to engage extensively and critically with what he saw as the ills of Egyptian society. On the one hand, *'Alamuddin* captures more of the social reality of Cairo and Egypt, and renders important details of the historical changes that Mubarak himself had witnessed and implemented. On the other hand, his earlier khitat reflects the imaginary of Egypt and Cairo's built legacy through the lens of a planner. Though it does document Cairo's architectural heritage with great faithfulness, however, his khitat does not pay adequate attention to social reality, presenting its built fabric as a closed chapter of the city's history.

Mubarak's vision had major effects on the built environment of Cairo. Most importantly, old monuments and large portions of the old fabric were demolished to make way for long, linear arteries designed to move traffic more efficiently through the congested city. For this reason his relationship with the Comité de Conservation des Monuments de l'Art Arabe, of which he later became a member, was very tense. The Comité was an independent institution, originally formed by European members and partially supported by the government, concerned with the documentation and preservation of Islamic monuments in Cairo. Its membership, which included both Europeans and Egyptians of Mubarak's era, viewed architectural preservation as imperative for Egyptian culture. For modernizers like Mubarak, the fast pace of urban renewal was indicative of Egypt's progress; but for many members of the Comité it was precisely the destruction that came with this supposed renewal that signified Egypt's inability to be a sovereign nation.[36] Such a view contrasted with Mubarak's paternalistic vision of changing Egypt and Cairo for the greater good, but it certainly perpetuated a similar fallacy—the assumption that Egypt still required European guidance to appreciate its own civilization.

The Comité's agenda and programs were dedicated to physically preserving structures by restoring them to a presumed original state. But in their efforts to conserve the "authentic" medieval parts of Cairo, the architects of the Comité operated under the assumption that only Mamluk architecture was truly representative of medieval Cairo. They did not see the Ottoman architectural legacy to be worthy of preservation, nor did they possess a general, let alone thorough, understanding of

Cairo's complex architectural history. They hence engaged in the restoration and rebuilding of several mosques using this narrow template. The Comité was generally blind to the fact that the variety of styles and forms present in the fabric of Cairo derived from centuries of local traditions, social forces, and adaptive changes that were as meaningful for Cairo as its Mamluk past.[37] The Comité's aim was not to only restore the authenticity of Cairo's architectural past, but to reify an image of medieval Islam that resonated with European travelers and matched the Orientalist depictions of Egypt. In a sense, the Comité was engaged in the project of making Cairo medieval, based on what it had imagined Cairo to be in the past. In reality, the Comité was inventing a new tradition, a tradition that gave Cairo's historic core what is now some of its current form. By contrast, for the progressive Mubarak, the historic fabric was part of a living tradition that needed to regenerate itself to stay alive. Thus he saw demolition not as a loss but as part of an ongoing and necessary process of change—part of daily life rather than a dwelling in the past.

While Egypt was being transformed by modernization and Cairo was being Westernized, European travelers to Egypt, motivated by the same zeal as the European members of the Comité, still sought out Egypt's ancient and medieval sites. With the advent of photography, travelers to Egypt increasingly began returning with photographic documentation in place of paintings and sketches. Cairo of the early nineteenth century was documented in paintings while Cairo of the second part of that century was captured in photographs. One of the most notable photographers to visit Cairo in this period was the Englishman Francis Frith (1822–1898). Frith was born into a Quaker family and as an entrepreneur made a fortune that allowed him to travel and dedicate himself entirely to photography later in life. After retiring from business, Frith declared: "Following my bent toward the romantic and perfected past, rather than to the bustling and immature present, I went East ... I would begin at the beginning of human history."[38] His expeditions to Egypt and the Holy Lands were motivated by a desire to explore the sites upon which the stories of the Bible were supposedly based. However, his photographs also satisfied a public avid for romantic accounts of travels to the Orient.

Figure 10.6   *Tombs in the Southern Cemetery,* by Francis Frith, 1857. ▬▬▬

Frith first arrived in Egypt in 1859 and immediately began photographing mosques in Cairo. Embarking from Bulaq, he then sailed up the Nile to Nubia, stopping in Thebes along the way. He returned to Egypt in 1857 and again in 1859, after the work from his first trip made him a name in photographic circles in England. Frith's photographic works and writings show an unmistakable Orientalist view of the places he documented, contrasting Western cultural norms with the supposed embedded traditions of the Orient. Although noting with disappointment that the signs of modernity and European imperialism were already present in Egypt and Palestine, Frith purposely turned his camera to the "perfected past." And much like Orientalist artists before him, he attempted to turn Ismail's rapidly modernizing Egypt into the mythical and imaginary Orient that the Victorian public so much desired.[39]

Although Ismail left Egypt's finances in disarray, the public works he undertook for more than a decade prepared Egypt for a new phase of technological development. The British occupation, which began in 1882, brought Egypt under colonial rule for more than half a century. Technically Egypt was still part of the Ottoman Empire, headed by Khedive Tawfiq. However, for the next fifty years the position of British consul carried great authority. During the initial phase of this period, the transformation of Cairo continued, albeit at a slower pace given the economic stagnation caused by British occupation. After the first decade of colonialism, Cairo began to experience a dramatic increase in population, which eventually had a positive effect on the country's economy and its political influence in the region.[40] This population growth could be attributed to foreign immigration, but also to a surge in Egypt's agricultural production. A major expansion of irrigation systems, canals, and barrages such as the Qanater barrage and the Aswan Dam, completed in 1902, greatly increased Egypt's agricultural output. The British also reorganized the country's agricultural sector and reoriented it chiefly toward the cultivation of cotton, much of which was shipped to textile mills in England. The American Civil War greatly reduced cotton shipments to these mills, and Egypt soon became Great Britain's source of raw material.

The railroad built under by Abbas and the road network put in place during Ismail's time were followed by the introduction of automobiles and a tram system in Cairo. Together these technologies allowed the city to expand significantly along its main transportation arteries to accommodate an unprecedented population boom. By century's end the Isma'iliya district was fully urbanized and densely populated, with villas on its southern side and higher-density dwellings around Opera Square.[41] The Museum of Egyptian Antiquities—commonly known as the Egyptian Museum—was moved to Bulaq in 1858 and involved Auguste Mariette, who helped grow and assemble its collection. It was relocated again in 1902 to its present location near the Qasr al-Nil barracks.[42]

Meanwhile the Dawawin area came to be the epicenter of government buildings and ministry headquarters.[43] Housing for government staff was developed in this area, consisting of luxurious villas for foreigners and

Figure 10.7 The Egyptian Museum.

apartments for Egyptian officials.[44] The area north of Azbakiya developed extensively as well, with a new business district that grew alongside
contemporary Parisian-style apartment blocks occupied by Christian traders and European expatriates. Finally, previously vacant land was designated by Khedive Tawfiq to be a new district to compete with Isma'iliya.
Named al-Tawfiqiyya, it was subdivided into parcels for purchase and
quickly developed, given its location next to the wealthy districts of the city.

The increasing numbers of foreign investors in Cairo also led to a
boom in property development. Much of the shoreline along the Nile
was now suitable for construction because the dam at Aswan prevented
seasonal flooding. Most land along the Nile, previously owned by Egyptian nobility, was now open to urban development. The Swiss company
Baehler purchased land in the northern part of Gezira and between 1905
and 1907, subdivided the land and built high-end villas.[45] Located along
the shores of the Nile, south of the Isma'iliya district, a new area called
the Garden City had a master plan that followed the picturesque British

Figure 10.8 ▪ Suleyman Pasha Square. ▬▬▬▬▬▬▬▬▬▬▬▬▬

model of the same name, with curved streets and residences set among gardens. Districts on the western edge of the Nile, such as Imbaba in the north and Giza in the south, also grew rapidly.

Responding to the need to accommodate an increasing number of residents, European investors also developed the northern part of the city. Baron Édouard Empain, a Belgian industrialist who made a considerable fortune from building the Paris Metro and undertaking business in the Congo, obtained a large area of desert in 1905. It was a grant from the government to build an experimental new community. On the site of ancient Heliopolis, his Heliopolis Oasis Company planned an upscale satellite residential town, ten kilometers away from Cairo and connected to it by high-speed tram. By 1930 Baron Empain's investment had proven very successful—the city of Heliopolis numbered 28,544 residents and had fully functioning infrastructure and public transportation.[46] Heliopolis was supposed to be divided into two sections—one containing luxury residences for Europeans, including a unique villa in a "Hindu style" for

Figure 10.9 Heliopolis.

the Baron himself, the other containing light industry and working-class housing for the native population. But ultimately only the area with luxury residences was built, with only a zone dedicated to service workers.

During the British colonial period, the deep cleavages between the western and eastern parts of Cairo, which had first appeared during Ismail's time, became even more pronounced. The tax revenue yielded by the western parts of the city, where most expatriates lived, was tenfold what was paid by the residents of the old quarters of eastern Cairo.[47] This reflected the fact that while Cairo's population was growing at an unprecedented rate, its two social spheres were growing increasingly apart: the Europeanized quarters to the west were prospering while the old city remained stagnant and untouched by modernity. It thus became apparent that Mubarak's projects had penetrated the old city core without changing its character or its living conditions. Nevertheless, during this period Cairo was developing into a cosmopolitan city, becoming worldly and modern through the advent of new ideas and peoples. By

Figure 10.10 The palace of Baron Empain. ▬▬▬▬▬▬

the first decade of the twentieth century, one-eighth of the city's population was foreign-born, and in the western districts one-third of the residents were foreigners.[48] This expatriate population consisted largely of businessmen and diplomats, but there were many outcasts among them as well.

The minimal contact that did exist between the two parts of the city derived largely from the need of expatriates living in the new city for employed native servants and helpers from the old city. Indeed, for foreigners the medieval quarter became an invisible part on the social map—a place sought after only occasionally for its exotic aura and medieval sights; meanwhile, for high-ranking Egyptians it was a place that signified Egypt's backwardness. The privileged position of expatriates created antagonisms with the local population. Upper-middle-class Egyptians coveted the privileged social standing of the Europeans, and saw Western education for their children as a prerequisite for upward social mobility. The old city—composed of Jamaliya, Bab al-Sha'riya, Muski, and Darb al-Ahmar—suffered from almost complete divestment. Its streets were rarely cleaned, the infrastructure was dilapidated, and utilities were virtually nonexistent. The populations living in these quarters were impoverished, and as the middle class and most businesses began leaving the old city, its decline accelerated.

When World War I broke out in Europe in 1914 and the Ottoman sultan declared his support for Germany, Egypt, which was still under nominal Ottoman authority, became part of the alliance against the British. The British in turn promptly removed the last khedive, Abbas Helmy II, from power and replaced him with another son of Ismail, Husayn Kamil. Proclaiming him sultan, Britain declared Egypt to be its protectorate.[49] British troops in Egypt thus assumed the role of an occupying army, which not only increased the rate of resource extraction during a time of severe shortage but also was used to justify the forcible mobilization of thousands of Egyptians into the war effort.

Egypt had already seen nationalism rising among its native population in the face of pronounced inequalities between foreign residents and Egyptians. But in 1918, when the British banned the Egyptian delegation from the Versailles peace talks, discontent among Egyptians became stronger than ever. In the spring of 1919 a popular uprising overtook the entire country; it lasted more than three years, with much of the unrest occurring in Cairo itself. Eventually, in 1922, the British had no choice but to acquiesce. Egypt was declared independent, and in 1924 Saad Zaghloul Pasha was elected prime minister.[50] Despite the political transition, Britain continued to station troops in Cairo, both in the Citadel and in the Qasr al-Nil barracks, which lay to the west of the Egyptian Museum. Britain also maintained control of the Suez Canal. Following Husayn Kamil's death, another son of Khedive Ismail, Fouad I, became the first monarch of Egypt—declaring the country a kingdom, with British support, in face of the demise of the Ottoman Empire.

Educated in Europe, where he had moved with his exiled father, the new king did not initially have a strong attachment to Egypt. However, his nephew, the sitting khedive, had invited him back to the country, where he served in a variety of positions before assuming power when he was in his fifties. Although he presided over a regime whose main objective was the extraction of wealth from Egypt's cotton crops for the landed elites, he nevertheless developed an effective government, allowing the development of political parties, and encouraged the founding of various cultural and educational institutions. Among the many important projects completed during his long rule was the building of an Egyptian university, for which he served as its principal trustee.

Upon King Fouad's death in 1936, his sixteen-year-old son, Farouk, who was very popular with the public, became the new king. But the British were still in control of Egypt. In February 1942, wishing to persuade Egypt to take an openly anti-German stance, the British, led by ambassador Sir Miles Lampson, surrounded Abdin Palace with tanks. They ordered Farouk to name their ally, Mustafa al-Nahhas Pasha, who had negotiated the 1936 Egyptian-British treaty, as prime minister.

The handsome boy-king Farouk continued to rule the country with the full support of the Egyptians, who invested hope and national pride in him. Farouk showed great respect for religion, and unlike his father, he was fluent in Arabic, which contributed to his popularity. But as a somewhat spoiled teenager, Farouk seemed never to mature as a leader over the following years after he ascended to the throne. His excesses— his passions for automobiles, women, and poker parties—were seen as reckless at a time when Egypt and the rest of Europe were engulfed in World War II. After several years of his rule, Egyptians began to lose faith in their king, particularly after a 1948 war in which the Egyptian army lost to the newly established state of Israel, resulting in the loss of Palestine. As popular unrest grew, so did the influence of the Muslim Brotherhood, who began to organize against the government after the government outlawed it.

In 1951, unrest and nationalistic sentiment grew to unprecedented levels in Cairo and turned into riots, strikes, and guerilla attacks against British forces. Following their objective to keep control of the Suez Canal, British troops launched a series of clashes with the local population, which culminated in the massacre of fifty Egyptian police conscripts. The next day angry crowds hit the streets of Cairo protesting the murders committed by the British. Arsonists stormed the European district and set fire to villas, bars, theaters, and luxury stores. The Shepheard Hotel was looted and set on fire, along with other landmarks in the European quarters and most of downtown Cairo. In the events that became known as Black Saturday, thousands of Cairenes lost their lives. Finally, in July of 1952, a bloodless coup led by a group called the Free Officers Movement, removed Farouk from power. He was subsequently sent into exile along with his entire family, while his court was sent to prison. Among those free officers who were to declare Egypt a republic two years later were Gamal Abdel Nasser and Anwar al-Sadat.[51]

One of the few surviving landmarks of the city's cosmopolitan and khedival age is a palace that had been taken over by the army. In an attempt to erase Egypt's royal past, the palace was turned into a hotel. As a reference to its opulence, rather than its history or its architectural style, the officers named the hotel Omar al-Khayyam Hotel, in the tradition of the mythical *One Thousand and One Nights*. The name of the hotel was also a reference to the Persian poet whose writings of love and wine were thought to be a more appropriate allusion to the building's royal origins, now detested in a new nationalist Egypt. Today it is simply the Cairo Marriott, the hotel from which we started our story.

The Arab Republic and the City of Nasser

ONCE DOMINATED BY towering minarets, the skyline of Cairo dramatically changed in the 1950s when a new structure rose on the horizon. Not only did it mark a new era of development, it also came to symbolize the advent of a new political age. At 187 meters tall, the Burj al-Qahira, or Cairo Tower, on Gezira Island rivaled in height the Great Pyramid at Giza. Shaped like a lotus plant and wrapped in a concrete lattice shell, it was lit at night in spectacular colors to shine like a beacon over the waters of the Nile.

Today the Cairo Tower bears witness to the birth of Egypt as a republic under the presidency of its most charismatic twentieth-century leader, Gamal Abdel Nasser. Looking south from its circular observation deck, a foreign observer in the 1960s would have seen the site of the former Helwan baths, recently transformed into an industrial complex.[1] To the southwest was Giza, which extended all the way to the Pyramids at the border between the city and the desert. Looking north close to Gezira were the gardens, designed by Barillet-Deschamps, and the Gezira Palace that Khedive Ismail had built to host his guests. Looking west was the modern City of Engineers, known as Mohandeseen. And northwest, the drab concrete apartment blocks of Imbaba, the vanguard of the government's social housing program, would stand out from the organic fabric of the city. Looking northeast, Medinat Nasr, the vast City of Victory, extended toward the eastern desert. Most importantly, such an observer looking out from the Cairo Tower would have seen, on the other side of the Nile directly east, two structures that are more than twenty stories

Figure 11.1   Cairo Tower in Gezira.

high: the Nile Hilton Hotel and the headquarters of the former Arab Socialist Union, the single party that ruled Egypt for almost two decades and brought great change to the capital city.

Built on the site of the old British army barracks at Qasr al-Nil, these two modernist structures from the 1950s make a proud statement about Egypt and its recovery from decades of European colonization. Yet, while they originally featured similar building masses and façade schemes, they expressed two diametrically opposed political principles. The Arab Socialist Union, with its louvered windows, monotonous façade, uniform proportions, and impenetrable institutional aesthetic, bore a strong similarity to the government buildings of the Soviet Union. It was, in ways, the very emblem of Nasser's nascent socialism and, later on, a metaphor for his authoritarian rule. By contrast the Nile Hilton, the outpost for American diplomats and foreign visitors in Cairo, featured eleven stories of balconies overlooking the river. Despite its capitalist origins, its tall, lustrous lobby and mezzanine were the venues chosen by Nasser

Figure 11.2   The Nile Hilton and former headquarters of the Arab Socialist Union. ▬

Figure 11.3   The Arab League.

for summits and meetings with visiting heads of state.[2] Meanwhile, to the south of the two structures and to the north of Garden City, the former upscale neighborhood of previous decades, was a slightly older modernist structure with unmistakable Arab iconography. It was the headquarters of the Arab League, an institution that will play an important role in our story here.[3]

The rise of the new Egyptian republic cannot be understood without first telling the story of Egypt and Gamal Abdel Nasser. Indeed, if Cairo is the venue through which the history of Egypt can be narrated in earlier periods, then Egypt as a nation-state is the instrument through which the history of Cairo under the Arab Republic can be told.

Nasser was born in Bani Mor, a small village in Upper Egypt, to a family of Arab origin. As a child he moved to Alexandria and following the death of his mother was sent to Cairo to live with relatives. As a boy, Nasser was influenced heavily by one of his uncles, a member of the Egyptian nationalist movement who had been imprisoned on numerous occasions for his activism. In the early 1940s Nasser decided to pursue a military career, based on his conviction that only the army was in a position to bring about change in Egypt.[4]

Six months after the fire that engulfed Cairo on Black Saturday, on January 25, 1952, Cairo's daily life was disrupted once again—this time by a quiet coup that overthrew the monarch. This brought to power a military group called the Free Officers in July 1952. The Egyptian army, disgruntled by continued British influence in the region as well as the establishment of the state of Israel and its loss of the 1948 war, finally took action by deposing King Farouk and forcing him into exile. The group appeared to have the support of the Egyptian people, who after years of colonization seemed ready to invest their hopes in an indigenous government run by well-spoken, young, and confident men who had been born and educated in Egypt and who would serve as new role models. The officers' coup quickly gained popular acceptance, but it was not a revolution in the fullest sense, because it did not involve the mobilization of Cairo residents or the involvement of the Egyptian masses. Rather, the officers managed to topple the regime simply by surrounding the royal palace and taking over the national radio station. Following their coup, they formed a provisional government controlled by a Revolutionary Command Council (RCC), which promised to establish a constitutional government within three years. But by June 1953 the officers decided to abolish the monarchy and recast their takeover as a revolution.

The first member of the group to emerge as a political leader was General Muhammad Naguib. Though he had not been directly involved in organizing the coup, he was designated prime minister by the RCC and later became the first president of the new Republic of Egypt. By contrast, Nasser, the behind-the-scenes leader of the Free Officers, began his political career as deputy prime minister and minister of the interior.[5]

Naguib began by reforming the administration and consolidating his power base. But his rapid rise and growing popularity among Egyptians soon posed a threat to the other members of the RCC, who, as members of the provisional government, were not eager to let go of their quasi-absolutist power. This was particularly true for Nasser. In addition, while Naguib supported the reform of political parties and a return to parliamentary democracy, Nasser favored one-party rule. For two years the outcome of the power struggle between the two men hung in the balance. The arrest of several politicians and the abolishment of political parties supported by Nasser prompted Naguib to announce his resignation. However, given the support he had enjoyed within the army and among the people, he soon returned to power, reviving the prospects of a democratically elected parliament.[6] But his return was short lived, as Nasser quickly mobilized opposition within the trade unions and the army, and worked to marginalize Naguib's allies and supporters of parliamentary democracy.

In 1954 Nasser began a new offensive against Naguib. After staging strikes and demonstrations, the RCC, from its headquarters now located in a palace at the southern tip of Gezira, proclaimed that elections would not take place, and that the RCC would continue to rule. Later that year, Naguib was definitively removed from power and placed under house arrest, where he remained for most of his life. This cleared the way for Nasser to take over as interim president and then as the official president of Egypt. In later years Nasser managed in effect to erase the memory of Naguib from history.[7] The only commemoration of Naguib in Cairo that survives today is a metro station in the downtown area, named after him long after he and his rival had died.

Nasser's prominence as a major figure in Egypt's history was to grow quickly. After becoming the sole candidate in Egypt's presidential election in 1956, he took a series of dramatic political measures to strengthen his rule, the first of which was to crush rival political parties. Shortly after coming to power, he abolished all political organizations and had their leaders detained. One of his targets was the Muslim Brotherhood, a conservative religious organization that posed a threat to the RCC. When a member of the Brotherhood tried to assassinate Nasser in October 1954 during a speech in Alexandria, the RCC considered this hostile act legitimate grounds to destroy the organization. Thousands of people connected to the Brotherhood were arrested, its leaders were tried, and six of its members were executed. The press was equally quashed, and all media that sided with the opposition were closed. Given the absence of other political parties in the government, Nasser nominally shared power with the RCC and soon assumed almost full control of the military and the civilian administration. To further secure his rule, he surrounded himself with only a few loyalists.[8]

Despite his despotic propensities, Nasser remained beloved by the Egyptian population. He was a well-read intellectual with a fondness for Voltaire and a refined taste in music, but he was still able to connect to the general public through speeches that electrified and captivated the masses.[9] After a long string of leaders whose foreign education and affectations precluded them from relating to ordinary Egyptians, Nasser spoke with a compelling simplicity, and he shared his nationalistic vision in ways that allowed all Egyptians to feel as if they were stakeholders in that vision. The fact that Nasser succeeded in removing British troops almost completely from Egypt also contributed to national pride and to the faith that ordinary Egyptians invested in him.

Nasser moved beyond the borders of the Arab world onto the global political stage, particularly through his involvement in the Non-Aligned Movement. In April 1955, Nasser attended a conference of nonaligned nations in Bandung, Indonesia, organized by Sukarno. The Indonesian leader's objective was to create a consortium of non-Western nations that could stand apart from the emerging superpowers, the United States and the Soviet Union. Nasser saw an opportunity in this transnational effort for sovereignty, and Egypt became a founding member of the Non-Aligned Movement. However, Nasser's role in this group was not seen favorably by the United States, given the movement's critical position toward the "cultural imperialism" of the West and U.S. control over the media.[10] At the Non-Aligned Conference, Nasser met Nehru, of India, whom he considered to be a hero of all third-world nations. He also secured an important political alliance with China and Yugoslavia after he met premier Chou En-Lai and President Josip Broz Tito. Among other issues, Chou facilitated an arms deal between Egypt and the Soviet

Union. Meanwhile Nasser offered diplomatic recognition to Communist China, an act that created further tensions with the United States.[11]

But Nasser's foreign diplomatic successes meant little if they could not be matched by domestic achievements. In particular, Nasser realized that Egypt needed to enter a phase of accelerated industrial development in order to maintain its geopolitical influence. Significantly stunted by the British, who were unwilling to invest in Egypt's infrastructure, Egypt's industrial base needed a major infusion of capital and resources. This was particularly the case as the country continued to be subject to the whims of the Nile floods. Moreover, Egypt had no real source of power, despite the Nile's vast potential for hydroelectric generation.

The project that was identified as being the most capable of addressing these needs was the High Dam at Aswan. It was estimated that this massive infrastructure project could triple Egypt's agricultural production and provide ample electrification for industrialization. Initially Nasser turned to the World Bank to fund the construction of the dam. But his alliance with the Chinese premier and his opposition to the Baghdad Pact, a strategy to maintain Britain's influence in the region, was now working against him. Opposition by the United States, led by Secretary of State John Foster Dulles, brought negotiations to a halt. Stymied by conditions he thought threatened Egypt's independence, Nasser initially abandoned the negotiations. When he reluctantly agreed to the terms of the loan, the United States decided to withdraw its support and the negotiations fell through. In response, Nasser made one of his boldest political moves: on July 26, 1956, he announced the nationalization of the Suez Canal.

Nasser's goal was to build the High Dam at Aswan with revenues obtained from the operation of the canal. Having withdrawn its military from Egypt after the ratification of the British-Egyptian Treaty in 1954, there was nothing more that the British government could do except express its indignation. Despite the departure of European pilots and technicians, the canal continued to operate with an Egyptian staff that was about a quarter of its former size. The British, however, began looking for a pretext to seize the canal and remove Nasser from power. To achieve their goal they soon formed an alliance with France and Israel. The mastermind of the alliance was British prime minister Anthony Eden. His plan was for Israel to attack Egypt, seize the Sinai Peninsula, and advance toward the canal. This would give Britain and France a reason to intervene and demand the withdrawal of Egypt and Israel from the canal zone. Israel would agree to withdraw, but Egypt would predictably not, as it would have been forced to relinquish territory to Israel. The standoff would serve as the premise to remove Nasser from power.

Israel's attack on Sinai came on October 29, 1956. This was followed by an attack by British and French forces on Port Said, located at the entrance to the canal, beginning a conflict that became known as the Tripartite Aggression. But British and French efforts soon backfired. Once Eden's plot was revealed, there was an outpouring of international support for Egypt. The United Nations condemned the attack; the United States refused to support Britain; and the Soviet Union threatened to attack England in return. Soon Eden was forced to withdraw British forces from the region, and without a key ally, France and Israel soon had to do the same.[12] In response, the Egyptian government confiscated all property owned by British and French citizens residing in the country and these residents were then ordered to leave Egypt immediately. Nasser famously declared that Eden was the last prime minister of Great Britain as the country would be referred to as merely "Britain" from then on. Support for Egypt during the crisis made Nasser a larger-than-life figure. Egypt's most famous singers of the time, Umm Kulthum and Abdel Halim Hafez, sang popular melodies about his victory, and these were broadcast repeatedly on the Voice of Cairo and the Voice of the Arabs, the main radio channels of the Republic of Egypt.

Following the resolution of the Suez Crisis, however, Nasser's plans to build the High Dam at Aswan did not go forth as hoped. Revenues from the nationalization of the canal did not prove sufficient to pay for its construction. Eventually funding and engineering expertise had to be sought from the Soviet Union, which was eager to expand its influence in Egypt. Construction of the High Dam at Aswan did finally begin in 1960. The dam, which remains the largest in the world, at 3,600 meters long and

111 meters high, was completed one year after Nasser's death. The dam would stabilize the banks of the Nile and forge its topographic outlines, particularly in the area around Cairo. However, the project also required the relocation of much of the population in the southern region of Nubia. The dam's reservoir, which was named Lake Nasser, also submerged ancient monuments, such as the temple of Abu Simbel, which had to be dismantled and relocated piece by piece to a nearby site with UNESCO's assistance.[13] The construction of the dam significantly increased the amount of arable land and national agricultural production, but it came at a high environmental cost. Increasing rates of water evaporation and salinity, the deterioration of the Nile Delta, and a declining fish industry were just a few of its attendant effects.

Later in his life, Nasser's significance as a political figure spread far beyond Egypt's borders. From the very beginning of his presidency, he was an advocate of pan-Arabism, declaring himself and Egypt to be leaders of the Arab world. In the constitution of 1956, Egypt was declared an "Arab" country. This was an unprecedented domestic political turn, one that would shape Egypt's national discourse for the decades to follow. After centuries of foreign rule, Arab ethnicity was now proclaimed as the principal marker of Egyptian identity. Although Egypt's strong association with the Arab world preceded Nasser—as evidenced by the location of the headquarters of the Arab League in Cairo—the pan-Arabism that spread throughout the region in the 1950s and 1960s was a testament to Nasser's will. The Arab League had been established in Cairo in 1945 by Egypt, Lebanon, Syria, Iraq, Saudi Arabia, Yemen, and Jordan, with other states joining in later years. But in the postwar period, it was Nasser who renewed the role of the League as a forum to promote the interests of its member states, as he was able to capitalize on its presence in Cairo.

Nasser's pan-Arabist message quickly spread to the rest of the Arab world. As the principal advocate of Arab nationalism, Nasser also became an immensely popular figure in Egypt and much of the so-called third world, which was newly liberated from centuries of colonial rule. His ideas were welcomed by countries such as Syria, Lebanon, and Palestine, but other Arab nations such as Saudi Arabia, Jordan, and Iraq initially opposed his vision. Nasser's pan-Arabism was not well received by this group of pro-Western countries, particularly because Nasser was opposed to the Baghdad Pact, which included Britain, Turkey, Pakistan, and Iran. Trying to minimize the influence of the Soviet Union in the region, the United States also favored the Baghdad Pact, and it considered Nasser's political moves hostile to its interests there.[14]

Nasser's pan-Arabism culminated in an event that attracted great attention in the Middle East and the West alike. In February 1958, Egypt and Syria formed the United Arab Republic, with Nasser as its leader and Cairo as its capital. In response, Iraq and Jordan—kingdoms where the British maintained strong influence—formed a rival union. This later dissolved when a coup removed Iraq's pro-Western monarchy from power.[15] The union between Egypt and Syria ultimately dissolved in 1961, as well, due to a military coup in Syria and growing discontent over its relatively weak role in the Egypt-dominated alliance.

At home, Nasser's economic reforms were implemented in several phases. The period after the Suez Crisis was characterized by increased state involvement in the economy. As noted before, the property and assets of British and French citizens, as well as some large businesses, were seized immediately following the crisis. The country's economy was mixed, however, allowing for both state ownership and private enterprise. Initially the Economic Development Organization, established in 1957, was tasked to oversee only industrial activity and investments in large projects. But after the country announced its first five-year plan in 1959, state control over private business and commerce increased significantly. The national economic development program called not only for the creation of state-owned enterprises, but also for additional restrictions on the private sector. Soon these policies started to manifest themselves in the physical appearance of Cairo. State-owned stores began to appear in the downtown area, and new commercial establishments with Arab names became increasingly common.

It was before all of these changes, however, in 1956, that the Cairo Tower began its ascent in Gezira. The source of funds to build this symbol

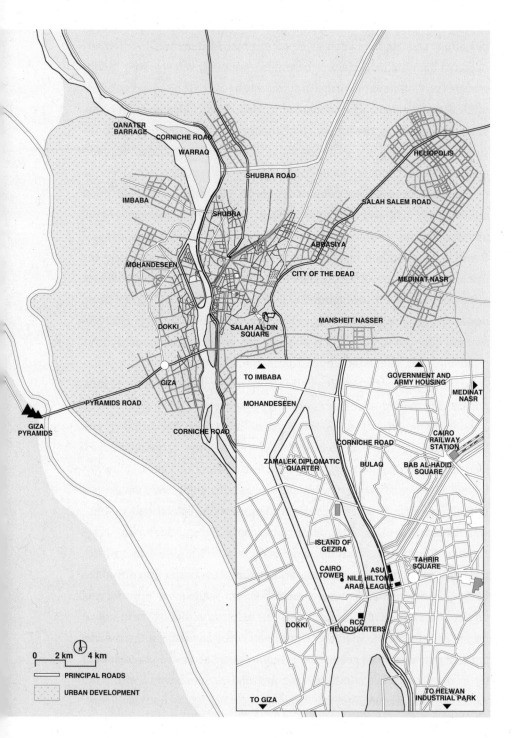

Figure 11.4   Map of Cairo during Nasser's rule.

of Egypt's soon-to-be socialist age still remains unclear. In 1953 Nasser negotiated for aid money from the United States in exchange for a pledge to reach an agreement with the British over the Suez Canal. After complex and difficult negotiations, the two parties, it is assumed, came to an agreement. But in addition to acceding to a specific amount of aid, it is alleged that the Americans under Secretary of State Dulles delivered an additional $3 million as a personal gift to Nasser. The details and purpose of this exchange remain shrouded in mystery; a CIA operative involved in the exchange later suggested that Nasser diverted this "personal gift" to building a landmark that was meant to send a message to the Americans. It was "something unidentifiable, but very large, very conspicuous, very enduring."[16] The tower was intended to express defiance against foreign influence in Egypt. As it was sited to face the Nile Hilton, American guests would see the structure from their balconies.[17] Designed by Egyptian architect Naoum Chebib along with an Italian structural engineer, the tower was also intended to demonstrate Egypt's ability to complete large-scale projects, such as the Aswan High Dam. The concrete tower, with its ancient Egyptian-inspired form, was visible from miles away. It was the tallest structure of its time in all of Africa and the Middle East, with a circular deck and a rotating top floor that offered panoramic views of Cairo.[18]

The Cairo Tower was built in what was already becoming the most significant district in the city—the ten-square-kilometer area composed of the central business district and the island of Gezira. These two areas were once home to most of the country's expatriates and for many years remained largely inaccessible to ordinary Egyptians. However, the area changed dramatically in the years after the 1952 coup. The departure of foreign nationals brought a large number of government workers and bureaucrats to the area, making it the playground of the Egyptian middle class. As the population of these districts increased, the villas that were once the area's predominant building type started to be replaced by apartments that could accommodate higher densities.[19] The district also ceased being the exclusive realm of the elites. Residents from poorer neighborhoods in the eastern and northern parts of Cairo now came to window-shop and frequent downtown cinemas and theaters.[20]

In 1956 Nasser appointed 'Abd al-Latif el-Baghdadi as the minister of public works and infrastructure. El-Baghdadi was sometimes referred to as "the dangerous minister" because he was the most influential government agent in the development of Cairo.[21] One of his most notable projects was a forty-kilometer road called the Corniche on the east bank of the Nile, which connected the southern suburb of Helwan with the northern suburb of Shubra and the Qanater barrage. Shaded by lush trees, the Corniche soon became a promenade for Cairo's middle classes. Business and commercial activity sprung from it, expressing a new level of urban vitality.[22] El-Baghdadi also replanned most of Cairo's public spaces, including Tahrir, Opera, Azbakiya, Bab al-Hadid (later named Ramses), and Muhammad Ali (later named Salah al-Din) squares. He also ordered construction of the University Bridge (connecting Cairo University in Giza with Rawdah Island), the Cairo stadium, and the government administrative center known as the Mugama'a—or "the complex."[23]

The Mugama'a, with its multiple ministerial functions, particularly the issuance of official documents and identity cards, became a major institu-

Figure 11.5   The Mugama'a Complex.

tion symbolizing not only the Egyptian bureaucracy but also the power of the Egyptian state over its citizens. During the last decade of Nasser's rule, no Egyptian could travel abroad or move freely around the country without a trip to one of the Mugama'a's offices, whether to acquire the necessary documents or simply to obtain written permission from relevant authorities. The building was designed in 1951 and completed in 1953. Its architect, Mohamed Kamal Ismail, had been greatly influenced by his training in Islamic architecture. Some see architectural similarities between the Mugama'a's composition and the form of Mamluk mosques. Interestingly, a few years later Ismail would also lead the restoration of the Prophet's mosque in Medina and employ a similar visual language. Over time, however, the Mugama'a came to represent the excess of Egyptian governmental bureaucracy.

In 1962 Nasser established the Arab Socialist Union (ASU), a single ruling party that he modeled after the Soviet Politburo. The ASU governed Egypt for less than a decade, but it was a decade that changed the entire social landscape of Egypt and had a profound effect on the city of Cairo. The ASU was the base from which Nasser launched his political initiatives. Among these was *Al-Mithaq,* a political manifesto intended to serve as a manual for official government ideology and practice. A few years later, it would be taught in all Egyptian schools under a new subject called "Arab Rhetoric."[24] The building that housed the ASU was originally designed by the Egyptian architect Sayed Karim in the late 1950s for the recently established Municipality and Governorate of Cairo. But the national government appropriated the building soon after its completion, and designated it as the headquarters of the ASU.[25] Fittingly located in the heart of Cairo on the shores of the Nile, the new structure redefined the city skyline, a paradigmatic example of modern socialist architecture that would transform Cairo for years to come.

Nasser's grand ambition during the 1960s was to double national revenue over the decade. To achieve such accelerated growth, he decided to steer Egypt into yet another phase of economic reform. In 1961 he nationalized all private property and individual assets in excess of ten thousand pounds—equal to roughly the same amount of U.S. dollars at the time. The move essentially dispossessed Egypt's elite. The assets of former landowners and industrialists were expropriated and managed by the state. After 1964 a total takeover of the economy was made virtually complete with the establishment of several new government bodies. Egypt declared itself an Arab socialist country, in which the state would not only run a massive industrial complex, but also centralize and infuse all cultural production with its ideology.[26] Cairo became the epicenter of this political transformation.

In addition to offering an inspiring vision, Nasser's socialist rule ensured to a great extent that the ideals of the officers' revolution were materialized. Social benefits were put in place for every Egyptian, particularly every Cairene, and the country was given a distinctly Arab and unmistakably modern identity.[27] To embody these ideals in physical forms, Nasser's administration imagined Cairo as the locus of rational planning and social engineering, and went further to establish a cabinet-level Ministry of Planning. Nationalist discourse and social reform came together in the administrative center. From there, social planners began molding not only the urban structure of Cairo but also the countryside through land reclamation. The larger targets were Egyptian society and the formation of an industrial working class.

Nasser's government also implemented novel education policies. An unprecedented number of people who had no previous access to education became high school and university graduates, adding to Nasser's popular support. This can be seen clearly in the large number of public educational facilities built by the government in and around Cairo. Cultural production during Nasser's time was also in the vanguard, although it suffered from the departure of Cairo's former cosmopolitan elites. From that point forward, the theater, opera, and the symphony were no longer seen as the sole forms of entertainment. Socialist-realist artistic production took center stage, glorifying the working classes and elevating the peasant to the status of national hero.

Egyptian national consciousness was not only refashioned during Nasser's time, as the city of Cairo also took on a new appearance. The Egyptian revolution of 1952 was in part a project to rewrite the history of Egypt, selectively invoking the past to construct a future for the city. Much like the pharaohs of ancient Egypt, who erased the names and histories of those who came before them, Nasser's administration changed the names of important urban landmarks and arteries. Thus, Isma'iliya Square became Tahrir, or Liberation, Square, and King Fouad Avenue was renamed 26th of July Avenue, after the date of Farouk's abdication.[28] Because the Free Officers were opposed to the dynasty of Muhammad Ali, the names of city streets and landmarks associated with the khedival family were all changed as well. As an open area, Muhammad Ali Square had existed since the time of Salah al-Din, and throughout Mamluk and Ottoman times it had been used for a variety of activities, including entertainment, military parades, and recreation. During Muhammad Ali's reign its edges were redefined by residential development, and during Ismail's time it had been replanned as a public square and named after Muhammad Ali. Now, under Nasser, Muhammad Ali Square was renamed Salah al-Din Square, despite the fact that it had not been a public square during Salah al-Din's time. Ironically, Salah al-Din, who was of Kurdish origin, was recast and promoted by the Egyptian revolution as the first Arab to advocate pan-Arabism. Indeed, many Egyptians and Arabs saw Nasser as the new Salah al-Din, and Nasser may have seen himself as Salah al-Din's successor, albeit ten centuries later.

Under Nasser, the concept of a Greater Cairo also began to crystallize. In essence Cairo became the spatial arena that stood in for all of Egypt; to act in the interest of Egypt was to build in Cairo. Unlike Muhammad Ali, Nasser considered Cairo his domain, and his rule left a significant imprint on the city. Prompted by rapid urbanization, Nasser's time was also the beginning of an era in which comprehensive planning linked systems of production and collective consumption, transportation infrastructure, and housing.[29] Social welfare was the chief aim of governance, and every effort was made to manage the city's population and create vast new sites of economic production, under an import substitution industrialization model.

Nasser's industrialization policies created new jobs and brought about abrupt demographic changes to Cairo. In 1956 demographers predicted that by the year 2000, Cairo's population would grow to 5.5 million. But this figure was surpassed in 1965, when the Cairo metropolitan area reached a population of 6.1 million.[30] Between 1960 and 1966, Cairo underwent intense urban in-migration, accounting for 80 percent of total migration nationwide. More than a third of the city's population at that time was born outside the city.[31] Most migrants had minimal education and few skills, and hence limited earning abilities. Nasser's regime promoted housing for the poor, but Cairo's population grew faster than new structures could be built. And under these demographic pressures, the city began to increase in density by expanding both horizontally and vertically. Thousands of hectares of farmland were converted to urban areas.[32] To deal with the looming pressures on the city's infrastructure, planners adopted a variety of additional strategies to cope with rapid urbanization. Their first master plan, for example, proposed the creation of several industrial satellite cities: Helwan in the south, Shubra al-Khayma in the north, and Imbaba and Giza in the west. The area around Helwan, which was emerging as Egypt's principal industrial complex, was also the target for vast new public housing estates.[33]

Another way in which Cairo absorbed great numbers of rural migrants was through the transformation of the City of the Dead, the former medieval cemetery, into a residential area. Its elaborate courtyard structures, and the tombs and funerary complexes of the Mamluk and Ottoman nobility, were taken over by squatters. Living in the cemetery was not a new phenomenon; since Mamluk times, tomb custodians had offered shelter to pilgrims and Sufi mystics.[34] And in the early twentieth century, the tombs in northern Cairo were occupied by men who worked in the limekilns, while quarry workers occupied the tombs in the city's southern areas. Prior to World War II, Cairo's cemeteries housed a population of more than fifty thousand. Despite efforts by the regime to resettle and relocate these people, the number of cemetery residents grew to more than one hundred thousand before the end of Nasser's two decades in power. Many of these squatter families lived in mud huts in the courtyards of the historic tombs. Such dwellings had no connection to municipal utilities such as water, sewers, or electricity, although some resourceful residents connected illegally to electrical lines. Increasingly, the cemetery population came to consist of migrants from rural Egypt who could not afford to live elsewhere in Cairo.[35]

The departure of the foreign population from the city during the 1950s also left several urban areas vacant and open for occupation by Egyptian nationals. But it was Nasser's social-welfare policies and socialist politics that were most responsible for opening Cairo to its native population. Such policies brought about not only massive social change, but also change to the physical form of the city. Reflecting upon the makeup and character of the built environment during Nasser's time, the architect Muhammad Hammad wrote, "Socialism has guided the architecture style that combines both solid massing and efficient standardization to achieve social justice."[36] Indeed, Nasser's socialism offered the chance for a generation of architects to realize their ideas through Egypt's public housing program.

As was the case in other socialist countries of that era, building new housing for a growing urban population was at the core of not only national identity but also the socialist ideological platform. To serve its poor and middle classes, the Egyptian state began a massive program of investment in infrastructure and public housing. In 1963 the Ministry of Public Works was renamed the Ministry of Housing and Public Utilities. Public housing efforts first appeared early in Nasser's rule, when newly nationalized companies and industries started to provide housing for their employees. Two other factors contributed to the extensive involvement of the government in the housing sector. The first was a vast program of slum clearance, begun by the new Ministry of Planning and Local Governments; the second was the debut of the prefabrication industry. In return for supplying the Soviet Union with cotton and textile products, Egypt bought prefabricated building components from several Russian and East European factories. These materials were then used in early public housing projects, before they were abandoned as expensive and inefficient.[37]

During Nasser's regime, thousands of housing units modeled after the Soviet modernist typology were built in Cairo for people of all classes.

Much of this production consisted of cramped, substandard four- to five-story walk-up structures. Such buildings were an unmistakable ideological tool of socialism; and along with the movement toward pan-Arab nationalism they became a primary vehicle for Nasser's ambitious project of nation building. Constituting a ring that surrounded metropolitan Cairo, this public housing helped maintain urban order and popular allegiance to the regime.

The population of Cairo during this period was roughly divided into three groups, distributed geographically according to occupation as well as urban development trends. A large segment had peasant origins and continued to engage in a rural way of life, while many others had begun work at the lowest levels in the industrial complexes founded by Nasser. A second major constituent was composed loosely of those who engaged in a range of economic activities and relations, as well as trades and crafts that had been part of Cairo's economy since medieval times. Much transformed and restructured since Egypt's modernization, these activities had been preserved while adapting their preindustrial economic activities to the new age. The third group was composed of urbanites—managers, technocrats, and intellectuals—who worked in the modern sector of Egypt's economy and resided in upper-income areas such as Heliopolis, the downtown district, or emerging outlying housing districts.[38]

As the city grew, modernist urban developments such as Mohandeseen, or the City of Engineers, began to appear on fields beyond Imbaba. Technocrats and middle-class residents there began to replace the existing farming population. Few areas were as indicative of the different worlds that collided in the city of Nasser than Imbaba and its adjacent Mohandeseen. Here one could find rural, mud-brick shacks next to modern, well-designed apartment buildings. The juxtaposition between the past and the future, an impoverished Imbaba and a middle-class district growing alongside the Nile, also rendered visible the trend toward high-density apartment buildings in both areas. Similarly, the medieval district of Islamic Cairo evidenced the contradictory forces of modernization. Its fabric began to gradually deteriorate, and many historic structures were lost to urban upgrading projects.[39] Sahafeyeen, or the City of Journalists, on the Giza side of the Nile, and Medinat Nasr, or the City of Victory, on the eastern side of Cairo, were products of the state's monumental efforts to deal with the pressures of urbanization.[40]

The character of each new district was largely determined by the occupations of its residents. For example, Nasr City, planned in 1958 between the edge of the desert and Heliopolis, attracted white-collar professionals and members of an expanding government bureaucracy. Only a small fraction of its housing was planned for low-income occupants, so it became a middle-class area. The new district turned out to be a success, and expanded to a population of five hundred thousand by 1970.[41]

Nasr City was also intended to be emblematic of Cairo's modern era of rational and technocratic planning. Its architects and planners, such as Muhammad Riyad, former chief of the Cairo municipality, conceived it to follow a typical modernist, functionalist scheme, organized into distinct functional zones. One zone included administrative and institutional units, such as ministerial offices, stadiums, and convention centers. A second zone coupled industrial areas with schools, universities, and recreational facilities. A third was reserved for residential development, in the form of multifamily housing estates for low- and middle-income residents.[42] The relocation of many government offices to Nasr City intensified its rapid growth. But existing districts such as Heliopolis also received a significant influx of upper-middle-class residents due to the increased use of private automobiles, which had previously been the privilege of the aristocracy.[43]

During the two decades of Nasser's rule, the building of new housing was almost entirely government led. However, with the urban population doubling every eighteen years, government spending ultimately could not keep up with demand.[44] Nasser's ministries engaged in massive public spending to alleviate overcrowding and improve living conditions in the city. But many poor, low-skilled people and new migrants had no alternative other than to live in decaying districts such as Bulaq and Imbaba.

Nasser's policies of centralization and social provision brought deep change to Egyptian society and closed the socioeconomic gap between the aristocracy and ordinary Egyptians. This had concrete spatial manifestations in the fabric of Cairo. For example, Ibrahim Pasha Street,

Figure 11.6   Public housing in Imbaba.

renamed Republic Street, the avenue that once divided Cairo between a city of the privileged on the west and a city of the destitute on the east, was no longer a social or spatial barrier. And, as mentioned earlier, Nasser opened the city of the privileged few, who included many foreigners before the revolution, to the middle class.[45] Although most families could

Figure 11.7 Tahrir Square during Nasser's time, 1962.

not afford to live in existing elite quarters, they could still find jobs there, and some poor were even able to squat in neighboring open spaces. Most urban interventions during Nasser's time also carried clear symbolic meaning and political overtones. One such project was the renovation of Tahrir Square, where the Mugama'a, a massive government complex, was built on the site of what had once been the garden of the residence of the British commissioner, the principal agent of Egypt's colonization.[46]

But the years of growth and enthusiasm came to an abrupt end by the close of the decade. The causes were both economic, as a result of Nasser's pursuit of socialism, and external, due to pressures and complex political conflicts on the world stage. The internal dimension of this time was incisively captured by the great Egyptian novelist Naguib Mahfouz, author of the *Cairo Trilogy*. The Cairene elite considered Mahfouz's books to be pedestrian novels, written in dialect form to appeal to the masses.[47] But in 1966 Mahfouz wrote *Adrift on the Nile*, a blunt probe into the social emptiness of Nasser's era, and it became one of his most popular novels. It tells the story of an Egyptian government bureaucrat disgruntled with what he sees as the hypocrisy of his ministry and the illiteracy and disengagement of the Egyptian public. He decides to escape these problems by hanging out on a boat moored in the Nile, smoking hashish in a *shisha,* a popular kind of water pipe. As he gets to know his companions on the boat, who represent diverse segments of Cairene society, he concludes that they are all also trying to escape the hegemony and corruption of Nasser's regime.

On July 5, 1967, after some political maneuvering by Egypt, Israel launched a surprise attack against Egypt.[48] Initially Egypt announced that it had succeeded in fending off Israel, but on July 9 a humiliated Nasser had to appear on national television to declare the contrary— that Egypt had been defeated and that he was resigning as president. In six days, Israel had not only decimated Egypt's air force and killed and captured thousands of its soldiers, but it had also taken the entire Sinai Peninsula and Egypt's richest oil fields, reaching the eastern side of the Suez Canal.[49] The citizens of Cairo played a crucial role in the events that ensued. Despite Egypt's crushing military defeat, thousands of Cairenes flooded the streets in both spontaneous and organized demonstrations, demanding that Nasser stay in office. What followed were a string of purges and arrests and the demotion of several army generals in a search for those responsible for the catastrophic loss, which Egyptians called the *naksa,* or the diversion. After a United Nations resolution ordering Israel to retreat from the occupied territory yielded no results, Nasser initiated what he called the War of Attrition, which led to the destruction of the towns of Isma'iliya and Port Said and the evacuation of millions of refugees in 1969.[50] This political crisis ended in 1970, when Nasser accepted the American-backed Rogers Peace Plan, which, in return for a cease-fire, promised the start of negotiations to discuss the return of lost territory.

But while Nasser's efforts brought about the resolution of this external crisis, the country's internal state of affairs led to another disaster. A global economic downturn produced such severe repercussions in Egypt that essential goods, such as food items, had to be rationed. The state enterprises that had become the foundation of the Egyptian economy, ensuring jobs for the working class, had also become largely unprofitable, requiring heavy subsidies. All of which set the stage for a possible economic collapse. As the impact of the crisis was felt throughout Egypt, popular revolts by student groups and unions erupted in Cairo.

The shortages were visible on the face of the city, particularly its housing stock. Most Cairenes lived in rented apartments in privately owned buildings. But in 1961, as part of his socialist measures, Nasser imposed a rent freeze that fixed rents at 1944 levels. This form of rent control had been designed to prevent speculation during World War II.[51] But continuing this policy had a disastrous effect on the housing market, as it eliminated incentives for future private investment. Indeed, feeling they could no longer earn enough in rent to maintain their properties, landlords stopped all spending on them.

Other aspects of the socialist promise—from housing to education—were also starting to sour. The blocks of five-story walk-up public housing that had once been at the vanguard of the socialist project began to decay throughout the city. Although Nasser's educational reforms made schooling available to those of humble means, the nation's universities were flooded with students and severely understaffed.

The state also became heavily involved in civil affairs through the increased presence of its secret service in daily life. Known as the *mukhabarat,* the intelligence service was initially charged with preventing the organization of political opposition or possible conspiracies against Nasser within the army. But following the Soviet big-brother model, the organization soon took on a more pervasive and disciplinary role, infiltrating almost every aspect of daily life and turning Egypt into a police state. Civilians were required to report the activities of their neighbors, and such reports often led to arbitrary arrests and groundless interrogations. Fear replaced the popular enthusiasm that characterized the beginning of Nasser's rule.[52]

When Nasser died suddenly in 1970, millions of Egyptians gathered in Tahrir Square to mourn his death and walk behind his coffin until it reached his final resting place. There was no tradition in Egypt for the burial of presidents—as Nasser was the first Egyptian president to have died while in office—and the government was initially at a loss as to where to bury him. The rulers of Egypt from the Muhammad Ali dynasty were all buried in the mosque of Rifa'i. Muhammad Ali himself was buried in his mosque atop the Citadel. Eventually, following the earlier monarchic tradition, the government decided to bury Nasser in a recently completed mosque, which was close to his private residence in Mansheit al-Bakri. Ironically, Nasser never had a comfortable relationship with Islam, as evidenced by his enmity toward the Muslim Brotherhood. Fate would have it, however, that Nasser would be buried in a mosque, just like the khedives and kings of the Muhammad Ali dynasty whose rule he had brought to an end.

Escaping the Present, Consuming the Past

ON OCTOBER 6, 1981, President Anwar Sadat sat in an outdoor grandstand across from the Monument to the Unknown Soldier in Heliopolis, watching a long military procession. The day was meant to commemorate the crossing of the Suez Canal during the 1973 war known to Egyptians as the Ramadan War and to Israelis as the Yom Kippur War. While most were engrossed by a military aviation performance taking place directly above the parade, some did notice a truck pull up to the grandstand and a group of soldiers run from it toward the area where Sadat was seated. Thinking that the soldiers were part of the official parade, the president rose to salute them. But as soon as the men reached the stands, they opened fire and threw hand grenades into the area where the president was sitting.[1] These men were later identified as Islamic militants. Sadat was killed along with seven others.

Ironically, one of the last things Sadat would see during his final moments was the Monument to the Unknown Soldier, which would become his tomb and final resting place. Because he died suddenly, and without plans for a place of burial appropriate for an Egyptian head of state, the government decided, with the approval of his family, to inter him under this landmark, which replicated a shape that had become emblematic of Egypt as a nation: the pyramid. Designed with a cruciform plan, the monument commemorated the fallen soldiers of the October 6, 1973, war, and consisted of four inclined pillar-like walls rising to a point forming the tip of the pyramid. The pillars marked off a void at ground level that also took the shape of a pyramid, at the center of which Sadat's body was buried under a black granite cube.

Figure 12.1   Sadat's tomb, also the Monument to the Unknown Soldier.

Sadat's Muslim fundamentalist enemies, who eventually became his assassins, had long opposed his resolute attempts to revive Egypt's pharaonic past at the expense of what they considered Egypt's true Islamic identity. In a twist of irony, Sadat was laid to rest under a pyramid, the most recognized symbol of ancient Egypt. For the Egyptian public, the inadvertent use of this form was charged with additional irony, given that the fundamentalists claimed Sadat to be the last of Egypt's modern pharaohs.[2] Cairenes were shocked by the brazenness of the attack, which took place in front of thousands of spectators and television cameras, but they did not take to the streets to mourn Sadat. Thousands of Egyptians turned out for Nasser's funeral eleven years before, but the masses did not come out this time, and Sadat's funeral was attended primarily by foreign heads of state and politicians.[3] Apathy had overtaken the public after the wars with Israel subsided, but the promises of prosperity made by Sadat's regime had gone unfulfilled.

Looking back, it is now possible to see that Egypt's era of socialism, and to some degree that of pan-Arabism, came to an end in 1970 after Gamel Abdel Nasser's death. When Sadat (1970–1981) rose to power, he brought a set of liberalization policies that became known as *infitah*. An original member of the Free Officers, Sadat was a charismatic leader, a master at dealing with the media, and an excellent public speaker who used his carefully constructed public persona to build credibility on the international diplomatic stage. His autobiography opens, "I, Anwar Sadat, a peasant born and brought up on the banks of the Nile," consciously pointing to his *fellahin,* or peasant, origins—a fact that Sadat believed distinguished him from Nasser, who was brought up in a middle-class household in Alexandria.[4] Yet, while Sadat might have been born in a village, he did not grow up a peasant. He was the son of an English-speaking military clerk and was brought up in Cairo, far from the village life described in his autobiography. A precocious child who read avidly, Sadat first received a religious education centered on the memorization of the Quran, and later was sent to school in the city to study with the children of the middle class.[5] In his memoirs, Sadat describes his formative years and the early development of his political awareness. From this upbringing he developed several traits and cultivated viewpoints that would later define his public stance on life: his engagement with Islam, his contempt for the British, his connection with the fellahin, his erudition and love of reading, an impeccable sense of style, and a charismatic presence that elevated him to the pinnacle of political success. Unlike Nasser, whose modest personal life emphasized the difference between his regime and the excesses of his predecessor, King Farouk, Sadat had no problem indulging in luxury and living in multiple elegant residences. He also surrounded himself with some of Egypt's wealthiest men who had survived Nasser's purges. Many of them became his advisors, and he made familial alliances with a few of them as a way to ensure his place among Egypt's elite.

Nasser had appointed Sadat as vice president a few months prior to his death, but he likely never intended for Sadat to succeed him as president of Egypt. Yet Sadat had always been loyal to Nasser, and he was rewarded for his loyalty by being given other high-level political positions. Sadat's rise to power was not without its difficulties, as other members of the

Arab Socialist Union vied with him for power immediately after Nasser's death. Sadat waited until 1971 to confront these political adversaries directly. In an action that became known as the Corrective Revolution, he arrested his Nasserite opponents and had them convicted of treason for attempting a coup.[6] Thus, Sadat not only brought an end to Nasser's political legacy of pan-Arabism, but he also took a stance against the old regime with its socialist ideology and centrally planned economy.

At first Sadat appeared to embrace some of Nasser's policies, especially his predecessor's pan-Arabist agenda. But in May 1971, through a presidential decree, Sadat changed the state's name from the United Arab Republic to the Arab Republic of Egypt, signaling the end of the pursuit of pan-Arabism and reinserting "Egypt" in the name of the nation-state. Another critical issue that extended to the international stage was the continuing Israeli occupation of the Sinai Peninsula, a legacy of the 1967 war. In 1971 Sadat asked for the United States' involvement by proposing the reopening of the Suez Canal in return for an Israeli withdrawal. But given a lack of diplomatic relations with the United States, Egypt's proposal fell through, forcing Sadat to hint at the possibility of war. At the time, the Soviet Union was still heavily involved in Egypt's economy and political affairs, a legacy of Nasser's political alliances, and it was also Egypt's main supplier of weapons. It therefore came as a huge surprise when Sadat ordered all Russian experts and workers out of the country, leaving Egypt without needed allies. This was followed by a series of events that began in the early hours of October 6, 1973, when Sadat ordered Egyptian troops into action. By the end of that day, the Egyptian army had succeeded in catching Israel off guard by installing pontoon bridges crossing the Suez Canal into Sinai. Syria simultaneously attacked Israel in the north, taking control of much of the Golan Heights. After the intervention of the United States and the Soviet Union, a cease-fire agreement was reached under the auspices of the United Nations. Following this agreement, diplomatic relations between Egypt and the United States were restored. Although Israel remained in control of the eastern portion of Sinai, Egypt reopened the Suez Canal in June 1975.[7]

In the period following the war, Sadat turned his attention to Egypt's

economy, which remained weak since the end of Nasser's regime. In
October 1974 he launched his economic initiative called infitah, or "the
opening," a major policy overhaul that aimed to pull Egypt out of its dire
financial straits. Infitah was intended not only to reestablish a market
economy and rebuild the private sector in Egypt, but also to establish an
entirely new direction for Egypt's international relations. Major shifts in
the global economy played a major role in the country's economic decline
at the end of Nasser's rule. Sadat's new regulatory framework was an
attempt to respond to these new global market conditions and once again
attract foreign capital to Egypt. Infitah policy interventions in the domestic economy entailed a process of liberalization and decentralization,
including a new law on investment and concessions on foreign trade to
attract investors as well as international aid.[8] Some of the measures that
came with Sadat's economic policy were specifically focused on transforming Cairo. These measures included the dismantling of many public-
sector institutions and the state's withdrawal from the construction of
public projects, particularly housing.

If Nasser was an Alexandrian by virtue of his upbringing, Sadat was
an aspiring Cairene who wanted to claim a place in the city. Under Sadat,
Cairo became the locus of free-market restructuring—on the one hand
providing a preferred location for new private initiatives and capitalist
enterprises, and on the other offering a prime site for land speculation.
Under Sadat's reforms, land values in Cairo rose dramatically, almost
quadrupling in less than a decade. Sadat's administration also brought an
unprecedented construction boom to Egypt. The government financed
only a fraction of this activity; its funds were mostly reserved for construction that served those with the lowest income, while the private sector
was encouraged to undertake most of the new construction.[9] More than
half a million housing units were eventually built in a decade—although
many were completed without permits from state authorities. However,
because speculation and inflation caused prices to rise, many households
could not afford these new units and many apartments remained vacant.
In contradictory fashion, as private developers were overbuilding, housing demand continued to grow—as did the number of the urban poor

living in the cemeteries of the City of Dead east of the old city, and in decaying old neighborhoods. The government was not able to enact a policy that could adequately address the housing needs of the poor, nor did it attempt to control speculation.[10]

The decentralization of planning administration in Cairo did not mean the end of large-scale urban projects. The policy of the first master plan drawn up during Nasser's rule, that of developing industrial satellite cities, continued during Sadat's administration, but in a different direction. Drafted by the Cairo Planning Commission, a new master plan emphasized the expansion of Greater Cairo. But it also clearly expressed the advent of a new age, one that encouraged urban development and capital accumulation. The new government inherited a city struggling with uncontrolled growth, inadequate infrastructure, deteriorating housing conditions, and ever-expanding informal settlements, or *ashwaiyyat* (the term conveys the seemingly ad hoc nature of their development). The government did attempt to tackle many of the factors that contributed to Cairo's urban crisis, such as rural migration, loss of agricultural land, and the use of topsoil to produce bricks—the city's main construction material. In particular, new efforts were made to protect arable land around the Nile, whereas the vast desert areas around Cairo were developed into new towns, as opposed to adjacent satellite communities.[11] By encouraging residents to move to the periphery, the government strategy was meant to address the overagglomeration and traffic congestion that was affecting Cairo.

Eighteen new towns were planned between 1975 and 1979 under the aegis of the New Urban Communities Authority.[12] Some of these were classified as satellites of Cairo, such as Sixth of October and Fifteenth of May; others were planned to be self-sufficient new towns, such as Sadat City and the Tenth of Ramadan. All were named after the dates of key events that occurred during Sadat's rule. Developed in 1976, Tenth of Ramadan City marks the day, according to the Hijri calendar, when the 1973 war began. Designed for a population of five hundred thousand, it was planned to include industrial areas that would create jobs and attract residents.[13] Sixth of October City—which also commemorates the day in

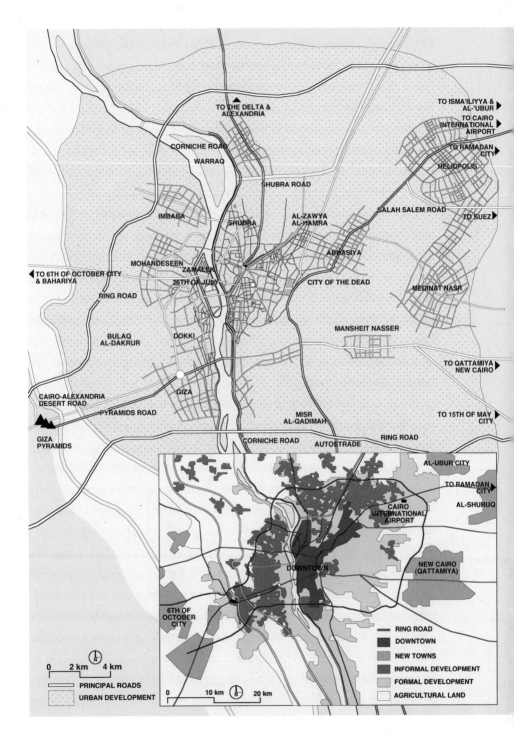

Figure 12.2   Map of the Greater Cairo region.

1973 when the war started, but according to the Gregorian calendar—
was, on the other hand, planned from the start as a satellite city to serve
Cairo. Both developments were private-sector initiatives on public land.
But in line with trends occurring across cities on the management of
urban space, the government was also involved in these so-called private
developments, designing incentives to attract people to them, such as
rent subsidies, significant salary raises for government employees who
chose to live there, and tax exemptions for industry and business.

Such policies contained contradictions. Building satellite cities often
hindered attempts to populate the new desert towns, which contributed
to the overconcentration of a sprawling Cairo. As such, these policies were
not able to solve Cairo's overcrowding problems. However, the new model
of planning and the scale and scope of these projects did help control
additional loss of agricultural land and shift much of Cairo's expansion to
desert areas. Cairo's existing informal settlements and slums were also
approached with a new strategy, one that encouraged slum improvement
rather than slum removal.[14]

These more sensitive approaches were always applied in places where
land is most valuable, as in areas close to Cairo's center. While Nasser's
approach was to make Cairo available to all, including the poor, Sadat's
strategy had the effect of driving the poor out of areas marked for development. Sadat's reforms were centered in the same impetus to modern-
ize Cairo as Nasser's earlier restructuring of urban space. However,
for Sadat's administration, efforts to "upgrade" housing conditions and
"rehabilitate" the city center are perhaps better characterized as cleanup
operations that aspired to put a prosperous Cairo on the global map, as
had been the case during Ismail's time. Under Sadat the city was made
more presentable and accessible to tourists, and more attractive to foreign
capital. But the process of globalizing Cairo was also a project of exclusion, as many working-class families residing in areas like Bulaq were
relocated to low-income public housing projects at the northern periphery
of the city.[15] Such moves not only placed these families far from the city
center but also reconfigured their relationship with the city at large.[16] In
order to legitimize such a strategy, the government framed this process

as an "upgrading," not only of houses, but also of people. Thus, the slum dwellers of Bulaq were stigmatized in government discourse as unproductive, backward members of society, who lived in unsanitary conditions, committed illegalities, and were in urgent need of "civilizing."[17]

After Sadat's assassination in 1981, his vice president, Hosni Mubarak, became head of state and was elected president a few months later. An unglamorous man known for his stoicism and simplicity, Mubarak's rise to power was largely uncontested, unlike Sadat's in 1970. His first presidential term (1981–1987) was marked by challenges on the domestic rather than the international front. Despite strong opposition, Mubarak has been able to maintain peace with Israel. But since the beginning of the 1980s, there has been growing disenchantment with infitah, and with the many promises it has failed to deliver. Nevertheless, Mubarak has continued the process of liberalization initiated by his predecessor. While he has kept intact many of the forms of government put in place by Sadat, he has allowed the opposition greater freedom to organize politically and tolerated the return of the opposition press. Unlike Nasser and Sadat, Mubarak has a taken a political stance not of a visionary but of a technocrat, concerned with the economic welfare of the Egyptian people.[18] He has allowed for some independence of the judiciary, and claimed that his administration governs on the basis of democratic principles. In the thirty years since Mubarak became president, Cairo has almost doubled in population and physical size. Economically, the city has also witnessed a level of prosperity that could not have been imagined half a century earlier. But such outcomes have been achieved at the high cost of income disparities unheard of in Cairo in the previous half century.

Under Mubarak a new master plan for Cairo was developed in 1983 in collaboration with foreign experts. It divided the city into sixteen units, each with an independent administrative apparatus.[19] Connecting all of these new areas, away from areas of arable land, is a seventy-three-kilometer automotive beltway, called the Ring Road. Despite the fact that Cairo's experts have tried to direct growth to planned developments, informal settlements, or ashwaiyyat, continue to expand unfettered in agricultural areas around the city. These settlements are not fundamentally illegal, given that their residents hold tenure to the land. But these areas violate regulations of the planning authority in that they occupy arable areas that have been converted into urban housing. Moreover, many of the structures located in such settlements do not satisfy city building codes. Despite these violations, the government has rarely resorted to demolition and eviction. These settlements have mostly remained in place. More significantly, ashwaiyyat constitute the only viable means through which residents of Cairo have been able to access affordable housing. That is, the informal sector has been fundamental to the provision of housing in recent decades. In general these expansions resemble other multistory inner-city housing quarters, even if most construction is substandard and initially lacks vital utilities.[20] Many residents have been able to obtain utilities by making illegal connections to electric and water lines. And because the new subdivisions had been plotted between existing irrigation channels, these channels were gradually turned into sewers, while existing dirt roads were turned into city streets. The loosening of regulations on private construction has fueled this development,

Figure 12.3 An informal settlement, or ashwaiyyat, in Cairo. ━━━━━━━

and remittance money from migrants, who work mainly in the Gulf region, has helped to fund it.

By the end of the twentieth century, more than 50 percent of Cairo's built environment consisted of such ashwaiyyat districts, which had come to satisfy most of the housing needs of the urban poor and the expanding lower middle class.[21] In the last two decades of the twentieth century, the informal sector produced as much as 40 percent of nonagricultural employment in Cairo. This condition may be common in many cities of the global south, but because of its extent in Cairo, the city has become known as the "informal city" par excellence. The presence of informal neighborhoods, however, is not a new phenomenon in Cairo. The ashwaiyyat have always been present in one form or another, and their expansion in recent decades is as much a product of economic liberalization started under Sadat as the neoliberalization that has taken hold under Mubarak. The unprecedented growth of ashwaiyyat has also been associated with the dismantling of the public sector in Egypt and with processes of globalization that have swept through Egypt and most of the countries of the Middle East. In particular, migrants who had sought work in the Gulf states began to send money home to their families, who could not otherwise afford the rising costs of housing. For many young Egyptian men, manual labor in the Gulf has become the only way to accumulate enough savings to marry and start a family.[22]

A growing concern with the ashwaiyyat did arise in the later years of the twentieth century, coupled with a will to "civilize," reform, upgrade, and provide services to these areas. This coincided with the rise of Islamist movements and the social upheavals in the 1980s and 1990s that resulted in violent confrontations with the state. Seen as both a threat and an opportunity, the ashwaiyyat and their millions of residents suddenly became of great interest to the government and experts. This newfound interest was not just based on unease over the rise of religious organizations there but reflective of the fact that urban residents who live in such precarious conditions began to acquire a collective voice and put forth claims to the government to ask for infrastructure and social services. After a major earthquake in 1992 caused hundreds of deaths in these poorly built neighborhoods, the government also took note of the fact that Islamist organizations were quicker to respond to the needs of the urban poor than its own bureaucratic apparatus was.[23] In neighborhoods such as Imbaba, constituted of dilapidated public housing surrounded by informal settlements, militant Islamic organizations like Al-Gama'a al-Islamiya have succeeded in penetrating and reorganizing the area's social fabric. They began as parallel institutions and internal systems, a phenomenon some have called "a state within a state."[24] Then, when residents and some of the foreign press started to refer to the area as the "Islamic Republic of Imbaba," ruled by an amir who governs in the name of Islam, the government had no choice but to send in the army to restore its authority.

In response to this perceived threat, government discourse eventually came to frame the ashwaiyyat as spaces of violence and destitution. This paved the way for new disciplinary techniques to penetrate the daily life of these neighborhoods and bring them under control.[25] One example is Bulaq al-Dakrur, an ashwaiyyat in northwestern Cairo, in the Governorate of Giza. Originally an agricultural area, over time it had slowly been converted to residential use by virtue of illegal construction that began in the 1970s. As with other ashwaiyyat, Bulaq al-Dakrur housed many migrants and poor residents, but because it bordered the upscale districts of Mohandeseen, near the center of Cairo, its social composition and environmental conditions were made starkly visible. The disparity between it and its surroundings was spatially reinforced by a railroad track and a fence that separated it from the rest of the formal city. As elsewhere in Cairo, the absence of government involvement and enforcement of regulations had allowed Bulaq al-Dakrur to become autonomous and to develop its own social institutions and networks. In the late 1980s and early 1990s, Islamist organizations began to establish roots there, and the government's laissez-faire approach changed to one of hostility and repression, culminating in confrontations between residents and the state. Eventually what had been regarded as a marginal and inconsequential area of the city was deemed criminal, framed through a discourse of urban pathology, and subjected to police violence, oppressive regulations, and constant surveillance. In the end rules regarding the enforcement of building regulations and the proper use of public space were used to justify massive intervention in these settlements.[26]

As Cairo's ashwaiyyat have expanded, so have exclusive residential areas and enclaves of leisure and consumption. Deeper divisions have thus appeared in the changing social and urban fabric of an already divided city. Cairo's global aspirations are reflected in its international hotels and office towers along the Nile, as well as in its gigantic luxury malls. While the "other" Cairo of impoverished neighborhoods and old quarters struggles to offer a viable living environment for a majority of the city's residents, luxury hotels incorporate motifs of Cairo's Mamluk architecture, such as *mashrabiya* screens, and cafés that cater to tourists, with low-slung seating areas and menus with "Oriental food."[27]

Figure 12.4   World Trade Center, Bulaq. ▬

One of the most paradigmatic examples is the gated community of Dreamland, west of the Pyramids of Giza. Dreamland is representative of not only Egypt's global aspirations but also Cairo's uncontrolled expansion. While the capital city has faced austerity measures and a rollback of state services, Dreamland and other projects like it have been underwritten by private capital. Built in the desert in the 1990s, this enclave of spectacular Tuscan villas and luxury multifamily walk-ups, and the lifestyle it promises, immediately distances itself from Cairo not only physically but also socially. Its villas are equipped with fiber-optic cable and wireless systems, and it offers "civic" amenities like shopping malls, a theme park, a golf course, and polo grounds. Like other gated communities in Cairo—such as Rehab, Hyde Park, and Beverly Hills (and much like the first example of its kind, Heliopolis, built in 1905 by Baron Empain)—Dreamland came into being through the sale of vast areas of public land to a handful of private developers.[28] In this case the builder and developer is Ahmed Bahgat, an Egyptian engineer with a doctorate from an American university, who returned to Egypt to become successful in the electronic manufacturing world. Bahgat hired foreign architects to design Dreamland in the fashion of North American suburbs, with eclectic and neoclassical pastel-colored villas, pitched roofs, and curved roads.[29] Similar formal characteristics can be found in Rehab, a recently built gated community northeast of Cairo.

In the Cairo of today, as in the Cairo of the past, such exclusive enclaves have responded to the desire for leisure, consumption, and security—and perhaps such spaces have even created such desires. "Sign now for a future value beyond any dreams ... before it's too late," reads one developer's pitch. "No factories, no pollution, no problems," it promises to its target audience, including those workers in the Gulf states who are saving for their dream home.[30] Much like Disney World in Florida, a source of inspiration for Dreamland's planners, advertisements like these portray Dreamland as a tourist destination where one can experience Europe's cities in the atmosphere of a medieval bazaar. Beyond that, this gated community in the desert was designed to be a consumer oasis that offers a sanitized physical environment, a leisurely lifestyle, and the illusion of escape from a polluted and overcrowded Cairo.

Figure 12.5   The gated communities of Dreamland and Rehab. Luxury apartments in Dreamland (above). Entertainment and shopping amenities in Rehab (below).

Modeled after suburban America, however, Dreamland does not have a clear center for its nominally "public" amenities. Rather, these are scattered throughout, divided between a theme park, shopping center, and golf course. Nor does it offer any sites for productive functions or labor, because its neighborhoods are almost exclusively zoned for residential use, consumption, and leisure.[31] Ironically, the so-called town center is marked by the minaret of a small mosque that combines the architectural language of Mamluk madrasas with Disneyfied brightly colored "Oriental" motifs. The green dome above its arched entryway was perhaps designed in homage to the lapis-colored dome of al-Nasir Muhhamad's madrasa at the Citadel. However, when in 2000 the Cairo stock market collapsed, so did the stock in the Dreamland company. The speculators who had extended Cairo into the desert had overbuilt their luxury enclaves and discovered overnight that the value of their "dreams" had dropped by more than half.[32]

In contemporary Cairo, luxury shopping malls have also sprouted up, right alongside the city's slums. This archipelago of luxury, built with

Figure 12.6   The mosque in Dreamland.

Gulf financing and connected by high-speed arteries, is the domain of Cairo's elite. Other city residents remain excluded, for their appearance betrays their social background. By 2005, twenty-four luxury shopping malls had been built in Cairo, the largest of which was City Stars Mall, at the border of Heliopolis and Nasr City. This mall, the largest in the Middle East at 150,000 square meters, was built by the Golden Pyramid Plaza Company owned by two Saudi investors. If the ashwaiyyat are "states within a state," the massive size of the City Stars Mall has earned it the description "a city within a city."[33] Besides its ten stories of shopping facilities, it houses luxury apartments, office spaces, and three five-star hotels.

Figure 12.7   City Stars Mall, Heliopolis.

The façade of the shopping complex employs the bold language of post-modern architecture, and its aesthetic blends aspects of the Las Vegas strip's architectural typologies, including the "decorated shed" and "the duck."[34] Two pharaonic statues flank its main entrance, suggesting that one is entering a temple, albeit one of a very different persuasion. Once inside, visitors can easily get lost among the many cafés, game arcades, restaurants, and a labyrinth of four hundred shopping outlets. At all times the mall is packed with thousands of people, many of them middle-class, wandering around or window-shopping for goods they cannot afford.

Despite the fact that many of these luxury mall projects have had short lives and wane in popularity only a few years after opening (perhaps with the exception of City Stars), and that only a small fragment of Cairo's population can afford to shop in them, their construction has continued apace.[35] Upscale coffee shops that tolerate mixed-gender socializing have similarly become a popular type of space for the privileged upper middle class. Some of these developments are based on a business model predicated on the spatial and social exclusion of the lower classes.[36] This separation has symbolized the struggle between *baladi,* as the "uncouth" lower classes are called, and the privileged patrons of luxury enclaves. But the middle class has its own divisions as well, with the "educated" members of the upper social class serving as the gatekeepers of what constitutes middle-class propriety.[37] These symbolic contestations have had major consequences and spatial manifestations, as most of Cairo's population has been relegated to its crowded older districts and informal areas. Ironically, however, the City Stars Mall has turned an entire wing into a facsimile of Khan al-Khalili in an effort to replicate the shopping experience of Cairo's old medieval core. Complete with a main *qassbah* bearing the name of its referent, al-Mu'izz Street, this "Oriental" shopping-cum-theme park is unambiguous in its exclusivity as a space for high-end clientele. For this neoliberal elite, the majority of Cairo's population is increasingly inconsequential to the city's global aspirations.[38] It is the city's spaces of consumption and leisure, such as City Stars Mall, and its gated communities, like Dreamland and Rehab with their golf courses and surfeit of amenities, that represent Cairo's global dreams.

Al-Azhar Park, completed in 1994, is one of the few projects that reflects an effort to counter the privatization of urban space. Built on a piece of land that had served for more than half a millennium as the city's garbage dump, this park attempts to create new green space in a city with little of it. It is funded by the Aga Khan Trust for Culture, a major philanthropic foundation that supports cultural projects in the Muslim world. Today the park, running along the remains of the old city walls, stands supreme, affording tourists and residents magnificent views of the old city, a reminder of Cairo's reputation as the city of a thousand minarets. Designed by an American landscape firm, the park includes features inspired by Andalusian and Mughal garden forms. These have been widely appreciated by the park's visitors, who have also frequented its restaurants and cafés, designed in a Mamluk style, that impart a sense that they have always been there. But the park, which borders many of Cairo's slum neighborhoods and was

Figure 12.8 Al-Azhar Park, Cairo.

initially designed to serve its lower classes, now primarily serves wealthy residents and foreign dignitaries. A somewhat steep entrance fee has made it difficult for the city's poor to access it, except during special occasions, such as for wedding photographs, when the cost of admission is reduced. In addition, many embassies have used Al-Azhar Park for formal receptions in a manner that undermines its original intent but nevertheless serves to enliven the area while providing revenue for the park's upkeep. Like many other venues in Cairo, what had been built for the poor has ended up serving the rich.[39]

Outside the borders of such oases has been a growing discontent in the city. In the 1980s and 1990s, Cairo saw the rise of Islamic movements and social unrest. Religion has grown in prominence in people's lives, a phenomenon wholly inconceivable during Nasser's time. Sadat's mixing of politics with religion allowed numerous religious organizations to become involved in previously secular government and national institutions: the military, schools and universities, bureaucratic offices, and political parties. Such a shift has been amplified by the fact that religion is one of the few channels through which citizens can openly express opposition to the government.[40] Small community mosques began to appear in a number of neighborhoods in the capital city and elsewhere in Egypt. In contemporary Cairo, it is now not unusual at Friday prayer time for mosques to lay prayer rugs in the streets to accommodate the overflow of worshippers. In Islam, any space, including a room, a courtyard, or even a street, can serve as a mosque, and at prayer time the city itself is turned into a mosque. This can at times block traffic and restrict the freedom of movement of non-Muslim residents, such as Cairo's sizable Coptic minority.[41] The growing importance of religion in daily life, perhaps triggered by Sadat's assassination at the hands of Muslim fundamentalists, has been theorized by some as an alternate form of postcolonial modernity, one that rejects the secular curtailment of religion in the conduct of daily life.[42] The spatial articulation of these movements has been analyzed by scholars as a new medieval modernity.[43] Others have seen the rise of fundamentalism as a response to the recent regime's drastic measures against the Islamist movement, and its attempt to prevent the movement's participation in political life and its rise to power.[44]

Cairo has been a cosmopolitan city throughout its long history. That cosmopolitanism reached its zenith during a period that began with the rule of Khedive Ismail and ended with King Farouk. This drastically changed during Nasser, when restrictions were imposed not only on the circulation of people but also on the circulation of information and capital. With the advent of infitah, however, Cairo opened its doors to the world once again to regain a degree of its urban vitality. Today Cairo is once more a cosmopolitan city, but with a very different character, oriented to the region and the countries of the Persian Gulf rather than its former European colonizers in the north. Against this notion of first-world cosmopolitanism, Cairo is increasingly looking back to its religious traditions and its past to negotiate the terms of its present. Perhaps the idea of a "borrowed" cosmopolitanism allows us to interrogate not only Cairo's articulation of that model, but also the notion of cosmopolitanism itself and its relevance for the cities of the global south. Cairo and its residents bring to light a form of cosmopolitanism that is not about unbounded openness, but rather about diversity within place. Cosmopolitanism is a relational process that involves social networks that are transnational in form; but it is also a process that is fundamentally urban and based in a territory.

Today Cairo is a large and diverse metropolis with global aspirations. As in its medieval past, it is once again a crossroads of transnational commerce and migration and a hub of cultural diversity. Two myths about the capital city continue to persist in the popular imagination, however: one imagines Cairo as a tomb—a dead or hyperpassive city that consists of a submissive population residing in an open-air museum of monuments; another imagines Cairo as a bomb, which stands in ironic contrast to the metaphor of the tomb.[45] This second myth imagines Cairo as a city marked by grave contradictions of an ever-expanding population, social upheavals, religious riots, and pollution—harboring a rebellious "Arab element" that can detonate at any moment. Such myths allow us not only to interrogate how Cairo is seen by those who study it, but also to peek into the imagination of those who live in it and give it life.[46]

Perhaps the fragility of Cairo and its neighborhoods—as a place whose momentary essence teeters between that of a tomb and that of a bomb—is best captured in *The Yacoubian Building,* the now-famous novel by Alaa Al Aswany. Al Aswany, who is a dentist by trade, was inspired by the real eighty-year-old building in Cairo in which his clinic was located. Following the tradition established earlier by Naguib Mahfouz with his focus on the self-contained Cairene *hara* as his setting, Al Aswany uses the *imarah,* an apartment building with mixed functions, as his stage. Such buildings became the standard mode of habitation in Cairo in the second half of the twentieth century.

The novel beautifully catalogs the transformations of Cairene society over five decades through a careful engagement with the changes occurring in the space of the building and the life of its inhabitants. We learn about how army officers who were empowered by the revolution unlawfully took over apartments that used to belong to the wealthy, who lost much of their wealth as a result of nationalization during Nasser's time. We learn about the small rooftop rooms that were once storage facilities for the apartments below and how, due to Cairo's housing shortage, they became populated by communities of servants and other rural migrants. These migrants brought with them not only their way of life but also their animals; consequently, the raising of chickens and ducks on rooftops became common during Sadat's time. Although the residents of the building and those of the rooftop seem worlds apart, the narrative of Al Aswany's novel reveals how their lives intersect in ways indicative of the new inequality brought about by the neoliberal economy under Mubarak.

We also learn about Taha, a rooftop resident who is the son of the building's doorman. He is in love with Busayna, another rooftop neighbor, who is obliged to give up her college education in order to support her family by consorting with a wealthier resident in the building. When Taha's dreams of upward social mobility and of marrying Busayna are crushed by the corruption of the state and the oppression of the economy, he becomes unhappy with the political regime and chooses to participate in public demonstrations. He is ultimately arrested and violated in jail, which leads him to engage in a suicidal terrorist attack against the state and police after his release. Throughout the book, Al Aswany tells a story of how the decadence of the wealthy and the misery of the poor have converged, leading to the rise of religious fundamentalism and the invocation of religion as the only means to save the city. Al Aswany's Cairo is indeed a truer depiction of the city at the beginning of the twenty-first century than anything one could have anticipated from a novel.[47]

Many authors who wrote about Cairo in the twentieth century, often fascinated by the city and enchanted by its spell, emphasized its name, al-Qahira, which could be translated from Arabic as "the victorious." But ironically, al-Qahira also means "the oppressor," a meaning that gives a whole new dimension to "the City Victorious." Thus, the great city at the beginning of the twenty-first century and in the era of neoliberalism turns out to carry a name with a loaded double meaning. What turns out to be victorious in the end is not the city, nor its lower- and middle-class residents, but rather the forces of capital that seem to exist outside Egypt altogether. In reflecting on its recent past, one may argue that the city was "liberated" from its rich landlords during Nasser's era and handed over to its poor. The city was later "liberalized" under Sadat and opened its gates to foreign capital. Now, half a century later, under Mubarak's government, it has been returned to the wealthy and its new elite.

But something else was happening in Cairo in the late twentieth century that has firmly reshaped it into the city we know today. The nineteenth-century project of medievalizing the old quarter—the invention of a sanitized historic urban environment that had never existed—has now taken hold as an official preservation strategy. Preserving Cairo for tourists, and possibly for future generations of Egyptians, now gives the government free license to restore old structures, and in the process to outfit them with an invented aesthetic that requires the abandonment of the structures' traditional functions. The old core is now being cleared of many of its craftworkers and small shops, replaced by cafés and tourist rest houses. What is left today are only the hollow names of the vibrant quarters—the spice and coppersmith bazaars—once dedicated to communities of craftsmen and traders.

The old quarter is quickly becoming a museum, and with this museumification has come a loss in trades, changes in people's lifestyles, and the fundamental transformation of the city into a Disney-like theme park. Indeed, Cairo is now starting to resemble its fictional image. Ironically, however, it also seems to be gaining sustenance from it. In the late nineteenth century, the architect Max Hertz was commissioned to design a replica of a Cairo street for the Chicago Columbian Exposition. To ensure the authenticity of one of its structures, a replica of a *sabil-kuttab*, Hertz went about removing the windows and tile work from the original sabil-kuttab of 'Abd al-Rahman Katkhuda without any qualms. He then had them shipped to America and installed them on the replica in uniform fashion. But the replica did not resemble the original. In a twist of fate, when the real sabil-kuttab back in Egypt underwent restoration in the early twentieth century and then later again that century, the restorers had little to rely on other than the images of the replica at the Columbian Exposition and the drawing produced to build it. Cairo now began to resemble its imagined self, and had come to derive its new authenticity from its copy.[48]

Figure 12.9   The sabil-kuttab of 'Abd al-Rahman Katkhuda after restoration.

It is not a wholly new phenomenon that Cairo is beginning to mirror its copy, as this is likely to have happened several times before in the city's long history. But arguably what is now new is how these copies are influencing the perception and appreciation of the real city. A decade ago I organized a large conference in Cairo that dealt with the "consumption of tradition," a theme on which I have written extensively about elsewhere. Many of the conference participants were foreigners from the United States and Europe, so the conference included the standard tourist trips to famous Cairo sites, including the Giza Pyramids. Standing close to American conference participants who were gazing down at the pit where the Sphinx lay, I overheard one say in a tone of disappointment, "Oh, it is small. Really small." His comments puzzled me for a while. Why was the Sphinx small? And compared to what? When I checked the participant's nametag and asked why he had made this comment, the story became much clearer. It turned out that he was a resident of Las Vegas, Nevada, the biggest casino-turned-city on earth, and that he often

Figure 12.10 View of the Sphinx in front of the Luxor Hotel and Casino in Las Vegas. ▬

lectured in one of its colleges. He regularly parked his car in a lot in front of the Luxor Hotel and Casino, built in the form of a pyramid, and whose entrance lobby and car drop-off areas form the replica of the Giza Sphinx. To accommodate the multi-lane entrance road underneath, however, that Sphinx had to be much bigger than the original from which it was copied. When our participant looked at the real Sphinx in Giza, he indeed had to be disappointed when its reality did not match his mental image of it. He was already acculturated to the size and the proportions of the Vegas Sphinx, and for him the original ceased to be relevant, as the image—the modern-day replica—was now his main frame of reference.[49]

In a globalizing era when cities no longer belong exclusively to their people, the image of the thing may come to replace the thing itself. Will that happen to Cairo? Will it transform itself using its invented tradition, employing its imagined historical aesthetic—mainly attempting to appeal to those who come to visit? Or will it continue to be the messy and diffi-cult but often vibrant and innovative city that its citizens will continue to shape though their actions and inactions? Only time will tell.

Appendix

Notes on Transliteration and Dates

Transliteration of words from standard Arabic follows a simplified version of the system used in the *International Journal of Middle East Studies*. There are no diacritical marks, and *ta marbuta* is rendered "a" and "ah" depending on common accepted English spellings. The *'ayn* has been retained when it appears within a word and is indicated by ('). The *hamza* has not been retained, with the exception of place and personal names. *Jim* has generally been transliterated as *j* except in cases of dialectical Egyptian use, in which case it is transliterated as *g*. Spellings common in English have been used, particularly for personal and place names. In some cases where dialectical Egyptian Arabic appears, the words have been translated phonetically.

Dates cited in the book are principally based on the Gregorian calendar. In specified instances, both Gregorian and Hijri dates are given. The first Hijri year is assumed to correspond to Friday, July 16, 622 AD.

Glossary

'alim	Singular of *ulama*.
ablaq	Alternating bands of dark and light masonry.
agha	Ottoman military title meaning ruler or leader of janissary militia; later used of civil officers and as a title of distinction.
amir	Military officer, prince or governor of a province under a sultan; historically, used in title for caliphs; in modern times, denotes a member of a ruling family.
amsar	Plural of *misr*.
arif	Inspector; literally means "one who knows."
asabiyah	Social solidarity with emphasis on group consciousness, cohesion, and unity.
Ashura	A festival commemorating the martyrdom of the Shi'ite Imams.
ashwaiyyat	An ad hoc or informal housing development; or areas considered such.
a'tfa	Small cul-de-sac.
bab	Gate or door.
baladi	Rural, local, or traditional.
basilica	A large oblong hall or building with double colonnades and a semicircular apse used for a court of justice and a place of public assembly.
bey	Ottoman rank below pasha, similar to governor or lord.
bimaristan	Hospital.
burj	Fortified tower.
caliph	Title given to the chief civil and religious ruler; means "successor"; competing dynasties have claimed this title at the same time.

castrum	A military garrison town based on the Roman practice.
cenotaph	Tomblike monument to commemorate person(s) whose remains are elsewhere.
crenellation	Battlements of a building of a walled city or castle.
cruciform	Having the shape of a cross.
dar	A house or residence of high standing or wealth.
dar al-imarah	Governor's residence; palace complex.
darb	Connector road.
diwan	Court council or administrative bureau; also registry.
faience	Glazed ceramic ware.
faqih	Jurist or expert in Islamic jurisprudence; a major segment of the ulama.
fellahin	Plural of *fellah,* meaning "peasant."
finial	Ornamental device at the apex of a roof, pinnacle, or canopy.
firman	Imperial edict.
hadith	A collection of traditions of the sayings of the Prophet Muhammad that guide daily practice of Muslims.
hamam	Public bathhouse, considered essential to an Islamic city.
hara	Residential quarter; also alley.
haram	The sanctuary of a mosque; the private quarters of a house.
haramlik	Women's quarters.
hisba	Islamic conception of order.
hypostyle	A building roof or flat ceiling supported by pillars.
iltizam	A taxation system based on farming, practiced in Egypt and the Ottoman Empire; tax farms were assigned to holders who paid fixed annual sums to the empire's treasury in exchange for the right to collect taxes for the empire.
imarah	Apartment complex.
infitah	Liberalization policies under Sadat.
istibdal	Exchange of property.
iwan	Vaulted hall that is a standard unit of Islamic architecture.

karimis	Muslim merchants who controlled the Oriental trade between the Mediterranean and India.
katkhuda	Lieutenant of janissary militia.
khanqah	Monastery dedicated to Sufi rites that features a central hall.
khedive	The title of the viceroy of Egypt under the Ottomans.
khitat	Plural of *khita:* a concession, parcel of land, or a main road; also a monograph on a city.
khutbah	Friday congregation mosque sermon.
Kufic	Calligraphic style made up of straight lines and angles.
loggia	A gallery or room with one or more open sides supported by pillars or pierced openings.
mabkhara	Incense burner.
madhab	A school of Islamic law or jurisprudence.
madrasa	A school.
maq'ad	Loggia, open sitting room.
mashrabiya	Wooden lattice screen, oriel window.
mastaba	Seating area in front of a home or shop.
maydan	A large public square; often the largest open space for ceremonies in the city.
mihrab	Niche in the wall of a mosque indicating the direction of Mecca toward which prayers are made.
minaret	Tall slender tower, typically part of a mosque, with a balcony.
misr	Refers to Egypt; a popular name for Cairo.
muhtasib	Administrative officer responsible for public morals and market regulation.
mukhabarat	Intelligence police.
multazim	Titleholder of iltizam.
muntazahat	Promenade.
muqarnas	Pointed squinch used in dome construction.
naksa	Diversion.
namus al-mulk	Rites and royal ceremonies.
narthex	Entrance or antechamber located behind the nave.

Naskhi	Calligraphic style replacing Kufic; the style most commonly used for printing Arabic, Farsi, and Pashto.
nave	The main body of a religious building, used to accommodate the congregation.
pasha	A title used from the beginning of Ottoman rule for governors.
pendentive	A curved triangle of vaulting formed by the intersection of a dome and its supporting arches.
qa'a	Reception hall in Cairene houses.
qadi	Judge who rules according to Islamic law.
qahwa	Coffee; also café.
Qanunama	Law prohibiting istibdal.
qassbah	Thoroughfare, spine, or central part of a citadel.
qaysariyya	Another term for wekala.
qibla	The direction toward Mecca, which Muslims face during prayers.
rab	Multistory apartment building, sometimes with shops on the ground floor.
rahbah	A medium-size square or other city space.
riwaq	Arcade or portico.
sabil	Water fountain; small kiosk with such a fountain.
sabil-kuttab	A structure housing a fountain and a nursery school.
sahah	An open square, often inside or outside the city gates.
sahn	Courtyard or interior central court of a mosque.
salamlik	Public reception space for guests; men's quarters.
soffit	Underside of an architectural structure, such as an arch, a balcony, or an overhanging eave.
squinch	A precursor to the pendentive; an arch placed across an angle to transition between a square compartment and a dome above.
suq	A market; sometimes a specialized commercial activity.
tahtabush	Seating area for the head of household to receive guests.
tariq	Main road.
tiraz	Epigraphic band on a wall or textile.

transept	Either of the two wings of building that intersect at 90 degrees, projecting at right angles from the nave.
ulama	Scholars of Islamic law, religion, and tradition; in general refers to the religious elite.
vizier	High-ranking political advisor or minister in a Muslim government.
waqf	Religious endowment or institution based on Islamic law.
wekala	Caravanserai, or roadside inn for sojourners; urban building that functions as a warehouse, market, or khan.
zawiya	Small convent for prayer.
ziyada	Outer enclosure or extension of mosque.
ziyaret	Special pilgrimage to a shrine.
zuqaq	Alleyway that connects to a major thoroughfare.

Endnotes

Preamble

1 Naguib Mahfouz, *Palace Walk* [*Bayn al-Qasrayn*], trans. W. Hutchins and O. Kenny (New York: Doubleday, 1990), 35–36.

2 The two other novels in the trilogy are *Palace of Desire (Qasr al-Shawq)* and *Sugar Street (Al-Sukkariyah)*. All three novels were published between 1956 and 1959.

3 Nezar AlSayyad, "Virtual Cairo," *Leonada* 32, no. 1 (1999): 99–100.

4 Italo Calvino, *Invisible Cities*, trans. W. Weaver (New York: Harcourt Brace Jovanovich, 1978).

1. Memphis

1 Auguste Mariette wrote for the local newspaper, *l'Annotateur Boulonnaise.*

2 Brian M. Fagan, *The Rape of the Nile: Tomb Robbers, Tourists, and Archaeologists in Egypt* (Boulder, Colo.: Westview Press, 2004), 181–184.

3 A modern-day observer may not be able to see all of these monuments directly from the Giza Plateau. However, Google Earth will show an image similar to that described here.

4 Alan Henderson Gardiner, *Egypt of the Pharaohs: An Introduction* (London: Oxford University Press, 1964), 325–326.

5 Max Rodenbeck, *Cairo: The City Victorious* (New York: Vintage, 1998), 8.

6 The term *Upper* is used to designate the southern part of Egypt, consisting mainly of the narrow Nile Valley. It is upper in reference to its moderately higher elevation, but mainly for being closer to the source of the Nile. Hence, Lower Egypt is actually in the northern part of Egypt, or the lower lands of the Nile Delta.

7 Gardiner, *Egypt of the Pharaohs,* 325–326.

8 James Henry Breasted, *A History of the Ancient Egyptians* (New York: Scribner's Sons, 1923), 39–51.

9 Leslie Greener, *The Discovery of Egypt* (London: Cassell, 1966), 3.

10 Ibid., 11.

11 Ibid., 10.

12 Ibid., 176–187.

13 Until 3100 BC, Egypt was divided into two kingdoms. The king of Upper Egypt wore a white crown, and the king of Lower Egypt, a red crown. Menes, the king of Upper Egypt, unified the two kingdoms, became its first pharaoh, and wore a crown of both colors.

14 The dates for the periodization of ancient Egypt are taken from the Carnegie Museum of Natural History website, www.carnegiemnh.org. These dates should be treated as approximate.

15 Breasted, *Ancient Egyptians,* 39–51.

16 Rodenbeck, *Cairo,* 10.

17 For more on ancient Egyptian houses, see Alexander Badawy, *A History of Egyptian Architecture: The Empire (the New Kingdom) from the Eighteenth Dynasty to the End of the Twentieth Dynasty, 1580–1085 B.C.,* vol. 1 (Berkeley: University of California Press, 1968).

18 Ibid., 2:35, 128.

19 Gardiner, *Egypt of the Pharaohs.*

20 For more on the travelers to Memphis in ancient times, see Dale M. Brown, ed., *Egypt: Land of the Pharaohs,* Lost Civilizations Series (Alexandria, Va.: Time-Life Books, 1992).

21 Gamal Mokhtar, "The Pharaonic Era," in *Cairo: The Site and the History,* ed. Morsi Saad El-Din and Harri Peccinotti (London: Stacey, 1988), 30.

22 Ibid., 31.

23 Breasted, *Ancient Egyptians,* 39–51.

24 Mokhtar, "The Pharaonic Era," 35.

25 Ibid., 31.

26 Mariette in a statement made to Maspero, found in Greener, *The Discovery of Egypt,* 177.

27 Ibid., 177–202.

2. From Ancient Egypt to the Coptic Enclave

1 Donald Malcolm Reid, *Whose Pharaohs? Archaeology, Museums and Egyptian National Identity from Napoleon to World War I* (London: University of California Press, 2002), 258.

2 Donald Malcolm Reid, "Excerpts from the Memoirs of Markus H. Simaika Pasha, C.B.E., F.S.A. (1864–1944)," unpublished, 258.

3 Ibid., 258.

4 Judith McKenzie, *The Architecture of Alexandria and Egypt, 300 BC to AD 700* (New Haven: Yale University Press), 39.

5 Ibid., 42.

6 Jason Thompson, *A History of Egypt: From Earliest Times to the Present* (Cairo: American University in Cairo Press, 2008), 118–119.

7 McKenzie, *Architecture,* 78.

8 Ibid., 124.

9 The origins of the name of Babylon have been extensively debated by historians. Bishop John of Nikiu, whose chronicles speak of Babylon, tells us that the foundations of the fortress were laid by Nebuchadnezzar, who invaded Egypt and named the fortress Babylon after his capital city. Nikiu also relates that Emperor Trajan, in 98, erected the walls on this foundation in order to create a defense against a Jewish rebellion that was simmering in Alexandria. The Greek Egyptian historian Strabo, however, notes the existence of a fortress where Babylonians had taken refuge, well before Emperor Trajan came to Egypt.

10 Richard Yeomans, *Art and Architecture of Islamic Cairo* (Reading, UK: Garnet, 2008), 9.

11 Ibid., 122–125, 143.

12 Ibid., 142–145.

13 Alfred J. Butler, *The Arab Conquest of Egypt, and the Last Thirty Years of the Roman Dominion* (Oxford: Clarendon Press, 1978), 71.

14 Ibid., 181.

15 André Raymond, *Cairo* (Cambridge, Mass.: Harvard University Press, 2000).

16 Yeomans, *Art and Architecture,* 7.

17 Butler, *Arab Conquest of Egypt,* 439.

18 Yeomans, *Art and Architecture,* 11.

19 Ibid., 12.

20 Butler, *Arab Conquest of Egypt,* 444.

21 Yeomans, *Art and Architecture,* 13.

22 Butler, *Arab Conquest of Egypt,* 245.

23 Ibid., 247.

24 Ibid., 239.

25 Yeomans, *Art and Architecture,* 10; as also described by Wladyslaw Kubiak in *Al Fustat: Its Foundation and Early Urban Development* (Cairo: American University in Cairo Press, 1987).

26 For a detailed description of the siege of the fortress of Babylon by 'Amr and his army, refer to John, Bishop of Nikiu, *The Chronicle of John, Bishop of Nikiu,* trans. R. H. Charles (Merchantville, N.J.: Evolution, 2007), 180–187.

27 Butler, *The Arab Conquest of Egypt,* xviii.

28 Ibid., 244.

29 Ibid., 242.

30 Ibid., 241.

31 Ibid., 247.

32 Ibid., 248.

33 Reid, *Whose Pharaohs?* 275.

34 Alaa El-Habashi, "Athar to Monuments: The Interventions of the Comité de Conservation des Monuments de l'Art Arabe" (Ph.D. diss., University of Pennsylvania, 2001), 87.

3. Fustat-Misr

1 The chronicler Ibn Duqmaq mentions this story in his *Kitab al-Intisar li-wasitat 'iqd al-amsar* in 1406. For more detail, refer to Caroline Williams, *Islamic Monuments in Cairo* (Cairo: American University in Cairo Press, 2008).

2 André Raymond, *Cairo* (Cambridge, Mass.: Harvard University Press, 2000), 10.

3 Nezar AlSayyad, *Cities and Caliphs: On the Genesis of Arab Muslim Urbanism* (New York: Greenwood Press, 1991), 45–46.

4 Ibid, 60.

5 Ibid., 72–73.

6 Wladyslaw Kubiak, *Al Fustat: Its Foundation and Early Urban Development* (Cairo: American University in Cairo Press, 1987), 111.

7 Ibid., 90.

8 Alfred J. Butler, *The Arab Conquest of Egypt, and the Last Thirty Years of the Roman Dominion* (Oxford: Clarendon Press, 1978), 229.

9 Kubiak, *Al Fustat,* 76.

10 Ibid., 106.

11 The figure recorded in the Egyptian *diwan* does not accurately reflect the population at that time, because women and children were not counted. For a description of the demographic transformations of Fustat in this period, see Kubiak, *Al Fustat,* 76–84.

12 Ibid., 83.

13 Contrary to the widely held belief that the mosque of 'Amr was initially built as a congregational mosque *(al-dajami')*, its original size indicates that it was meant to serve only the Ahl al-Raya quarter. For a discussion on source material concerning the founding of the mosque and its evolution to an *al-dajami'*, see Kubiak, *Al Fustat,* 129.

14 Ibid., 62.

15 Ibid., 130.

16 None of the original mosque of 'Amr survives today, and what we see is an accumulation of successive restorations and additions made over time by a series of rulers. Eventually the monument expanded to almost ten times its original surface area due to these changes. This accounts for the fact that while its historical importance has been universally acknowledged, its aesthetic qualities have been largely ignored, and it has been dismissed as a piecemeal accumulation of architectural elements, many of them dating from the nineteenth century.

17 Raymond, *Cairo,* 20.

18 Maslama ibn 'Abd al-'Aziz was the brother of Caliph 'Abd al-Malik and a patron of architecture. As the governor of Egypt, he was the first in Islamic history to found a satellite residence town, Hulwan, thus instituting a tradition followed by numerous subsequent rulers in the Islamic world. 'Abd al-'Aziz's legacy is essential to Islamic architecture. During his rule, at the peak of the Umayyad dynasty, he encouraged the building of many monuments in the Fustat area and undertook the rebuilding of the mosque of 'Amr.

19 Kubiak, *Al Fustat,* 11.

20 Keppel Archibald Cameron Creswell, *Short Account of Early Muslim Architecture* (New York: Penguin Books, 1958), 301.

21 Raymond, *Cairo,* 26.

22 Although Samarra was a new city, having just replaced Baghdad as the capital of the caliphate, architectural historians believe that it was the cradle of Islamic architecture, given the extensive building that took place under Caliph al-Mu'tasim.

23 Creswell, *Short Account,* 304.

24 Raymond, *Cairo,* 26.

25 Richard Yeomans, *Art and Architecture of Islamic Cairo* (Reading, UK: Garnet, 2008), 33.

26 The most lavishly decorated prayer niche probably dates from the Fatimid period, one built by vizier al-Afdal Shahinshah. The original niche is now located at the Museum of Islamic Art in Cairo. The replica that has taken its place is decorated in stucco and bears inscriptions dedicated to the caliph who ordered it built.

27 Williams, *Islamic Monuments in Cairo,* 49.

28 Creswell, *Short Account,* 308.

29 Only three of the window stucco grills contain original stucco enclosures. They are the fifth, sixth, and sixteenth openings on the left side of the qibla wall. Another six openings have been identified as dating from the thirteenth-century restoration conducted by Sultan Lajin. More information can be found in Williams, *Islamic Monuments in Cairo,* 49.

30 The washing facility was replaced in the thirteenth century by a domed foun-

tain built by Lajin, who ordered restoration work on the structure in later times.

31 The stone minaret located on the north side of the *ziyada* is also attributed by some historians to Lajin. Other sources, however, indicate that it was built by Ibn Tulun. The debates stem from a lack of evidence on the exact date of the original structure.

32 The anecdote concerning Ibn Tulun and the creation of the stone minaret is described in Creswell, *Short Account,* 315; Creswell cites the writings of Ya'qubi, Ibn Duqmaq, and Maqrizi.

33 Ibid.

34 Williams, *Islamic Monuments in Cairo,* 48.

35 Doris Behrens-Abouseif, *Cairo of the Mamluks: A History of the Architecture and Its Culture* (London: Tauris, 2007), 19.

36 Although there are no surviving stucco decorations in extant mosques in Samarra, the adornments of Ibn Tulun's mosque are reportedly adaptations of the style of stucco ornamentation found in archaeological excavations conducted in other parts of Samarra.

37 Raymond, *Cairo,* 27.

38 Jason Thompson, *A History of Egypt: From Earliest Times to the Present* (Cairo: American University in Cairo Press, 2008), 172.

39 Yeomans, *Art and Architecture,* 41.

40 William Edward Burghardt Du Bois, *W. E. B. Du Bois: A Reader,* ed. David Levering Lewis (New York: Henry Holt and Co., 1995), 223.

41 Yeomans, *Art and Architecture,* 41.

42 Ibn Hawkal as cited in Deborah Manley and Sahar Abdel-Hakim, eds., *Traveling through Egypt: From 450 B.C. to the Twentieth Century* (Cairo: American University in Cairo Press, 2008), 46.

4. Al-Qahira

1 The Shi'ites (which in Arabic means "partisans") constitute the second-largest denomination of Islam. Their primary difference from the Sunnis, the largest branch of Islam, is in the Shi'a emphasis on the importance of the family of the Prophet and his descendants, whom the Shi'ites accord a special spiritual and political authority over the community.

2 The Ismailis constitute the second-largest segment of the Shi'ite community. The Bohras are an Ismaili Shi'ite community originally from western India. They are of Hindu descent but trace their spiritual lineage to the Fatimids. For an ethnography of the Bohras, see Jonah Blank, *Mullahs on the Mainframe: Islam and Modernity among the Daudi Bohras* (Chicago: University of Chicago Press, 2001), 184.

3 Paula Sanders, *Creating Medieval Cairo: Empire, Religion, and Architectural Preservation in Nineteenth-Century Egypt* (Cairo: American University in Cairo Press, 2008).

4 A later-day Mamluk tomb, the Tomb of Qurqumas, at the entrance of the al-Hakim mosque, is a main casualty of this approach.

5 Janet Abu-Lughod, *Cairo: 1001 Years of the City Victorious* (Princeton: Princeton University Press, 1971), 16.

6 Philip Hitti, *Capital Cities of Arab Islam* (Minneapolis: University of Minnesota Press, 1973), 110.

7 Abu-Lughod, *Cairo*, 18.

8 Marcel Clerget, *Le Caire*, vol. 1 (Cairo: E. and R. Schindler, 1934), 128.

9 Abu-Lughod, *Cairo*, 18.

10 Hitti, *Capital Cities*, 18.

11 Abdul Rahman Zaki, *Al-Qahirah, 969–1825* (Cairo: Al-Dar al-Mesriyah L-lta'lif wa al-Targamah, 1966), 10.

12 Taqi al-din al-Maqrizi, *Al-Mawa'ez wa al-I'tibar bi-Dhikr al-Khitat wa al-Athar* (Cairo: Bulaq Press, 1853), 2:179.

13 Zaki, *Al-Qahirah*, 10.

14 Maqrizi, *Al-Mawa'ez*.

15 Clerget, *Le Caire*, 7:123.

16 C. J. Haswell, "Cairo: Origin and Development," *Bulletin de Société Royal de Géographie d'Egypte* 3–4 (1933): 176.

17 Roger Le Tourneau in an interview with Janet Abu-Lughod, published as a footnote in Abu-Lughod, *Cairo*, 18.

18 R. E. Reitemeyer, *Beschreibung Ägyptens* (Leipzig: J. C. Hinrichs, 1903), 261.

19 The Arabic *al-Qahira* is often translated as "the victorious," but an equally valid translation is "the oppressor." Maqrizi, *Al-Mawa'ez*, 2:273.

20 Nezar AlSayyad, *Streets of Islamic Cairo* (Cambridge, Mass.: Aga Khan Program for Islamic Architecture, 1981), 16.

21 Maqrizi, *Al-Mawa'ez*, 2:275.

22 Hitti, *Capital Cities*, 114.

23 Maqrizi, *Al-Mawa'ez*, 1:377.

24 Ali Mubarak, *Al-khutat al-Tawfiqiyah al-Jadidah* (Cairo: Dar al-Kutub, 1969), 1:42.

25 Ibid., 1:36.

26 Maqrizi, *Al-Mawa'ez*, 2:273.

27 K. Paul Ravaisse, in 1890, recreated a contextual site plan in relationship to the palaces, city wall, and gates. A. C. Creswell, in 1952, first reconstructed the plan of the original mosque.

28 Doris Behrens-Abouseif, *Islamic Architecture in Cairo* (Leiden: E. J. Brill, 1989); Nasser Rabbat, "Al-Azhar Mosque: An Architectural Chronicle of Cairo's History," *Muqarnas* 13 (1996): 45–67.

29 The mosques of 'Amr and Ibn Tulun continued to accommodate Friday congregations, given their locations at a considerable walking distance from Fatimid Cairo. They continued the Sunni khutbah instead of the official Shi'ite khutbah sanctioned by the Fatimid caliphs.

30 After this period of neglect, al-Azhar emerged again around 1490 as a major institute of Islamic learning, as attested by the increased rate of restorations and additions in the latter stages of the Mamluk period. Between 1309 and 1340, the Mamluks restored al-Azhar and built madrasas attached to its outer enclosure as well as various gateways and passages between them. Elegant minarets were also added during that time. During the period when Egypt was a province and later a suzerainty of the Ottoman Empire, the main portal was added (in 1753) and the expansion behind the Fatimid mihrab was carried out (in 1894). For more on the al-Azhar mosque, see Rabbat, "Al-Azhar Mosque," 50, 56.

31 *Palace Walk*, a novel by the Egyptian Nobel laureate Naguib Mahfouz, pays tribute to the area between the Eastern and Western Palaces. For more,

see Nezar AlSayyad, "Cairo: Bayn al-Qasrayn, the Street between the Two Palaces," in *Streets: Critical Perspectives on Public Space,* ed. Zeynep Çelik, Diane Favro, and Richard Ingersoll (Berkeley: University of California Press, 1994), 71–82.

32 Mubarak, *Al-khutat,* 1:44.

33 Today the street is named Mu'izz Li Din Illah.

34 Jason Thompson, *A History of Egypt: From Earliest Times to the Present* (Cairo: American University in Cairo Press, 2008), 178.

35 Ibid., 178.

36 Ibid., 179.

37 Maqrizi, *Al-Mawa'ez,* 2:245.

38 Ibid.

39 At roughly 110 by 103 meters in plan. Jonathan Bloom, "The Mosque of al-Hakim in Cairo," *Muqarnas* 1 (1983): 15–36.

40 Zaki, *Al-Qahirah,* 20.

41 Bloom, "Mosque of al-Hakim," 25.

42 Mubarak, *Al-khutat,* 1:46.

43 Irene A. Bierman, *Writing Signs: The Fatimid Public Text (*Berkeley: University of California Press, 1998), 100–132; Caroline Williams, "The Cult of Ali Saints in the Fatimid Monuments of Cairo. Part I: The Mosque of al-Aqmar," *Muqarnas* 1 (1983): 37–52.

44 Bierman, *Writing Signs.*

45 Ibid.

46 Ibid.

47 Behrens-Abouseif, *Islamic Architecture in Cairo,* 76–77.

48 Nasir-i Khusraw and Wheeler M. Thackston, *Nasir-i Khusraw's Book of Travels: Safarnamah,* trans. W. M. Thackston (Costa Mesa, Calif.: Mazda, 2001), 60.

49 Ibid., 59, 67.

50 Abu-Lughod, *Cairo,* 24.

51 Yaacov Lev, "Army, Regime and Society in Fatimid Egypt, 968–1094," *International Journal of Middle Eastern Studies* 19, no. 3 (1987): 337–366.

52 Khusraw and Thackston, *Khusraw's Book of Travels,* 57.

53 Ibid.

54 Nezar AlSayyad, ed., *Forms of Dominance: On the Architecture and Urbanism of the Colonial Enterprise* (Aldershot, UK: Avebury, 1992), 34–40.

55 Abu-Lughod, *Cairo,* 23.

56 S. J. Staffa, *Conquest and Fusion: The Social Evolution of Cairo, 642–1850* (Leiden: Brill, 1977), 157.

57 Abu-Lughod, *Cairo,* 29.

58 G. Scanlon, "Recent Archeological Work in Fustat," paper submitted to the American Research Center in Egypt annual meeting, Boston, March 1981.

59 Maqrizi, *Al-Mawa'ez,* 2:28.

60 For a detailed discussion on the disintegration of the original Fatimid plan at the end of its rule, refer to Nezar AlSayyad, "Space in an Islamic City," *Journal of Architecture and Planning Research* 4, no. 2 (1987): 108–119; and AlSayyad, *Streets of Islamic Cairo.*

61 Ayman Fuad Sayyid, *La Capitale de l'Égypte jusqu'à l'époque fatimide Al-Qahira et Al-Fustat: Essai de reconstitution topographique* (Beirut: Orient-Institut der Deutschen Morgenländischen Wissenschaft, 1998), 285–290.

More information can be found in Wladyslaw Kubiak, "The Burning of Misr al-Fustat in 1168: A Reconsideration of Historical Evidence," *Africana Bulletin* (Warsaw) 25 (1976): 51–64. For a discussion that dismisses the extent of the Fustat burning, see André Raymond, *Cairo* (Cambridge, Mass.: Harvard University Press, 2000), *75–77.*

62 Sayyid, *La Capitale de l'Égypte,* 285–290.

63 Ibid.

5. Fortress Cairo

1 Winifred Holmes, *She Was Queen of Egypt: Hatshepsut, Nefertiti, Cleopatra, Shagaret el dor* (London: G. Bell, 1959), 137. *Shagarat al-Durr* is the transliteration of her name from Egyptian Arabic. Her name is also spelled *Shajarat al-Durr,* following the transliterated modern standard Arabic. Egyptian has a corollary to the consonant *g,* whereas in other Arabic dialects it is pronounced as a *j.*

2 Ibid., 140.

3 The origin of the name *Bahri Mamluks* is contested. *Bahri* might have meant "of the sea" in reference to the Nile. Alternatively, Gamal al-Shayal argues that the term could have indicated "the land behind the sea." His hypothesis rests on the fact that the Mamluks came from Turkey using marine routes. As further support for this view, al-Shayal argues that there were other groups existing in Yemen, also called Bahri Mamluks. For more details, see Gamal al-Shayal, *Tarikh Misr al-Islamiya* (Cairo: Dar al-Ma'aref, 1967), 2:145.

4 Ibid., 135.

5 Ibid., 149.

6 Max Rodenbeck, *Cairo: The City Victorious* (New York: Knopf, 1999), 58.

7 Today the house is a museum and cultural center open to the public, where possessions of Louis IX and other artifacts from the time of the Crusade are on display.

8 Holmes, *She Was Queen,* 167.

9 Ibid., 170.

10 Scholars believe that Shagarat al-Durr and her husband Aybak sponsored a public ceremony to move the body of al-Salih from the island of Rawdah to the mausoleum that Shagarat al-Durr had built for him in Bayn al-Qasrayn. For more details, see al-Shayal, *Tarikh Misr al-Islamiya,* 2:152.

11 Nasser Rabbat, *The Citadel of Cairo: A New Interpretation of Royal Mamluk Architecture* (New York: Brill, 1995), 5.

12 Ibid., 8.

13 Janet Abu-Lughod, *Cairo: 1001 Years of the City Victorious* (Princeton: Princeton University Press, 1971), 27.

14 Rabbat, *The Citadel of Cairo,* 9.

15 Ibid., 16.

16 Richard Yeomans, *Art and Architecture of Islamic Cairo* (Reading, UK: Garnet, 2008), 107.

17 Ibid., 118.

18 Rabbat, *The Citadel of Cairo,* 55.

19 Bab al-Qarafa and Burg al-Imam have undergone several restorations and today are both in relatively good condition. The original Bab al-Qarafa no longer exists, but an Ottoman gate bearing the same name has replaced it.

Burg al-Imam used to be connected to a bridge that spanned the moat. The principal gate, Bab al-Mudarraj, is today flanked by the mosque of Muhammad Ali, dating from the early nineteenth century, and by the original Ayyubid walls. For more, see ibid., 69.

20 Although it carries the same name, the Ottoman gate is not located in the same place as the original gate. It is unknown where the original Bab al-Qarafa was located. For more details, see ibid.

21 Yeomans, *Art and Architecture,* 108.

22 Ibid., 81, 109.

23 Rabbat, *The Citadel of Cairo,* 75.

24 Ibid., 74.

25 Al-Kamil chose to fortify the Citadel instead of the cities of Fustat and al-Qahira once he realized such an arrangement was more financially feasible. For more, see ibid., 75.

26 Today the Citadel is divided between its northern and southern enclosures, which were built in different periods, as evidenced in their distinctive styles and techniques of construction. Some portions include walls that date from the post-Ottoman period. Initially the walls extended from Burg al-Wastani to Burg al-Muqattam at the juncture between the two enclosures. Creswell, in *A Short Account of Early Muslim Architecture* (Beirut: Libraire du liban, 1958), suggests that the wall south of Burg al Muqattam, extending toward Yusuf's well, might be part of the original fortification. For more, see Rabbat, *The Citadel of Cairo,* 59.

27 The edifices are no longer extant, having been demolished later by Sultan al-Nasir Muhammad. For more, see Caroline Williams, *Islamic Monuments in Cairo: A Practical Guide* (Cairo: American University in Cairo Press, 2002), 197.

28 Maqrizi, *Al-Mawa'ez wa al-I'tibar bi-Dhikr al-Khitat wa al-Athar* (Cairo: Bulaq Press, 1853), 1:110.

29 Abu-Lughod, *Cairo,* 30.

30 Maqrizi, *Al-Mawa'ez,* 2:362.

31 Abd al-Latif ibn Yuśuf al-Baghdadi, *Kitab al-Ifada wa al-I'tibar fi al-Ummour al-Meushadhad wa al-Hawadith al-M'aiyana bi-Ard Misr* (Cairo: Al-Migala al-Gadida, n.d.), 40.

32 Ibn Sa'id, *Kittab al-Maghreb fi Hiyla al-Maghreb* (Cairo: Cairo University Press, 1956), 45.

33 Nezar AlSayyad, "Cairo: Bayn al-Qasrayn, the Street between the Two Palaces," in *Streets: Critical Perspectives on Public Space,* ed. Zeynep Çelik, Diane Favro, and Richard Ingersoll (Berkeley: University of California Press, 1994), 71–82.

34 Rahman Zaki, *Al-Qahira, 969–1825* (Cairo: Al-Dar al-Misriya L'al-ta'lif wa al-Targama, 1966), 72.

35 Yeomans, *Art and Architecture,* 26.

36 Rodenbeck, *Cairo,* 49.

37 Yeomans, *Art and Architecture,* 114.

38 Doris Behrens-Abouseif, *Islamic Architecture in Cairo: An Introduction* (Cairo: American University in Cairo Press, 1996), 12.

39 Yeomans, *Art and Architecture,* 112.

40 Ibid., 11.

41 Ibid., 56.

42 Ibid., 12.

43 Doris Behrens-Abouseif, *Cairo of the Mamluks: A History of the Architecture and Its Culture* (London: Tauris, 2007), 116.

44 Yeomans, *Art and Architecture*, 118.

45 Very little of the south wing of the madrasa has survived. There still remains a part of the façade that connects to the north wing, which is in much better condition. The north iwan of the madrasa had three mihrabs, as well as its original vaulted ceiling.

46 Behrens-Abouseif, *Islamic Architecture in Cairo*, 12.

47 Yeomans, *Art and Architecture*, 116.

48 The door is known today as Harat al-Salihiya.

49 Desmond Stewart, *Cairo: 5500 Years* (New York: Crowell, 1968), 106.

50 Holmes, *She Was Queen*, 174.

6. The Bahri Mamluks

1 Ibn Khaldun, as cited in Jason Thompson, *A History of Egypt: From Earliest Times to the Present* (Cairo: American University in Cairo Press, 2008), 200.

2 Ibn Khaldun, as cited in Gaston Wiet, *Cairo: City of Art and Commerce,* trans. Seymour Feiler (Norman: University of Oklahoma Press, 1964), 63.

3 Anne Wolff, *How Many Miles to Babylon? Travels and Adventures to Egypt and Beyond, 1300 to 1640* (Liverpool: Liverpool University Press, 2003), 14.

4 Ibn Khaldun, as cited in Mohammad Abdullah Enan, *Ibn Khaldun: His Life and Work* (Lahore: Shaik Muhammad Ashraf, 1944), 122, 123.

5 Janet Abu-Lughod, *Cairo: 1001 Years of the City Victorious* (Princeton: Princeton University Press, 1971), 32.

6 Thompson, *A History of Egypt,* 190.

7 Gamal al-Shayal, *Tarikh Misr al-Islamiya* (Cairo: Dar al-Ma'aref, 1967), 2:161–170.

8 Ibid., 191.

9 Richard Yeomans, *Art and Architecture of Islamic Cairo* (Reading, UK: Garnet, 2008), 127.

10 Doris Behrens-Abouseif, *Cairo of the Mamluks: A History of the Architecture and Its Culture* (London: Tauris, 2007), 119.

11 Abu-Lughod, *Cairo,* 32.

12 Yeomans, *Art and Architecture,* 127.

13 J. Bloom, "The Mosque of Baybars," unpublished paper submitted to the American Research Center in Egypt annual meeting, Boston, March 1981.

14 Behrens-Abouseif, *Cairo of the Mamluks,* 121, 122.

15 Ibid., 124.

16 Only fragments of Baybars's madrasa survive today, but some facts about its architecture are known through Maqrizi's accounts.

17 Yeomans, *Art and Architecture,* 130.

18 Behrens-Abouseif, *Cairo of the Mamluks,* 134.

19 Maqrizi writes that many religious buildings were brought to life through similarly controversial means. For more on Maqrizi's commentary, see Doris Behrens-Abouseif, *Islamic Architecture in Cairo: An Introduction* (Cairo: American University in Cairo Press, 1996), 96.

20 Behrens-Abouseif, *Cairo of the Mamluks,* 134.

21 Creswell, in *A Short Account of Early Muslim Architecture* (Beirut: Libraire du liban, 1958), connected the shape of Qalawun's windows to a similar example found in the Sicilian cathedral of Monreale, built during the Norman period. For more, see Behrens-Abouseif, *Cairo of the Mamluks,* 135.

22 Behrens-Abouseif, *Islamic Architecture in Cairo,* 98.

23 Only a portion of the monument exists today. Its current entrance was created out of an existing window; its former entrance was transformed in the eighteenth century by Amir 'Abd al-Rahman Kathuda.

24 Behrens-Abouseif, *Cairo of the Mamluks,* 140.

25 The present dome is a restoration from 1903, carried out by the Comité, the organization in charge of conserving Islamic monuments at the time.

26 During Maqrizi's time, this ceremony was still performed. For more, see Behrens-Abouseif, *Cairo of the Mamluks,* 138.

27 The area of the mausoleum is 21 meters by 23 meters; the area of the madrasa is 17.5 meters by 15.5 meters. See ibid.

28 The building has not survived, but a few remains indicate that it was located at the end of the passage separating the madrasa from the mausoleum.

29 Behrens-Abouseif, *Islamic Architecture in Cairo,* 96.

30 Rosskeen Gibb, Ibn Batuta, and Hamilton Alexander, *Travels in Asia and Africa, 1325–1354* (New York: R. M. McBride, 1929), 50.

31 The waqf deed of the hospital of Qalawun, as reproduced in Wiet, *Cairo,* 128.

32 Ibid., 50.

33 Wolff, *How Many Miles,* 17.

34 Ibid., 18.

35 Thompson, *A History of Egypt,* 192.

36 The restored house of the amir Taz is today located in the vicinity of the mosque of Ibn Tulun.

37 Thompson, *A History of Egypt,* 192.

38 Max Rodenbeck, *Cairo: The City Victorious* (New York: Knopf, 1999), 67.

39 Ibn-Battuta, *Travels in Asia and Africa, 1325–1354,* trans. Hamilton Alexander Rosskeen Gibb (London: Routledge, 2005), 50.

40 Maqrizi, *Al-Mawa'ez wa al-I'tibar bi-Dhikr al-Khitat wa al-Athar* (Cairo: Bulaq Press, 1853), 2:145.

41 Abu-Lughod, *Cairo,* 48.

42 Behrens-Abouseif, *Cairo of the Mamluks,* 152.

43 Ibid., 154.

44 Ibid.

45 The mosque of al-Nasir also served as the seat of government until the Ottoman period.

46 Abu-Lughod, *Cairo,* 37.

47 Maqrizi, *Al-Mawa'ez,* 2:95.

48 Maqrizi, as cited in André Raymond, *Cairo* (Cambridge, Mass.: Harvard University Press, 2000), 140.

49 Ibid., 141.

50 Ibid., 142.

51 Ibid., 140.

52 Only one of the original minarets has survived. The other collapsed in 1659; its dome collapsed two years later.

53 Yeomans, *Art and Architecture,* 157.

54 Rodenbeck, *Cairo,* 68.

55 Susan Jane Staffa, *Conquest and Fusion: The Social Evolution of Cairo, 642–1850* (Leiden: Brill, 1977), 221.

56 Maqrizi, *Al-Mawa'ez,* 2:95.

57 L. C. Brown, introduction to *From Medina to Metropolis,* ed. L. C. Brown (Princeton: Darwin Press, 1966), 35.

58 Ibid., 34.

59 Staffa, *Conquest and Fusion,* 161.

60 A. A. Al-Shami, "Urban Geography of the Arabs," *Alam Al-Fikr* (Kuwait) 11 (1980): 144.

61 Raymond, *Cairo,* 152.

62 M. M. Amin, *The Waqf and the Social Life in Egypt* (Cairo: Dar al-Nahada al-Arabia, 1980), 148.

63 Ibid., 316.

64 Abu-Lughod, *Cairo,* 37.

65 Brown, *From Medina to Metropolis,* 35.

66 Al-Shami, "Urban Geography," 148.

67 Nezar AlSayyad, *Streets of Islamic Cairo* (Cambridge, Mass.: Aga Khan Program for Islamic Architecture, 1981), 36.

68 Raymond, *Cairo,* 122.

69 Rahman Zaki, *Al-Qahirah, 969–1825* (Cairo: Al-Dar al-Mesriyah L-lta'lif wa al-Targamah, 1966), 160.

70 S. L. Mustafa, *Al-Turath al-Mi'emari al-Islami fi Misr* (Beirut: Arab University Press, 1977), 46.

71 Ibid., 39.

72 Abu-Lughod, *Cairo,* 31.

73 Ibn Khaldun, as cited in Enan, *Ibn Khaldun,* 69.

74 Morimoto Kosei, "What Ibn Khaldun Saw: The Judiciary of Mamluk Egypt," *Mamluk Studies Review* (Middle East Documentation Center, University of Chicago) 6 (2002): 109–131.

75 Enan, *Ibn Khaldun,* 69.

76 Ibn Khaldun, as cited in ibid., 107.

77 Nasser Rabbat, "Who Was al-Maqrizi?" *Mamluk Studies Review* (Middle East Documentation Center, University of Chicago) 7 (2003): 1–19.

78 Ibn Khaldun, as cited in Thompson, *A History of Egypt,* 201.

7. Governing from the Tower

1 Richard Yeomans, *Art and Architecture of Islamic Cairo* (Reading, UK: Garnet, 2008), 199.

2 Gaston Wiet, *Cairo: City of Art and Commerce,* trans. Seymour Feiler (Norman: University of Oklahoma Press, 1964), 101.

3 Max Rodenbeck, *Cairo: The City Victorious* (New York: Knopf, 1999), 86.

4 Nairi Hampikian, "Medievalization of the Old City as an Ingredient of Cairo's Modernization: Case Study of Bab Zuwayla," in *Making Cairo Medieval,* ed. Nezar AlSayyad, Irene A. Bierman, and Nasser Rabbat (New York: Lexington Books, 2005), 206.

5 Hasan Abdel-Wahab, *Derasat an al-Maqrizi,* On the House of Maqrizi, (Cairo: al-Dar al-Masriya, 1971), 75.

6 Nasser Rabbat, "Who Was al-Maqrizi? A Biographical Sketch," *Mamluk Stud-*

ies Review (Middle East Documentation Center, University of Chicago) 7 (2003): 10.

7 Maqrizi, as cited in Mohammad Abdullah Enan, *Ibn Khaldun: His Life and Work* (Lahore: Shaik Muhammad Ashraf, 1944), 101.

8 Rabbat, "Who Was al-Maqrizi?" 6.

9 Ibid., 7.

10 Ibid., 11.

11 Ibid., 4–5.

12 Abdel-Wahab, *Derasat an al-Maqrizi,* 41.

13 Ibid., 44.

14 Doris Behrens-Abouseif, *Cairo of the Mamluks: A History of the Architecture and Its Culture* (London: Tauris, 2007), 12.

15 Ibid., 20.

16 Ira M. Lapidus, ed., *Middle Eastern Cities* (Berkeley: University of California Press, 1969), 87.

17 Behrens-Abouseif, *Cairo of the Mamluks,* 225.

18 Yeomans, *Art and Architecture,* 199.

19 Leonardo Frescobaldi, cited in Leonardo Frescobaldi, Giorgio Gucci, and Simone Sigoli, *Visit to the Holy Places of Egypt, Sinai, Palestine, and Syria in 1384* (Jerusalem: Franciscan Press, 1948), 46.

20 Ibid., 44.

21 Ibid., 45.

22 Janet Abu-Lughod, *Cairo: 1001 Years of the City Victorious* (Princeton: Princeton University Press, 1971), 38.

23 Maqrizi, *Al-Mawa'ez wa al-I'tibar bi-Dhikr al-Khitat wa al-Athar* (Cairo: Bulaq Press, 1853), 2:95.

24 Behrens-Abouseif, *Cairo of the Mamluks,* 11–12.

25 Ibid., 225.

26 Ibid., 229.

27 Yeomans, *Art and Architecture,* 201.

28 Behrens-Abouseif, *Cairo of the Mamluks,* 227.

29 Yeomans, *Art and Architecture,* 208.

30 Behrens-Abouseif, *Cairo of the Mamluks,* 239.

31 Ibid., 241.

32 The mosque fell into disrepair in the nineteenth century, and only the structures on the southeastern side of the complex have survived.

33 Behrens-Abouseif, *Cairo of the Mamluks,* 241.

34 Hampikian, "Medievalization," 206.

35 Yeomans, *Art and Architecture,* 208.

36 The shops are still present today.

37 The hypostyle prayer hall is the only one of the four original *riwaqs* to survive today; the others are reconstructions.

38 Behrens-Abouseif, *Cairo of the Mamluks,* 244.

39 Wiet, *Cairo,* 66.

40 Behrens-Abouseif, *Cairo of the Mamluks,* 5.

41 Maqrizi, as cited in Wiet, *Cairo,* 67.

42 Nasser Rabbat, *The Citadel of Cairo: A New Interpretation of Royal Mamluk Architecture* (New York: Brill, 1995), 293.

43 Behrens-Abouseif, *Cairo of the Mamluks,* 63.

44 Ibid., 294.

45 Ira M. Lapidus, *Muslim Cities in the Later Middle Ages* (Cambridge, Mass.: Harvard University Press, 1967), 118–122.

46 Ibid., 123–127.

47 André Raymond, *Cairo* (Cambridge, Mass.: Harvard University Press, 2000), 173.

48 Ibid., 172.

49 Ibid., 173.

50 Jonathan Berkey, "The Muhtasibs of Cairo under the Mamluks: Toward an Understanding of an Islamic Institution," in *The Mamluks in Egyptian and Syrian Politics and Society,* ed. Michael Winter and Amalia Levanoni (Leiden: Brill, 2004), 254.

51 Ibid., 246. It is not known whether the Greek term was in use in the region prior to the Arab conquest.

52 Ibid., 248–249.

53 Ibid., 254.

54 Yeomans, *Art and Architecture,* 219.

55 P. M. Holt, "Literary Offerings, a Genre of Courtly Literature," in *The Mamluks in Egyptian Politics and Society,* ed. Thomas Philipp and Ulrich Haarmann (Cambridge: Cambridge University Press, 1998), 13.

56 Behrens-Abouseif, *Cairo of the Mamluks,* 275.

57 This dome typology is encountered in the star domes of Barsbay.

58 Behrens-Abouseif, *Cairo of the Mamluks,* 276.

59 Ibid., 290.

60 Desmond Stewart, *Cairo: 5500 Years* (New York: Crowell, 1968), 137.

61 Behrens-Abouseif, *Cairo of the Mamluks,* 295.

62 Yeomans, *Art and Architecture,* 229.

63 Ibid., 232.

64 The dome collapsed in the nineteenth century. Its lapis-blue tiles were described in waqf documents. For more, see Behrens-Abouseif, *Cairo of the Mamluks,* 297.

65 Ibid., 295, 296.

66 The roof no longer exists, but it is mentioned in the waqf deed. It is also pictured in an engraving by David Roberts in his portfolio *Travels in Egypt and the Holy Land.*

67 Two reconstruction efforts followed in later centuries after the last dome collapsed in the nineteenth century. For more, see Behrens-Abouseif, *Cairo of the Mamluks,* 297.

68 Yeomans, *Art and Architecture,* 229.

69 Behrens-Abouseif, *Cairo of the Mamluks,* 298.

70 Yeomans, *Art and Architecture,* 230.

71 Raymond, *Cairo,* 155.

72 Ibid., 158.

73 Yeomans, *Art and Architecture,* 230.

74 Ibid., 231.

75 Wiet, *Cairo,* 117.

76 Maqrizi, *Al-Mawa'ez,* 1:120.

77 S. L. Mustafa, *Al-Turath al-Mi'emari al-Islami fi Misr* (Beirut: Arab University Press, 1977), 46.

78 Nezar AlSayyad, *Streets of Islamic Cairo* (Cambridge, Mass.: Aga Khan Program for Islamic Architecture, 1981), 58.

79 Ibid.

80 Mustafa, *Al-Turath*, 92.

81 AlSayyad, *Streets of Islamic Cairo*, 58.

82 Behrens-Abouseif, *Cairo of the Mamluks*, 27.

83 Jason Thompson, *A History of Egypt: From Earliest Times to the Present* (Cairo: American University in Cairo Press, 2008), 205.

84 Yeomans, *Art and Architecture*, 232.

85 Wiet, *Cairo*, 156.

86 Thompson, *A History of Egypt*, 205.

87 Wiet, *Cairo*, 156.

88 Rabbat, "Who Was al-Maqrizi?" 17.

89 Ibid., 19.

90 Nasser Rabbat, "The Medieval Link: Maqrizi's *Khitat* and Modern Narratives of Cairo," in AlSayyad, Bierman, and Rabbat, *Making Cairo Medieval*, 31.

91 Ibid., 32.

8. A Provincial Capital under Ottoman Rule

1 Jason Thompson, *A History of Egypt: From Earliest Times to the Present* (Cairo: American University in Cairo Press, 2008), 213.

2 Paula Sanders, *Creating Medieval Cairo: Empire, Religion, and Architectural Preservation in Nineteenth-Century Egypt* (Cairo: American University in Cairo Press, 2008), 30.

3 Ibid., 208.

4 Doris Behrens-Abouseif, *Cairo of the Mamluks: A History of the Architecture and Its Culture* (London: Tauris, 2007), 312.

5 Ibid., 313.

6 On the mosque's northern side, a sabil-kuttab with a separate entryway was added by amir Janim al-Hamzawi, who enlarged the original endowment made by Khair Bey. See ibid., 312.

7 Ibid., 313.

8 Nezar AlSayyad, *Cities and Caliphs: On the Genesis of Arab Muslim Urbanism* (New York: Greenwood Press, 1991), 14.

9 Thompson, *A History of Egypt*, 209.

10 Doris Behrens-Abouseif, *Egypt's Adjustment to Ottoman Rule: Institutions, Waqf and Architecture in Cairo, 16th and 17th Centuries* (New York: Brill, 1994), 53.

11 Only Suleyman Pasha (1525–1538) and Dawud Pasha (1538–1549) managed to retain power for relatively longer periods of time. For more, see André Raymond, *Cairo* (Cambridge, Mass.: Harvard University Press, 2000), 192.

12 Ibid., 195.

13 Thompson, *A History of Egypt*, 211–213.

14 The Mosque of Sinan was restored in 1983.

15 Caroline Williams, *Islamic Monuments in Cairo: A Practical Guide* (Cairo: American University in Cairo Press, 2002), 228.

16 Ibid.

17 Thompson, *A History of Egypt*, 213.

18 Raymond, *Cairo*, 237.

19 The upper units were restored in 2003 by the Supreme Council of Antiquities.

Nicholas Warner, *The Monuments of Historic Cairo: A Map and Descriptive Catalogue* (Cairo: American University in Cairo Press, 2005), 156.

20 Over time, carpentry workshops took over the courtyard of the palace.

21 Warner, *Monuments of Historic Cairo*, 126.

22 Ibid., 214–215

23 Raymond, *Cairo*, 215.

24 Thompson, *A History of Egypt*, 217.

25 Abu al-Dahab and Ali Bey al-Kabir sought to restore Mamluk power. For more, see Williams, *Islamic Monuments in Cairo*, 156.

26 Ibid.

27 Thompson, *A History of Egypt*, 211.

28 Max Rodenbeck, *Cairo: The City Victorious* (New York: Knopf, 1999), 206.

29 Ibid., 188.

30 Williams, *Islamic Monuments in Cairo*, 173.

31 Janet Abu-Lughod, Cairo: *1001 Years of the City Victorious* (Princeton: Princeton University Press, 1971), 48.

32 Ibid., 51.

33 Susan Jane Staffa, *Conquest and Fusion: The Social Evolution of Cairo, A.D. 642–1850* (Leiden: Brill, 1972), 260.

34 Ibid., 268.

35 For a more detailed discussion of the haras, refer to Raymond, *Cairo*, 159.

36 This is an estimate made by the writers of *Description de l'Egypte*. For more, see Raymond, *Cairo*, 210.

37 Ibid., 211.

38 Ibid., 273.

39 The current entrance, along with a substantial part of the structure, is a nineteenth-century reconstruction. The house was restored by the Mission de Sauvegarde des Monuments du Caire Islamique of the Institut Francais d'Archéologie Orientale and by the Supreme Council of Antiquities. It is now open to the public for special events and concerts. Warner, *Monuments of Historic Cairo*, 156.

40 Williams, *Islamic Monuments in Cairo*, 201.

41 Ibid., 202.

42 Warner, *Monuments of Historic Cairo*, 269.

43 Ibid., 275.

44 Behrens-Abouseif, *Adjustment to Ottoman Rule*, 227.

45 Sanders, *Creating Medieval Cairo*, 31.

46 Ibid., 53.

47 J. Thevenot, *The Travels of Monsieur de Thevenot into the Levant*, trans. A. Lowell, part 1, vol. 2 (London: H. Clark, 1686), 128.

48 Warner, *Monuments of Historic Cairo*, 10.

49 Raymond, *Cairo*, 271.

50 Staffa, *Conquest and Fusion*, 264. There were some major streets, but for the most part thoroughfares were few and typically heavily congested. The minor changes in street composition that took place under the Ottoman regime indicate that the structure of the city had largely stabilized. Thus, Ali Mubarak's description of the streets of Cairo in his *Al-Khitat al-Tawfiqiyya al-Jadida*, published in 1888, differs little from the map produced for the Napoleonic *Description de l'Egypte,* or from a modern-day street map.

9. A Changing City

1 André Raymond, *Cairo* (Cambridge, Mass.: Harvard University Press, 2000), 195.

2 Geoffrey Roper, "Texts from Nineteenth-Century Egypt: The Role of E. W. Lane," in *Travelers in Egypt,* ed. Paul Starkey and Janet Starkey (London: Tauris Parke Paperbacks, 2001), 244.

3 Stanley Lane-Poole, the nephew of Edward William Lane, continued the latter's work on the *Arabic English Lexicon.* He later became a prominent Orientalist, and his brother, Reginald Lane-Poole, became a medievalist historian. For more, see Paula Sanders, *Creating Medieval Cairo: Empire, Religion, and Architectural Preservation in Nineteenth-Century Egypt* (Cairo: American University in Cairo Press, 2008), 93.

4 Napoleon's "Proclamation to the Egyptians," as cited in Raymond, *Cairo,* 215.

5 Max Rodenbeck, *Cairo: The City Victorious* (New York: Knopf, 1999), 118.

6 Napoleon, as cited in Desmond Stewart, *Cairo: 5500 Years* (New York: Crowell, 1968), 173.

7 Ibid., 119.

8 Al-Jabarti, as cited in Rodenbeck, *Cairo,* 119.

9 Ibid., 174.

10 Robert L. Tignor, introduction to Sheikh al-Jabarti, *Napoleon in Egypt: Al-Jabarti's Chronicle of the French Occupation, 1798* (New York: Markus Wiener, 1993), 7.

11 Desmond Stewart, *Cairo: Great Mother of the World* (Cairo: American University in Cairo Press, 1996), 177.

12 Juan Cole, *Napoleon's Egypt: Invading the Middle East* (London: Palgrave Macmillan, 2007), 127.

13 Abdal Rahman Zaki, *Al-Qahira, 969–1825* (Cairo: Al-Dar al-Misriya L'al-ta'lif wa al-Targama, 1966), 253.

14 Cole, *Napoleon's Egypt,* 126.

15 Napoleon, cited in ibid.

16 Ibid., 130.

17 Ibid., 257, 259.

18 Al-Jabarti, *Napoleon in Egypt,* 108.

19 Zaki, *Al-Qahira,* 151–152.

20 Today the remains of this building are part of a complex of government buildings occupied by the Egyptian consulate council.

21 Al-Jabarti, *Napoleon in Egypt,* 111.

22 Ibid., 109–111.

23 Rodenbeck, *Cairo,* 122.

24 Ibid., 107.

25 Ibid., 257.

26 Ibid., 264.

27 Jason Thompson, *A History of Egypt: From Earliest Times to the Present* (Cairo: American University in Cairo Press, 2008), 221.

28 Ibid., 221.

29 Ibid., 222.

30 Henry Laurens, Charles C. Gillispie, Jean-Claude Golvin, and Claude Traunecker, *L'Expédition d'Egypte: 1789–1801* (Paris: Armand Colin, 1989), 199.

31 Ibid., 278.

32 Letitia Wheeler Ufford, *The Pasha: How Mehemet Ali Defied the West, 1839–1841* (Jefferson: McFarland and Co., 2007).

33 Nevine Yousry, *Kismet: The Incredible Destiny of Muhammad Ali* (Cairo: L'Orientale, 2005), 20–36.

34 Ibid.

35 Thompson, *A History of Egypt,* 225.

36 Ibid., 226.

37 Raymond, *Cairo,* 306.

38 Agnieszka Dobrowolska and Khaled Fahmy, *Muhammad Ali Pasha and His Sabil* (Cairo: American University in Cairo Press, 2004), 50.

39 Edward William Lane, *Manners and Customs of the Modern Egyptians* (London: East-West, 1989), 115.

40 Rodenbeck, *Cairo,* 128.

41 Roper, "Texts," 246.

42 Edward Said has called into question Lane's ethics as an ethnographer; he also criticizes Lane's adoption of Egyptian customs and his position as a mediator and translator of Egyptian and Muslim behavior as an act of bad faith. For more, see Edward Said, *Orientalism* (New York: Vintage Books, 1979), 159–163.

43 Caroline Williams, "Nineteenth-Century Images of Cairo: From the Real to the Interpretative," in *Making Cairo Medieval,* ed. Nezar AlSayyad, Irene A. Bierman, and Nasser Rabbat (New York: Lexington Books, 2005), 102.

44 Ibid., 103.

45 Ibid., 105.

46 Florence Nightingale, *Letters from Egypt: A Journey on the Nile, 1849–1850* (New York: Weidenfeld and Nicholson, 1987), 32.

47 Ibid., 40.

48 Anthony Sattin, introduction to Nightingale's *Letters from Egypt,* 16.

49 Ibid., 113.

50 Ibid., 116.

51 R. R. Madden, as cited in Stewart, *Cairo,* 190.

52 Janet Abu-Lughod, *Cairo: 1001 Years of the City Victorious* (Princeton: Princeton University Press, 1971), 95.

53 Ibid., 96.

54 Ibid., 92–93.

55 Raymond, *Cairo,* 264.

56 Sanders, *Creating Medieval Cairo,* 31.

57 Thompson, *A History of Egypt,* 228.

58 Ibid.

59 Caroline Williams, *Islamic Monuments in Cairo: A Practical Guide* (Cairo: American University in Cairo Press, 2002), 200.

60 The second mihrab was a gift from King Faruq.

61 Napoleon Bonaparte, as cited in Stewart, *Cairo,* 172.

62 Roper, "Texts," 251.

63 Ibid., 252.

10. **Modernizing the New, Medievalizing the Old**

1 André Raymond, *Cairo* (Cambridge, Mass.: Harvard University Press, 2000), 315.

2 Ibid.

3 The cotton boom in Egypt was precipitated by the American Civil War. The war had cut off cotton supplies to Europe, creating a shortage that increased the price of Egyptian cotton. For a more detailed explanation, see Janet Abu-Lughod, *Cairo: 1001 Years of the City Victorious* (Princeton: Princeton University Press, 1971), 103.

4 Robert Hunter, *Egypt under the Khedives, 1805–1879: From Household Government to Modern Bureaucracy* (Pittsburgh: University of Pittsburgh Press, 1984), 70.

5 Abu-Lughod, *Cairo,* 95.

6 Raymond, *Cairo,* 307.

7 The original Shepheard's Hotel burned down in the great Cairo fire of 1952. See Abu-Lughod, *Cairo,* 100.

8 Ibid., 102.

9 These barracks were built on the site where Napoleon's troops had been stationed. It later became the site of the Nile Hilton Hotel.

10 Abu-Lughod, *Cairo,* 103.

11 Georges Douin, *Histoire du règne du Khédive Ismaïl* (Rome: Istituto Poligrafico dello Stato per la Reale Società di Geografia d'Egitto, 1933), 5–8.

12 Original correspondence between Ismail and Baron Haussmann is currently housed in the Cairo National Archive.

13 Raymond, *Cairo,* 312.

14 Timothy Mitchell, *Colonising Egypt* (Berkeley: University of California Press, 1988), 4.

15 Zeynep Çelik, *Displaying the Orient: Architecture of Islam at Nineteenth-Century World's Fairs* (Berkeley: University of California Press, 1992), 32–34.

16 Nezar AlSayyad, "Ali Mubarak's Cairo: Between the Testimony of 'Allamudin and the Imaginary of the Khitat," in *Making Cairo Medieval,* ed. Nezar AlSayyad, Irene A. Bierman, and Nasser Rabbat (New York: Lexington Books, 2005), 51–52.

17 Ibid., 53.

18 Ibid., 54.

19 Abu-Lughod, *Cairo,* 106.

20 Raymond, *Cairo,* 315.

21 Abu-Lughod, *Cairo,* 107.

22 For more, see Heba Farouk Ahmed, "Pre-Colonial Modernity: The State and the Making of Nineteenth-Century Cairo's Urban Form" (PhD diss., University of California, Berkeley, 2001), 110.

23 Raymond, *Cairo,* 315.

24 Nicholas Warner, ed., *An Egyptian Panorama: Reports from the Nineteenth-Century British Press* (Cairo: Zeitouna, 1994), 66.

25 Today the palace is flanked by two modern tower structures and is part of the Gezira Marriott Hotel.

26 Abu-Lughod, *Cairo,* 108.

27 Max Rodenbeck, *Cairo: The City Victorious* (New York: Knopf, 1999), 132–133.

28 Abu-Lughod, *Cairo,* 113.

29 Raymond, *Cairo,* 316.

30 Mitchell, *Colonising Egypt,* 137.

31 Text from the British periodical *Graphic,* July 1, 1882, as cited in Warner, *An Egyptian Panorama,* 105.

32 Abu-Lughod, *Cairo,* 113.

33 Warner, *An Egyptian Panorama,* 109.

34 AlSayyad, "Ali Mubarak's Cairo," 57.

35 Ibid., 62.

36 Paula Sanders, *Creating Medieval Cairo: Empire, Religion, and Architectural Preservation in Nineteenth-Century Egypt* (Cairo: American University in Cairo Press, 2008), 84.

37 Ibid., 38.

38 Francis Frith, as cited in Douglas R. Nickel, *Francis Frith in Egypt and Palestine: A Victorian Photographer Abroad* (Princeton: Princeton University Press, 2004), 10.

39 The travel notes, impressions, and photographs that resulted from his encounter with the Orient were later published in both Britain and the United States, giving him notoriety in the realm of photography. Frith became one of the most prominent professional photographers in Victorian England, and his nearly five hundred photographs resulting from his expeditions to Egypt, Palestine, Syria, and Lebanon were met with critical acclaim and great public interest, which brought him considerable financial reward. For a more detailed discussion, see ibid.

40 By the end of British rule, the population reached 1,312,000 inhabitants. For more, see Raymond, *Cairo,* 319.

41 Abu-Lughod, *Cairo,* 115.

42 Ibid., 142.

43 The Dawawin area runs along today's Shari al-Qasr al-Ayni.

44 Abu-Lughod, *Cairo,* 116.

45 This district later became the famed and fashionable area known as Zamalek.

46 Raymond, *Cairo,* 331.

47 Ibid., 318.

48 Rodenbeck, *Cairo,* 138.

49 Jason Thompson, *A History of Egypt: From Earliest Times to the Present* (Cairo: American University in Cairo Press, 2008), 274.

50 Ibid., 276.

51 Rodenbeck, *Cairo,* 157.

11. The Arab Republic and the City of Nasser

1 Max Rodenbeck, *Cairo: The City Victorious* (New York: Knopf, 1999), 171.

2 The Nile Hilton was designed by the American firm Welton Beckett.

3 The building that houses the Arab League was designed and built in the late 1940s. Although its aesthetic is unmistakably Arab and Islamic, some aspects of its forms and proportions are similar to Italian fascist buildings.

4 Robert St. John, *The Boss: The Story of Gamal Abdel Nasser* (New York: McGraw-Hill, 1960), 4–10.

5 Jason Thompson, *A History of Egypt: From Earliest Times to the Present* (Cairo: American University in Cairo Press, 2008), 293.

6 Ibid., 294.

7 Ibid., 294.

8 Ibid., 294–295.

9 Rodenbeck, *Cairo,* 171.

10 Akhil Gupta, "The Song of the Non-Aligned World," in *The Anthropology of Space and Place: Locating Culture,* ed. Setha Low and Denise Lawrence-Zuniga (Oxford: Blackwell, 2003), 324.

11 Thompson, *A History of Egypt,* 296.

12 Ibid., 299.

13 Ibid., 300.

14 Ibid., 296.

15 Ibid., 304.

16 Nasser, as cited in Miles Copeland, *The Game of Nations: The Amorality of Power Politics* (New York: Simon and Schuster, 1969), 177.

17 Ibid., 177–178.

18 Maria Golia, *Cairo: City of Sand* (London: Reaktion Books, 2004), 84.

19 Janet Abu-Lughod, *Cairo: 1001 Years of the City Victorious* (Princeton: Princeton University Press, 1971), 203.

20 Ibid., 204.

21 Shehata Issa Ibrahim, *Al-Qahira* (Cairo: Maktabit al-Ussra, 1999), 334.

22 Abu-Lughod, *Cairo,* 202.

23 Raymond, *Cairo,* 349.

24 Hrair Dekmejian, *Egypt under Nasir: A Study in Political Dynamics* (Albany: SUNY Press, 1971), 144–145.

25 Today the structure is somewhat run-down and serves as the headquarters of the National Democratic Party (NDP). This is the governing party and is as important in Egyptian contemporary politics as the ASU once was during Nasser's rule.

26 Thompson, *A History of Egypt,* 307.

27 Rodenbeck, *Cairo,* 176.

28 Ibid., 170.

29 Omnia El Sharki, "Cairo as Capital of the Socialist Revolution?" in *Cairo Cosmopolitan: Politics, Culture, and Urban Space in the New Globalized Middle East,* ed. Diane Singerman and Paul Amar (Cairo: American University in Cairo Press, 2006), 94.

30 Golia, *Cairo,* 84.

31 André Raymond, *Cairo* (Cambridge, Mass.: Harvard University Press, 2000), 342.

32 The urban planner Galila el-Kadi noted that between 1945 and 1982, urban development had taken over 8,900 hectares of farmland. See Raymond, *Cairo,* 343.

33 El Sharki, "Cairo," 84.

34 Abu-Lughod, *Cairo,* 196.

35 Ibid.

36 Muhammad Hammad, *Egypt Builds* (Cairo: Hansah, 1963), 64.

37 For more information on public housing in Cairo, see *The Housing Construction Industry in Egypt,* MIT/CU Technology Adaptation Program, multiple volumes, 1977–1982.

38 Abu-Lughod, *Cairo,* 218–219.

39 Ibid., 208.

40 Rodenbeck, *Cairo,* 172.

41 Raymond, *Cairo,* 348.

42 El Sharki, "Cairo," 85.

43 Abu-Lughod, *Cairo*, 217.

44 Raymond, *Cairo*, 348.

45 Rodenbeck, *Cairo*, 176.

46 Raymond, *Cairo*, 349.

47 Mahfouz wrote many novels about and set in Cairo. Indeed, an entire urban history of the city in the early part of the twentieth century can be told using his famous trilogy, whose novels are titled after actual streets in Cairo: *Palace Walk, Palace of Desire*, and *Sugar Street*. Mahfouz was awarded the Nobel Prize in Literature in 1988.

48 Thompson, *A History of Egypt*, 313.

49 Rodenbeck, *Cairo*, 171.

50 Thompson, *A History of Egypt*, 315.

51 Rodenbeck, *Cairo*, 173.

52 Thompson, *A History of Egypt*, 308.

12. Escaping the Present, Consuming the Past

1 Jason Thompson, *A History of Egypt: From Earliest Times to the Present* (Cairo: American University in Cairo Press, 2008), 338.

2 Nezar AlSayyad, "From Vernacularism to Globalism: The Temporal Reality of Traditional Settlements," *Traditional Dwellings and Settlements Review* 7, no. 1 (1995): 13–24.

3 Thomas W. Lippman, *Egypt after Nasser: Sadat, Peace and the Mirage of Prosperity* (New York: Paragon House, 1989), 220.

4 Anwar Sadat, as quoted in Lippman, *Egypt after Nasser*, 191.

5 Ibid.

6 Ibid., 318.

7 Ibid., 324.

8 Omnia El Sharki, "Cairo as Capital of the Socialist Revolution?" in *Cairo Cosmopolitan: Politics, Culture, and Urban Space in the New Globalized Middle East*, ed. Diane Singerman and Paul Amar (Cairo: American University in Cairo Press), 86.

9 André Raymond, *Cairo* (Cambridge, Mass.: Harvard University Press, 2000), 349.

10 Ibid., 350.

11 El Sharki, "Cairo," 87.

12 Ibid., 88.

13 Raymond, *Cairo*, 354.

14 El Sharki, "Cairo," 89.

15 Farha Ghannam, *Remaking the Modern: Space, Relocation and the Politics of Identity in a Global Cairo* (Berkeley: University of California Press, 2002), 2.

16 Farha Ghannam, "Keeping Him Connected: Globalization and the Production of Locality in Urban Egypt," in Singerman and Amar, *Cairo Cosmopolitan*, 254–255.

17 Ghannam, *Remaking the Modern*, 70.

18 Lippman, *Egypt after Nasser*, 221.

19 Raymond, *Cairo*, 351.

20 Ibid., 353.

21 Diane Singerman and Paul Amar, introduction to *Cairo Cosmopolitan*, 13.

22 Ibid., 16.

23 Diane Singerman, *Cairo Contested: Governance, Urban Space and Global Modernity* (Cairo: American University in Cairo Press, 2009), 7–8.

24 Asef Bayat and Eric Denis, "Who Is Afraid of Ashwaiyyat? Urban Change and Politics in Egypt," *Environment and Urbanization* 12, no. 2 (2000): 185–199.

25 Salwa Ismail, *Political Life in Cairo's New Quarters: Encountering the Everyday State* (Minneapolis: University of Minnesota Press, 2006), 32.

26 Ibid., 153–155.

27 Ibid., 123.

28 Singerman, *Cairo Contested,* 15–16.

29 Khaled Adham, "Cairo's Déjà Vu: Globalization and Urban Fantasies," in *Planning Middle Eastern Cities: An Urban Kaleidoscope in a Globalizing World,* ed. Yasser Elsheshtawy (New York: Routledge, 2004), 159–160.

30 A developer's promotional ad, as cited in Timothy Mitchell, *Rule of Experts: Egypt, Techno-Politics, Modernity* (Berkeley: University of California Press, 2002), 273.

31 Adham, "Cairo's Déjà Vu," 161.

32 Ibid., 302.

33 Mona Abaza, *Changing Consumer Cultures of Modern Cairo: Cairo's Urban Reshaping* (Boston: Brill, 2006), 30.

34 Robert Venturi drew a distinction between the "decorated shed" and "the duck" as architectural typologies of the Las Vegas strip. See Robert Venturi, Denise Scott Brown, and Steven Izenour, *Learning from Las Vegas: The Forgotten Symbolism of Architectural Form* (Cambridge, Mass.: MIT Press, 1977).

35 Mona Abaza, "Egyptianizing the American Dream: Nasr City's Shopping Malls, Public Order, and the Privatized Military," in Singerman and Amar, *Cairo Cosmopolitan,* 199.

36 Anouk de Koning, *Global Dreams: Class, Gender, and Public Space in Cosmopolitan Cairo* (Cairo: American University in Cairo Press, 2009), 119.

37 Ibid., 122.

38 Ibid., 28.

39 Philip Jodidio, *Under the Eaves of Architecture: The Aga Khan, Builder and Patron* (London: Prestel, 2008), 22–27.

40 Mohammed Heikal, an Egyptian journalist and author of *Autumn of Fury,* as cited in Maria Golia, *Cairo: City of Sand* (London: Reaktion Books, 2004), 198.

41 Nezar AlSayyad, ed., preface to *Cities and Fundamentalisms* (New York: Routledge, 2010), ii.

42 An example of this approach is Saba Mahmood, *Politics of Piety: The Islamic Revival and the Feminist Subject* (Princeton: Princeton University Press, 2005).

43 Nezar AlSayyad and Ananya Roy, "Medieval Modernity: On Citizenship and Urbanism in the Global Era," *Space and Polity* 10, no. 1 (2006): 1–20.

44 Golia, *Cairo,* 198.

45 Diane Singerman and Paul Amar, "Introduction: Contesting Myths, Critiquing Cosmopolitanism, and Creating the New Cairo School of Urban Studies," in Singerman and Amar, *Cairo Cosmopolitan,* 20–22.

46 Nezar AlSayyad, afterword to Singerman and Amar, *Cairo Cosmopolitan,* 539–540.

47 Samia Mehrez, *Egypt's Culture Wars: Politics and Practice* (New York: Routledge, 2008), 145–173.

48 Irene A. Bierman, "Disciplining the Eye: Perceiving Medieval Cairo," in *Making Cairo Medieval,* ed. Nezar AlSayyad, Irene A. Bierman, and Nasser Rabbat (New York: Lexington Books, 2005), 22–24.

49 Nezar AlSayyad, "Global Norms and Urban Forms in the Age of Tourism: Manufacturing Heritage, Consuming Tradition," in *Consuming Tradition, Manufacturing Heritage: Global Norms and Urban Forms in the Age of Tourism,* ed. Nezar AlSayyad (New York: Routledge, 2001), 26.

Figures and Credits

Photographs and maps accompanying the text are © Nezar AlSayyad except where specified otherwise.

1. Memphis

Fig. 1.1. *The Pyramids of Giza, from Egypt and Nubia,* by David Roberts, 1854. Library of Congress.

Fig. 1.2. Map showing Memphis, Dahshur, Saqqara, and Giza.

Fig. 1.3. The Step Pyramid of Djoser.

Fig. 1.4a. The Red Pyramid of Snefru. b. The Bent Pyramid of Snefru.

Fig. 1.5. The Great Pyramids at Giza in the nineteenth century. Weghat Nazar Magazine Archives.

Fig. 1.6. The Sphinx and the Pyramid of Khafra in the nineteenth century. Weghat Nazar Magazine Archives.

Fig. 1.7 Tomb of Auguste Mariette at the Egyptian Museum, Cairo.

2. From Ancient Egypt to the Coptic Enclave

Fig. 2.1. The Coptic Museum.

Fig. 2.2. Map showing the Fortress of Babylon.

Fig. 2.3a. The Fortress of Babylon during the time of the Napoleonic expedition. *Description d'Egypte,* vol. 5, *Antiquités,* plate no. 20, "Babylone Plan, Vue et Détails d'un Édifice de Construction Romain," 1829. Used with permission, The Bancroft Library. b. Remains of a circular tower at the Fortress of Babylon.

Fig. 2.4. The Church of al-Mu'allaqa.

Fig. 2.5. The interior of the Church of al-Mu'allaqa.

Fig. 2.6. The Church of St. George.

3. Fustat-Misr

Fig. 3.1. A map of Fustat and its surroundings.

Fig. 3.2. The Mosque of 'Amr ibn al-'As.

Fig. 3.3. The Mosque of Ahmad ibn Tulun.

Fig. 3.4. The interior of the Mosque of Ibn Tulun.

Fig. 3.5. The doorway connecting the interior of the Mosque of Ibn Tulun to his palace.

Fig. 3.6. The spiral minaret of the Mosque of Ibn Tulun.

4. Al-Qahira
Fig. 4.1. Map of Fustat, al-Askar, al-Qata'i, and al-Qahira.

Fig. 4.2. The Mosque of al-Azhar.

Fig. 4.3. The Mosque of al-Anwar, also known as the Mosque of al-Hakim. a. Before restoration, 1976. Used with permission, The Bancroft Library. b. After restoration.

Fig. 4.4. Gates of Cairo. a. Bab al-Futuh, 1976. Copyright John A. and Caroline Williams. All rights reserved. Used with permission. b. Bab al-Nasr, 2001. c. Bab Zuwayla, 2010.

Fig. 4.5. The Mosque of al-Aqmar. a. Before restoration, 1976. Copyright John A. and Caroline Williams. All rights reserved. Used with permission. b. After restoration.

5. Fortress Cairo
Fig. 5.1. Map of Cairo area during the Ayyubid period.

Fig. 5.2. The Citadel of Cairo.

Fig. 5.3. The minaret of al-Salih Najm al-Din Ayyub madrasa and funerary complex.

Fig. 5.4. The funerary mausoleum of Shagarat al-Durr.

6. The Bahri Mamluks
Fig. 6.1. Map of Cairo area during the Bahri Mamluk period.

Fig. 6.2. The Mosque of Sultan al-Zahir Baybars.

Fig. 6.3. The funerary complex of al-Mansur Qalawun.

Fig. 6.4. Madrasa and mausoleum of Sultan al-Nasir Muhammad.

Fig. 6.5. The Mosque of Sultan al-Nasir Muhammad at the Citadel.

Fig. 6.6. The Mosque of Sultan Hasan. a. Exterior view. b. View of the iwan.

7. Governing from the Tower
Fig. 7.1. Map of Cairo area during the Burji Mamluk period.

Fig. 7.2. Bab Zuwayla, also known as Bab al-Mitwalli.

Fig. 7.3. The madrasa and funerary complex of Sultan al-Zahir Barquq.

Fig. 7.4. The minarets of al-Mu'ayyad Mosque above Bab Zuwayla.

Fig. 7.5.The funerary complex of Sultan al-Mu'ayyad.

Fig. 7.6. The funerary complex of Sultan al-Ashraf Qaytbay.

Fig. 7.7. The Mosque and funerary complex of Sultan al-Ashraf Qansuh al-Ghuri. a. As portrayed in the nineteenth century by David Roberts in the *Bazaar of the Silk Mercers,* circa 1846. Library of Congress. b. Present day.

Fig. 7.8. The madrasa and khanqah of al-Ghuri viewed from al-Azhar overpass.

Fig. 7.9. The wekala of al-Ghuri.

8. A Provincial Capital under Ottoman Rule
Fig. 8.1. The funerary madrasa of Amir Khair Bey.

Fig. 8.2. Map of Cairo area during the Ottoman period.

Fig. 8.3. The Mosque of Sinan Pasha.

Fig. 8.4. The wekala and bazaar of Ridwan Bey.

Fig. 8.5. The Mosque of Abu al-Dahab.

Fig. 8.6. The sabil-kuttab of 'Abd al-Rahman Katkhuda.

Fig. 8.7. Courtyard view of Bayt al-Sihaymi.

9. A Changing City

Fig 9.1 The skyline of Cairo with the Mosque of Muhammad Ali.

Fig. 9.2. Map of Cairo at the end of Muhammad Ali's rule.

Fig. 9.3. Headquarters of the French army in Azbakiya. *Description de l'Egypte,* vol. 6, *État Moderne,* plate no. 40, "Vue du Quartier Général de l'Armée Française," 1822. Used with permission, The Bancroft Library.

Fig. 9.4. The Napoleonic expedition map of Cairo. *Description de L'Egypte,* vol. 6, *État Moderne,* plate no. 26, "Le Kaire: Plan Particulier de la Ville," 1822. Used with permission, The Bancroft Library.

Fig. 9.5. Muhammad Ali's Palace in Shubra.

Fig. 9.6. A view of Bab Zuwayla as portrayed by David Roberts in the nineteenth century in *Minarets and Grand Entrance of the Metwaleys at Cairo,* circa 1846. Library of Congress.

Fig. 9.7. *Prayer on the Rooftops of Cairo (La Prière au Caire)* by Jean-Léon Gérôme. Bildarchiv Preussischer Kulturbesitz / Art Resource NY.

10. Modernizing the New, Medievalizing the Old

Fig. 10.1. a. The Gezira Palace of Khedive Ismail as illustrated by the British journal, *The Graphic,* London. September, 30, 1882. b. The palace today as the Cairo Marriott.

Fig. 10.2. Cairo Railway Station, also known as Bab al-Hadid.

Fig. 10.3. Qasr al-Nil bridge.

Fig. 10.4. Abdin Palace in Cairo at the end of the nineteenth century. Weghat Nazar Magazine Archives.

Fig. 10.5. Map of khedival and royal Cairo.

Fig. 10.6. *Tombs in the Southern Cemetery,* by Francis Frith, 1857, from the book *Sinai, Palestine, the Nile,* circa 1863. Courtesy of George Eastman House, International Museum of Photography and Film.

Fig. 10.7. The Egyptian Museum.

Fig. 10.8. Suleyman Pasha Square.

Fig. 10.9. Heliopolis.

Fig. 10.10. The palace of Baron Empain.

11. The Arab Republic and the City of Nasser

Fig. 11.1. Cairo Tower in Gezira.

Fig. 11.2. The Nile Hilton and former headquarters of the Arab Socialist Union.

Fig. 11.3. The Arab League.

Fig. 11.4. Map of Cairo during Nasser's rule.

Fig. 11.5. The Mugama'a Complex.

Fig. 11.6. Public housing in Imbaba.

Fig. 11.7. Tahrir Square during Nasser's time, 1962. Weghat Nazar Magazine Archives.

Index